DIGGING SEDGEFORD
A people's archaeology

The SHARP Team

Further details of Poppyland Publishing titles can be found at
www.poppyland.co.uk
where clicking on the 'Support and Resources' button will lead to pages
specially compiled to support this title.

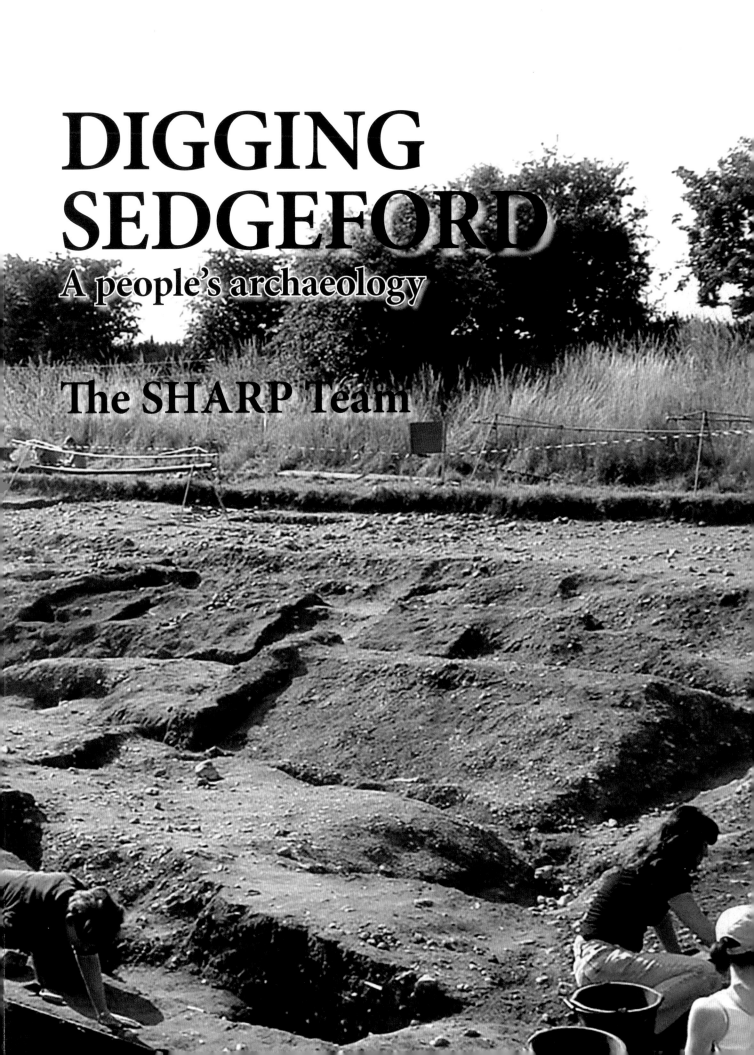

DIGGING SEDGEFORD
A people's archaeology

The SHARP Team

ISBN 978-1-909796-08-9
Published by Poppyland Publishing, Cromer NR27 9AN

A catalogue record for this book is available from the British Library.

Picture credits:

Dominic Andrews Figs. 1.2, 7.2, 7.3, 7.4, 7.5, 8.6
Ray Baldry Plates 2.6, 2.8, 2.9, 2.11, 2.13, 3.6, 6.1, 6.2, 6.3, 6.4, 6.5, 6.7, 6.8, 6.9, 6.10, 6.11, 6.12, 6.13, 6.14, 6.15, 6.16, 6.17, 6.18, 6.19, 6,20
Ray Baldry and Sue White Fig. 5.7
Valerie Booth, Gatwick Park Hospital, Plate 2.7 and the radiograph in Plate 6.15
Andrea Cox Fig. 7.1
Contains Ordnance Survey data © Crown copyright and database right 2014 Figs. 0.1, 0.2, 2.8, 3.1, 9.1, 9.2, 9.3, 9.4, 9.5, 9.6, 9.7, 9.8, 9.9, 9.10
Mike Page Front Cover, Plate 9.1
Norfolk Museums Service, Ancient House Museum, Thetford Plate 2.24
Norfolk Record Office Plate 1.6 (NRO LEST/OC 1), Plate 8.8 (NRO LEST/OC 1). Plate 8.9 (NRO CHC 11002), Plate 8.10 (NRO C/CA 3/2), Plate 8.11 (NRO DN/TA 309).
Hilary Snelling Plate 6.6
Royal College of Surgeons Fig. 4.2
All other pictures and photographs contributed by the SHARP team

Publication Editors:

Neil Faulkner, Keith Robinson, Gary Rossin

Printed in Turkey by Latitude Press Ltd.

Contents

The SHARP Team

This list could be much longer - the names of the team mentioned here have been taken from our annual reports published over the years. We might have listed everyone who has attended in any capacity since 1996. During that time hundreds of people – from around the world and from around the corner – have contributed to the project in countless ways. All of these people are part of the wider SHARP community.

John Ames, Dominic Andrews, William Armitage, Ray Baldry, Steve Barnett, Terry Baxter, Sophie Beckett, Andrea Beckham (née Cox), Pam Bent, Edward Biddulph, Mark Blagg-Newsome, Eleanor Blakelock, Dave Bonner, Darren Bowley, Ruth Buckley, Raoul Bull, Charlotte Burrill, Sophie Cabot, Kirsty Cairns (née Halifax), Stuart Calow, Greg Campbell, Peter Carnell, Mark Chapman, Pat Chapman, Nathan Chinchen, James Coles, Nicholas Cooke, Lorna Corr, Richard Coulton, Jon Cousins, Daniel Crampsie, Kathryn Creed, Matthew Cross, Kirsten Cutler, Erica Darch, Gareth Davies, Nicola Dennies, Megan Dennis, Mark Dodd, Adrian Donaghey, Jo Dullaghan, Mo Eeles, Neil Faulkner, Sally Faulkner, Charlotte Fenwick, Vi Ferrante di Ruffano, Susan Fielding, Hugh Ford, Angus Forshaw, Jonathan Fox, Val Fryer, Victoria Furneaux, Kim Garbutt, Andrew Gardner, Sarah Glover, Anna Gow, Roger Greaves, Timothy Haines, Lucy Hall, Janet Hammond, Steve Hammond, Claire Hannington, Michael Harvey, Martin Hatton, Jackie Heath, Stacey Hennessy, John Hensby, Angela Hibbitt, David Hibbitt, Matt Hobson, Richard Hoggett, Holly Holman, Lorraine Horsley, Bill Howard, Brenda Huggins, Peter Inker, James Insley, Lynn Jollans, John Jolleys, Mark Jordan, Chris Kelly, Zoe Knapp, Alice Larter, Nick Long, Ray Ludford, Alison MacFarlane, Chris Mackie, Claire Malleson, Bill Manners, Wendy Martin, Anthony Maynard, Jill Maynard, Marion McCabe, Jean McGinty, Katie Mckinnon, Michael Medlar, Stefania Merlo, Charlie Middleton, Doug Mitcham, Christine Morton, Gabriel Moshenska, Kathrine Murphy, Nicci Neilson, Darren Nicholl, Esmee Nicolson-Lai, Linda Nudds, Michael Nudds, Marion Ogden, Max Ogden, Jamie Owen, Katie Pack, Ruth Panes, Rebecca Parker, Jannine Parry, Gef Parsons, Vic Parsons, Naomi Payne, Brian Pfieffer, Monica Place, Mark Pocock, Kris Poole, Jennifer Potten, Jonny Price, Robin Putland, Piers Pye-Watson, Judith Quinn, Matt Ratcliff, Jim Reid, Pat Reid, Jerry Revell, Eve Richardson, Deborah Riches, Michael Rivett, Tegwen Roberts, Eleanor Robinson, Keith Robinson, Georgina Robotham, Gary Rossin, Zannah Salter (née Baldry), Jonathon Schub, Michael Seales, Richard Skinner, John Smallwood, Ann Smith, Kelvin Smith, Hilary Snelling, Tim Snelling, Brenda Stibbons, Peter Stibbons, Laura Stockley, Richard Swann, Luke Taylor, Valerie Teh, Zena Tett, Helen Thirkettle, Pauline Thirkettle, Ray Thirkettle, Gabor Thomas, Meredith Thompson, Melanie Van Twest, Peter Ward, Gay Watt, James Westoby, Russell Wigglesworth, Pippa Willcox, Liz Wilson, Pauline Wilton (née Fogarty), Tristan Wood-Davis, Luke Woodley.

Acknowledgements

Our deepest thanks are due to the landowners, farm managers, estate staff and householders of Sedgeford parish who have facilitated our work. Particular thanks are due to: Bernard, Susan and Charlie Campbell; Andrew and Katharine Ramsay; Harry Buscall; Janet Hammond and Tim Snelling; William Barber; David Lyles and John Austen.

Specialist analysis and advice which have contributed substantively to the results presented in this volume have been undertaken on a commercial or research basis by the following people: John Ames (worked flint); Julian Andrews (geological identifications); Michael de Bootman (geophysics); Greg Campbell (archaeo-environmental samples); Geraldine Crann (worked flint); Debbie Forkes (conservation); Val Fryer (archaeo-environmental samples); Adam Longcroft (education); Alice Lyons (pottery); Tim Pestell (small finds); Kris Poole (animal bones), Peter Robins (worked flint) and John Smallwood (specialist advice). Information and advice on human remains was freely provided by Don Brothwell and Tony Waldron.

Valuable assistance in facilitating research has been given by: Maggie Bellati and Mercedes Okumura (Duckworth Collection, Cambridge University); Louise King (Royal College of Surgeons); Theya Molleson (Natural History Museum) and Keith Rogers (Cranfield University).

Special thanks are due to Brian Ayers, David Gurney and Andrew Rogerson, all high-profile and long-serving Norfolk archaeologists, for their critical reading of an early draft of this monograph. It has, we hope, been much improved in consequence.

We would specifically like to thank the members of the North West Norfolk History Society for their support with the publication of this volume.

Foreword

This amazing project all began in the bar of the Europa Hotel in Sorrento! Together with my wife and our 11-year-old son Charlie (he is 30 now), I was chatting over a drink with our tour guide Neil Faulkner.

Neil had a dream – to direct an excavation, a 'dig' – that was open to all, preferably somewhere that held archaeological deposits of a range of periods.

My wife, Susan, was intrigued with the idea and immediately invited Neil to Sedgeford to view the archaeological potential of the Sedgeford Hall Estate. We had long known that the small pasture sloping down to the River Heacham and named 'Boneyard' since time immemorial was an ancient burial-ground. Human bones, hand-axes, Roman coins, pottery, even a beautiful Iron Age torc had all been found on the Estate over the years. Susan was sure that our home ground, with its rich archaeological deposits, was just the place to fulfil Neil's dream.

The rest, as they say, is history. Neil arrived, loved the place, and soon established a long-term, richly rewarding excavation.

Each year we learn a little more, both about our own Estate and about the fascinating village of Sedgeford. It is inspiring for us, as landowners and residents, to have our summers filled with enthusiastic archaeologists, historians and helpers. We feel very privileged to have attended conception and birth of this project, and to have seen it grow in strength and knowledge year by year.

This preface is an ideal opportunity to thank and congratulate the entire SHARP Team on this magnificent achievement, and to thank them on behalf of all the people of Sedgeford for revealing so much of the history of the village and its people.

Professor Bernard Campbell
April 2014

Preface

The Sedgeford Historical and Archaeological Research Project has its origin in a hotel bar overlooking the Bay of Naples in 1995. That was where Professor Bernard Campbell and his wife Susan told me about the archaeology on their Norfolk estate and invited me to come up and take a look.

There it might have rested, still-born, like many casual holiday exchanges of contact details. But I was a research student at UCL's Institute of Archaeology at the time and was eager to set up a big excavation project – without being too picky about what and where.

When I contacted Bernard and Susan shortly after getting back, I was at pains to stress the scale of what I had in mind: I wanted them to have the option of politely retreating. It turned out that they were as serious as I was. They have remained so ever since and consequently, over the last 18 years, the Campbell family has become the ever-willing patron of one of the largest and longest-running archaeological research and training projects in Britain.

When it started, in 1996, we had no money, no equipment, no staff and no formal research aims. Nonetheless, we aimed to put 50 people on site for six weeks that summer. And this we did.

Conditions were primitive. Tools were stored in an old trailer. Lunch was a cheese roll sitting on a log. The portaloos stank and were too close to the campsite. Much worse, it turned out that we disagreed about how archaeology should be organised.

Towards a democratic archaeology

The core of the supervisory team had been recruited from among UCL archaeology students. The team had been hastily assembled rather than carefully selected, and no real attempt had been made to talk through aims and methods. In consequence, the team came apart during the season, mainly because different people had different ideas about what sort of project they wanted.

The conflict became personalised and acrimonious – and, no doubt, there were private agendas in play – but the substance of the dispute was political, even if some of the less theoretically acute protagonists did not realise this. Conflict is often creative. It was on this occasion. The argument inside the supervisory team helped crystallise what I have since come to call 'democratic archaeology'.

A majority of the team wanted the project run on conventional lines, with a clear hierarchy of directors, supervisors and volunteers and with higher-level archaeological practice performed by 'specialists'. Perhaps this matched the expectations of young university archaeologists who were uncertain of their skills and their future: they wanted a traditional model that seemed to confirm their as-yet insecure status as 'professionals'. Perhaps, too, it reflected trends in archaeology at the time – towards greater standardisation and regulation of field practice – and in society more widely – where the 'neoliberal counter-revolution' was fast creating a more corporate, hierarchical and inhumane world.

I was older and belonged to a different tradition. I see labour as something potentially creative, democratic and empowering. I see it as a way in which people can develop their own skills and achieve self-enrichment in the context of a collective endeavour in which they share ownership. Usually work is not like that. In the factories, offices and call-centres of modern capitalism, it is experienced as drudgery, stress, humiliation and alienation.

It seems inexcusable to me that some archaeologists seek to replicate oppressive social relations in their own field practice. Do they really believe that this is how the world has to function? Even should function? Do they consider it 'efficient' and 'cost-effective'? Or what? It is, in fact, wholly counterproductive for humans to flourish in a democratic environment, and wither when they have to be bullied into working (Faulkner 2000).

I wanted to do different at Sedgeford. Norfolk has a tradition of doing this, not least in archaeology, where the county was one of the pioneers in forging close relationships between archaeologists and metal-detectorists, creating a model that has since been enshrined in a new Treasure Act and the associated Portable Antiquities Scheme and rolled out across the country (Portable Antiquities Scheme; Faulkner 2003, 173-182). The 1996 SHARP season had clarified the fact that relationships between 'professional' and 'amateur' archaeologists working on the same excavation could be equally problematic. So the following season, with a substantially new supervisory team, we began an experiment in public archaeology which has been developing ever since.

A democracy of volunteer workers

Things do not always run smoothly. The project has passed through two political crises, the first in 1996-1997 as described, the second in 2008-2009, when an attempt was made to take the project over and impose a formal top-down structure upon it.

The second crisis, played out over several months, went through three distinct phases: first there was a split between the project directors and most of the lay members of the SHARP committee; then the supervisory team was convened and confirmed its support for the directors; finally a general meeting of volunteers assembled in Sedgeford, many having travelled long distances to attend and this meeting, around 50 strong and the most representative in the history of the project, endorsed the position of the archaeological team by an overwhelming majority.

The 'democratic' looseness of the project's structure had left it exposed to ill-conceived attempts to make it conform to a traditional model. The lesson learned was that democracy needs structures, procedures and rules like any other kind of governance.

So we now have a formal constitution which defines a 'member of SHARP' as anyone who has contributed work of any kind over the preceding two years, and which grants all members an equal voice and vote in the running of the project. SHARP is, quite literally, a democracy of volunteer workers on an archaeological field project. The first-time student trainee now has the same decision-making power as directors, supervisors and veteran volunteers (Faulkner 2009).

This has implications for what is commonly called 'community archaeology'. This is one of those terms which, while implying 'A Good Thing', is in fact a portmanteau embracing a diversity of practice not all of which is in fact good.

Communities are not pre-existing givens; they are active processes of social construction. Good 'community archaeology' means creating opportunities for local people to become part of the socially constructed community that is an archaeological field project. Those who chose to do so may then be empowered as full members of the project community. This is to define community as a set of social relationships that arise in the context of collective activity. It is to make it something dynamic and creative.

But there is another, more common version of 'community archaeology'. In this version, members of the public are simply invited to consume certain archaeological experiences delivered to them by professional 'community archaeologists'.

These two versions of 'community archaeology', as various commentators have been at pains to point out, including former SHARP directors Gabe Moshenska and Pat Reid, are very different things: the former involves 'participation'; the latter is more a matter of 'performance' (Moshenska and Dhanjal 2012; Reid 2012). It is mainly for this reason that I value the term 'democratic archaeology': it leaves no room for doubt about what we intend.

Control over work

Crucial to democratic archaeology is demystification of the discipline and deconstruction of the dichotomy between 'experts' and 'amateurs'. Field archaeology is not theoretical physics. It is a set of practical skills that anyone can learn with time and effort, and the key requirement is attention, care and applied intelligence.

The rewards are high, and people usually come to archaeology well motivated. Embrace that, encourage them to engage fully with the material, keep them informed and give them ownership over their work, and you are likely to get quality excavation and accurate observation and recording.

Treat volunteers as 'trowel fodder' and morale will fall and minds disengage. Work will be messy and slow and stratigraphic distinctions may go unnoticed. My heart always sinks when an excavation team is sullen and silent: that means an alienated, switched-off workforce.

But democratic archaeology is not just about output and quality. It is also about the human experience as an end in itself. At one level, archaeology does not matter. Everyone whose bodies, houses and knick-knacks we dig up is long dead and past caring. Archaeology exists in the present, not the past; it involves living people, not dead ones. It is something of a luxury: we do it not because life depends on it but because we want to know about the past. We do it because a defining characteristic of our species is that we seek knowledge and understanding and because the quest itself is life-enriching. In view of this, to make excavation into drudgery is to destroy half its purpose. Archaeology is fun or it is largely pointless.

We have a golden rule at Sedgeford: the volunteer who first uncovers something gets to complete the excavation and help record it. When metal-detectorist, SHARP volunteer and RAF mechanic Kevin Woodward recovered a cow bone filled with gold staters in 2003, we set up an improvised lab in the Old Village Hall and he had the privilege of excavating the coins, one by one, from their container. A senior colleague at county level had proposed sending the cow bone to the British Museum for 'expert' excavation. Kevin, supported by a team making detailed records as the coins emerged, carried out the 'expert' excavation instead (Dennis and Faulkner 2005, 18-21).

Experts do not spring ready-made from the ether; they develop organically through education and experience. Not the least of SHARP's roles is to create its own organic experts – very many of whom have been successfully launched into careers in professional and academic archaeology.

Dialectical method

Also important has been my deliberate rejection of the bureaucratic apparatus of research aims and project designs. When we started, we dived straight into a site known from unpublished excavations in the 1950s. And that site has remained the main focus ever since, evolving into a major Middle Anglo-Saxon cemetery and settlement excavation. But true to our initial remit – to investigate settlement and land-use in the parish of Sedgeford throughout the past – we have carried out a series of secondary projects. Our experience now spans almost 5,000 years – everything from a Late Neolithic-Early Bronze Age crouch-burial to a First World War aerodrome.

We still have no overall 'project design'. Nor will we adopt one. Instead of a linear approach – research aims, evaluation, excavation, analysis, interpretation – we prefer a scientific method in which observation and interpretation are allowed to interact. At Sedgeford it is, as the late Peter Reynolds once described it to me, a matter of 'heads down, bums up, get digging'. Then, when we have some results, we think about what we have learned, frame new questions and plan fresh fieldwork to answer them. In that way, knowledge advances – not in linear fashion, but in a way that some have called 'hermeneutic' and I prefer to call 'dialectical' (Faulkner 2002).

What many colleagues fail to grasp is that the formal apparatus is not there to serve research but the requirements of grant applications and competitive tendering. Pure research is never linear. If we knew what we were going to find before we started, we would not need to dig it. Archaeology is inherently a journey into the unknown. Napoleon used to say that no military plan survives first contact with the enemy. No project design should survive first contact with the landscape.

'If we knew what we were doing, it would not be called 'research', would it?' Who said this? Einstein – who knew as much about scientific method as anyone ever did. Linear project designs are a bureaucratic barrier to the intelligent improvisation essential to scientific work in the field.

Organic experts

Project designs have another effect: they reinforce a division of labour and a hierarchy of expertise within archaeology. Instead of field practice being a craft in which 'reasoning and execution' are united, the two are separated, with lower grade personnel performing routine digging and recording tasks, and various higher grade personnel then carrying out the analysis, interpretation and publication.

'The idea of archaeology as a craft,' argue Michael Shanks and Randall McGuire, 'challenges the separation of reasoning and execution that characterises the field today.' Craft, for them, implies a rounded creative activity in which 'purpose' (research aims and relevance to society), 'viability' (the material remains and the methods used to explore them) and 'expression' (the many personal satisfactions to be had from archaeological work) interact (Shanks and McGuire 1996).

This is close to ideas we have developed independently, where a key feature of the contrast between traditional 'archaeology from above' and democratic 'archaeology from below' is that the latter creates a framework in which the three M's – material (the archaeological evidence), method (how we access that evidence) and meanings (how we interpret it) – do not follow a linear sequence but instead form a feedback loop (Faulkner 2002, 17-18).

SHARP's finest example of archaeology as craft is perhaps the work of our human remains team. Osteo-archaeology is unquestionably one of those mysterious specialisms that is remote from the experience of most professional archaeologists, never mind that of the humble amateur. Yet SHARP's work on an assemblage of around 300 skeletons has all been carried out in permanent and temporary buildings in Sedgeford, mainly during the annual summer excavation season, often with students and volunteers engaged in high-level research activities (Baldry, Burrill, Hatton and Snelling 2012).

The world in a field

One of my veteran colleagues at Sedgeford denies that SHARP is 'an experiment'; it is, he says, 'just the way we do things'. I think this is to underestimate the significance of SHARP's intervention in debates about public archaeology. We are challenging both the presumption that there is a single 'correct' way to do archaeology – that of commercial rescue archaeology – and the pretensions of a 'community archaeology' handed down from on high.

More than that, SHARP's experiment in ways of working together implies a critique of the social hierarchies prevalent in the modern workplace; it implies that people work better – more creatively and diligently – where they are part of a democratically structured collective.

Not the least of SHARP's academic roles is to construct and observe a tiny microcosm of human social organisation in a Norfolk field each summer. We are studying the Anglo-Saxons. But we are also studying ourselves.

Neil Faulkner
Founder-director

References

Baldry, S., Burrill, C., Hatton, M. and Snelling, H., 2012, 'Community Archaeology and Human Osteology: the Sedgeford experience', in G. Moshenska and S. Dhanjal (eds.), *Community Archaeology: themes, methods and practices*, Oxford, Oxbow, 90-99.

Dennis, M. and Faulkner, N., 2005, *The Sedgeford Hoard*, Stroud, Tempus.

Faulkner, N., 2000, 'Archaeology from below', in *Public Archaeology*, 1 (1), 21-33.

Faulkner, N., 2002, 'The Sedgeford project, Norfolk: an experiment in popular participation and dialectical method', in *Archaeology International*, 2001/2002, Institute of Archaeology UCL, 16-20.

Faulkner, N., 2003, *Hidden Treasure: digging up Britain's past*, London, BBC Books.

Faulkner, N., 2009, 'The Sedgeford Crisis', in *Public Archaeology*, 8 (1), 51-61.

Moshenska, G. and Dhanjal, S., 2012, 'Introduction: thinking about, talking about and doing community archaeology', in G. Moshenska and S. Dhanjal (eds.), *Community Archaeology: themes, methods and practices*, Oxford, Oxbow, 1-5.

Portable Antiquities Scheme, www.finds.org.uk/info/advice/aboutus.

Reid, P., 2012, 'Performance or Participation: the relationship between local communities and the archaeological domain', in G. Moshenska and S. Dhanjal (eds.), *Community Archaeology: themes, methods and practices*, Oxford, Oxbow, 18-27.

Shanks, M. and McGuire, R., 1996, 'The craft of archaeology', in *American Antiquity*, 61(1), 75-88.

Why we are here: Voices from Sedgeford

Kev Woodward, SHARP volunteer at the metal-detected discovery of the Sedgeford Hoard:

'Once it became clear the signal came from beneath the unexplored archaeological layer, our attitude changed. The machine indicated it was non-ferrous and 14 inches long. Terry removed two inches of soil with his trowel, and then I swept the area again. The signal had not changed, so more soil was removed. Two inches more down and I came across an animal bone lying on its side. I lifted the bone and dug some more. Once Terry and I had cleaned the area up, I swept over the hole again.

'This time things were different, and my mind went into overdrive: there were signals coming from both our little heaps of spoil and from the hole itself – lots of them. Within a few seconds I had an Iron Age gold coin in my quivering hand, and within a minute we had recovered four more identical coins from the spoil heaps. There were still signals from the hole, so I moved the detector-head away so that Terry could continue the excavation. In doing so, I passed it over the animal bone and the detector gave off a strong signal. To investigate this, I moved the bone, assuming it was in the way, but when I tried again the signal had disappeared.

'Only then did it dawn on me that maybe a coin had got lodged inside the bone, so I passed the detector-head over it and received a strong signal. I carefully picked out some of the mud inside the broken end of the shaft. Two gold coins appeared, wedged inside. It was then that I noticed how heavy the bone was. And as I tilted it, I could feel more coins moving around inside …'

Melanie Van Twest, SHARP volunteer during the project's first excavation season:

'Wake up at 8am and pull on my 'Invasion of the Bodysnatchers' T-shirt. The volunteers are camping on Chalkpit Field – only supervisors are allowed on Boneyard! The portaloos are due for emptying today, so they're a bit smelly! Breakfast is damp cereal, stale bread and spreads out of the tool shed. Then it's morning meeting.

'Different teams are working in a variety of areas, including mattocking back the Boneyard trench and digging test-pits in the Reeddam and along the river. I am working at the church, planning the stones on the exterior of the west wall. Sigh!

'Down on Boneyard the first skeleton is discovered. Someone put a mattock through the thigh bone. Whoops! Human Remains supervisor is reportedly both pleased to have a skelly to work on, but not impressed with the damage …

'I am on lunch duty today, so off I go to Hill Farm to collect the lunch meats and veggies from the fridge in Janet Hammond's barn. Walk down to site and slice tomatoes, lettuce, etc. near the trees.

'Everyone meets up under the trees at 12.30. Hungry hordes grabbing a convenient log to sit on. The tuck is brought out, so it's ham and salad sandwiches with coke.

Wasps are bad – I have to keep waving my sandwich around to keep them off, and a hand over my drink to stop them crawling in! The plan is to annihilate them tomorrow – if we can find the nest. Clouds building up, looks like we are in for a shower …

'… I jump in one of the showers at Hill Farm to beat the rush at the end of the working day. It's mainly volunteers here – the supervisors use the shower at Glovers Farm Cottage, which is their base. At least there's somewhere solid to work in other than the church. Not sure what they'll do next year when the cottage has been renovated and sold.

'Dinner at the King William means getting to meet a few of the locals – especially Bert, who has a special corner at the bar and Rik and Glenn, who own the pub. Good beer. Meal is okay too. Not sure about 'Angel Delight' for dessert – doesn't seem either angelic or delightful to me. Guess you have to be born here …

'Back to Hill Farm for the site meeting in the barn, chaired by Neil Faulkner. Heated discussion of the thin 'grey marl' layer that Gabs is finding in each test-pit section … Topic turns to what to do with the skellies now that we are finding them. Decision is made that one day they will be returned to the soil, rather than spending the rest of eternity gathering dust in some storage facility. All seem happy with that.

'Music night at the pub. Between us from site and people coming in from all around, it is filled to overflowing. Managed to get a few pints down before pub shuts. Take shortcut back to Boneyard through the building site for new cottages along the Heacham road next to the pub. Have to be sneaky – they don't like us doing that!

'Creep into bed at midnight. A good day, overall. Looking forward to punch party tomorrow night, though not sure about seeing Gabs Thomas gyrating to *The Prodigy* once again! Rather frightening. Wonder what I'll be doing tomorrow …'

David Crease, SHARP volunteer since 2007:

'Well, I am retired now. I began life as a chemist, I studied chemistry at the University of London, I did some research and then I went into teaching. I have always had an interest in archaeology, having done some very informal digging when I was a student. In 2007 my interest was revived and I came to SHARP and took the Basic Excavation and Recording Techniques (BERT) course, which was excellent.

'In terms of the digging, I find just the precision of taking something apart very carefully fascinating. I know it looks like people grubbing around in the mud, but it's like a lot of scientific things, a delightful mixture of practical work and theoretical technical stuff at the same time.

'You're down in a trench and you're digging when you find something that might be of interest, so you use modern electronics to locate its position on the surface of the earth to within a few centimetres.

'Only Harry Potter gets to be a wizard, but probably the next best thing to that is being a chemist or an archaeologist ...'

Stuart Calow, SHARP volunteer and supervisor since 2000:

'I had previously been a truck driver and I'd been reading books on archaeology for 15 years and I was desperate to break into it and I didn't know how. I met Neil Faulkner by accident and ended up paying for a whole summer here. He asked me to be a supervisor the next year, which was a great surprise seeing as I had virtually no experience, and I quickly realised that the ethos of SHARP was to give people a chance – no matter what their background, no matter how academic or non-academic.

'After being a supervisor here for two years I'd got enough experience to get work professionally. Since then I've worked all over the south of England, a couple of years in Ireland and I've been working the last four years for the Norfolk unit.

'I come back here each summer and spend three weeks of my annual leave actually doing archaeology for nothing precisely because of the contrast with the commercial world. SHARP is almost unique: it's possible to do the archaeology slowly. And the place itself is beautiful, and the people that come back here year after year have obviously got the bug and they love it as much as I do.

'We have a constant turnover of young people, a lot of students, but we get people from all walks of life. We get pensioners that come back year after year. Literally everybody, all types of people come here, and the atmosphere on the dig is completely non-hierarchical.

'Of course, we have leaders in the sense that the most experienced people are deferred to for making decisions about the archaeology, which of course is as it should be. But the structure of SHARP is that anybody that has ever contributed towards it is considered to be a member, every one of whom is entitled to come to the annual general meeting and vote, and create the leading committee that runs the organisation and in that sense I think the organisation is unique.

'I can't think of anywhere else in the country where this happens, and that's mainly down to Neil Faulkner's ethos, and the energy he originally put into setting up the organisation.'

Lynn Hollyer, SHARP volunteer since 1999:

'I originally come from New York and I first came to SHARP in 1999. I'd just done one previous training dig at Bignor Roman Villa. I didn't really know how interested in archaeology I was, but I saw the Human Remains course and I decided I wanted to do that, and I signed up for the extra week of digging

afterwards, and when I came it really was a cemetery dig.

'We had Old Trench and Reeddam and they were both still stuffed with skeletons, and the Human Remains course involved actually cleaning off and digging up your own skeleton. Ours was named Alex. We named her Alex because we wanted a neutral name as some people had given very feminine names to very masculine skeletons and vice versa. So Alex was our skeleton, and we lifted her and we cleaned her up and we learned all the bones – or not as the case might be!

'The next week we were out on the trench. I was in Old Trench, with another skeleton, and in those days I think they were coming up several a day. And I thought it was absolutely wonderful. I still don't know why I'm so interested in bones, but I am.

'Back then Reeddam was basically under water, so there was the pump constantly going and the minute it stopped everything got buried. I was physically not strong enough to excavate in Reeddam because the mud was so gloopy and it sucked everything. You tried to dig and it was absolutely black goo – but the skeletons that came out were in excellent condition.

'One of the things I do remember was that you had the very wet Reeddam skeletons and then higher up on Old Trench you had the skeletons that were very dry, and they were in good condition. Then you had middle ones that had been both wet and dry, and they would look absolutely beautiful in the ground and you would touch them and the bones would just disintegrate. You would see a beautiful thigh bone, try to lift it and it would come into four or five pieces. Which was very frustrating and rather sad!'

Tyler Mackie, SHARP volunteer on her first excavation experience:

'Before SHARP, I was a digging virgin. I had never used my shiny trowel. My clothes were not caked in dirt and my boots were fresh out of the box. I had never camped and never travelled alone, certainly not from my tiny village in Scotland to an equally tiny village in Norfolk. I had no idea what to expect, save from guesses based on the SHARP poster that advertised 'a cross between Glastonbury and Time-Team'.

And then I became a BERT (Basic Excavation and Recording Techniques) trainee, assigned my first excavation on the Anglo-Saxon settlement site on Chalkpit Field.

'I stand a very small five foot two and was the shortest person on site. Was it fate, irony, or the deliberate work of the site supervisors that I was given the largest pit in the trench to dig, thus beginning the legend of the Big Pit?

'I was excited by my first find – a mussel shell! I felt like Christmas had come, complete with rainbows and kittens … A few days later, I was sick of shells – particularly oyster shells. I think Anglo-Saxons ate ridiculous amounts of oysters purely to annoy future archaeologists.

'However, I began to find animal bones and soon uncovered a cow scapula. I was both thrilled and mesmerised. So thrilled and mesmerised that I attempted to yank the thing straight out of the ground and broke the poor scapula in half! I'm certain I saw a tear run down supervisor James 'Westy' Westoby's face! I was politely asked to handle animal bones more carefully and the subsequent finding of incomplete ones was always followed by: 'Tyler, did you break another bone?'

'By the end of the week the pit was so deep that I had given up lying on the surface and dangling my upper body and arms into the pit to excavate (I felt like I was doing handstands), and resorted to jumping inside the feature. There were major advantages to this: I got shelter from the wind and rain, and I got to wear a yellow hard hat!

'Clambering in and out of the pit required some real acrobatic skills. I'd always thought I was flexible, but I came out of the pit with my only pair of waterproof trousers torn on the backside after snagging them on a bone. Many jokes ensued. Sadly, I never finished excavating my pit, which I had grown so fond of over my three-week stay and I passed the torch (or burden, depending on your perspective) on to Westy.

'SHARP was more than excavations and research. The anthem of Toto's *Africa* proved to be very catchy and was either sung or played daily, becoming almost a mantra on site. I experienced first-hand several of the infamous punch parties, one extremely muddy one echoing Glastonbury's own muddy atmosphere, and another where I won musical chairs, the only sport I take seriously! I even took part in a cricket match against the team from the nearby village of Snettisham, which SHARP came close to winning! I had never played cricket before, but proved to be good at catching the ball with my forehead …

'Film nights with hot chocolate and outings to the beach meant that there was always something fun to do, and I never had time to read the book I'd brought.

'What I found to be integral and unique to SHARP is its ethos of community. After spending only a few weeks with people, I was pleased to call everyone there my friends, who feel like an unofficial extension of my family. A new volunteer's thoughts and ideas are valued as much as those of someone who has worked at the site for years, and everyone is willing to help without a second thought.

'SHARP has proven to be a truly rewarding experience on many levels, going beyond just fieldwork experience. I went home caked in mud, messy-haired, with a worn trowel and ruined clothes, extremely happy.'

Introduction

This volume is a summary of the results and ideas arising from our first 12 years of fieldwork in the parish of Sedgeford (1996-2007), together with provisional results from further excavations between 2007 and 2012. During the earlier period, the project centred on the excavation of a large part of a Middle Anglo-Saxon cemetery and a smaller part of the contemporary settlement associated with it. The site is known to us as 'Boneyard-Reeddam'.

In tandem with this, subsidiary projects explored Iron Age, Roman, Late Anglo-Saxon, Medieval and Modern remains, both on the Boneyard-Reeddam site and in other parts of the parish. In particular, considerable work was undertaken in the West Hall area, which lies at the historic centre of the modern village (Fig. 0.3).

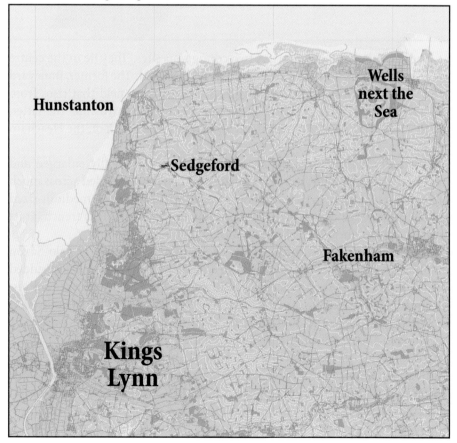

Fig. 0.1: Map of Britain showing location of Sedgeford.

Fig. 0.2: Map of north-west Norfolk showing the position of Sedgeford and major physical features.

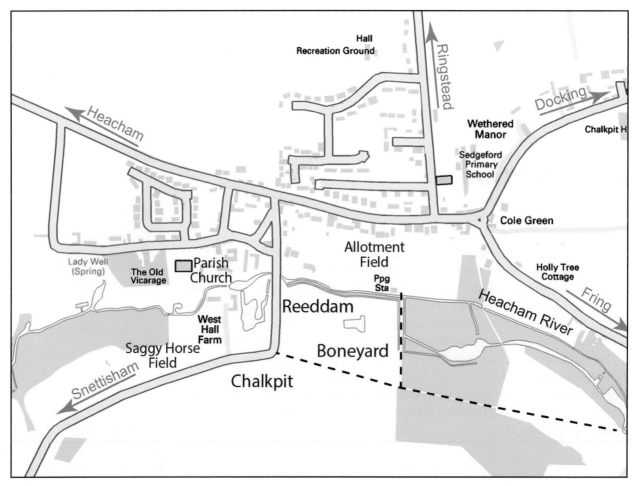

Fig. 0.3: Map of village of Sedgeford showing physical and human geography.

Boneyard-Reeddam comprises two contiguous sites. They lie in the centre of the parish on the southern side of the Heacham River. The former, Boneyard Field, is a small, irregularly shaped and steeply sloping field that rises from the base of the river valley and is nowadays under stewardship. The latter, the Reeddam, is an extensive wetland adjacent to, and south of, the Heacham River.

What were originally separate excavations were gradually enlarged and merged to create a single, roughly L-shaped trench that extended across much of the westernmost part of Boneyard Field and included a medium-sized 'nibble' at the edge of Reeddam immediately to the north. This trench, at its greatest extents, measured 50m east-west and 40m north-south.

We excavated 291 individually identifiable Middle Anglo-Saxon inhumation burials on the Boneyard-Reeddam site. To these must be added a further 126 other skeletons recovered from the site in earlier excavations, the great majority during investigations by Peter Jewell and Don Brothwell in 1957, 1958 and 1960. Our best guess is that this sample represents between a quarter and a half of the total cemetery population.

In addition, we excavated a sequence of boundary ditches and other features, including four structures, some contemporary with the cemetery, others post-dating it. Large quantities of pottery, worked bone, metalwork, animal bone, shell and other material were found in the fills of these features or in disturbed secondary deposits overlying them.

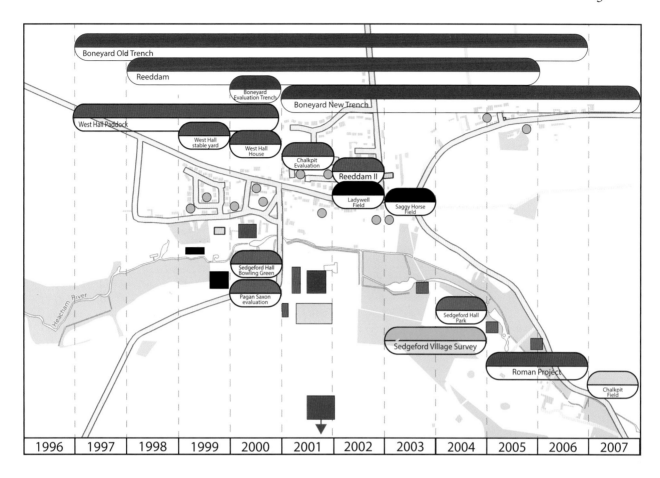

1996 | 1997 | 1998 | 1999 | 2000 | 2001 | 2002 | 2003 | 2004 | 2005 | 2006 | 2007

The Boneyard-Reeddam – Lower Chalkpit site

These discoveries provide the core of this report (Chapters 5 and 6). But it extends beyond them in two senses, one spatial, the other temporal. The wider spatial context is provided by discoveries in Lower Chalkpit Field, immediately north of Boneyard-Reeddam on the opposite side of a farm-track (Fig. 0.5), during excavations undertaken since 2007.

Unlike the Boneyard-Reeddam excavation, which became a single trench cut through deep layers of hillwash at the base of a slope, the Lower Chalkpit excavation has comprised a series of lateral trenches higher up the slope. The archaeological deposits here generally lie immediately below the modern plough-soil and have been heavily truncated by the plough. Their shallowness has made possible both strong geophysical survey results and rapid excavation of relatively large areas. Because of this, whereas our picture of Boneyard-Reeddam developed vertically, that of Lower Chalkpit is developing horizontally, giving us a clear picture of events across a large swathe of the site even before the excavations are complete.

Analysis of the main phases of activity on Lower Chalkpit is proceeding in tandem with the ongoing excavations. We are therefore able to provide a summary report of the Lower Chalkpit excavations from 2007 to 2012. Detailed analysis must await full reports on the finds, but the sequence of features, dated by pottery assemblages, are known, and these can be related

Fig. 0.4: Diagram showing SHARP's archaeological interventions in the parish of Sedgeford between 1996 and 2007. The bars span the years shown at the foot of the diagram; the colour of the bars links to the rectangles and dots showing the location of activity.

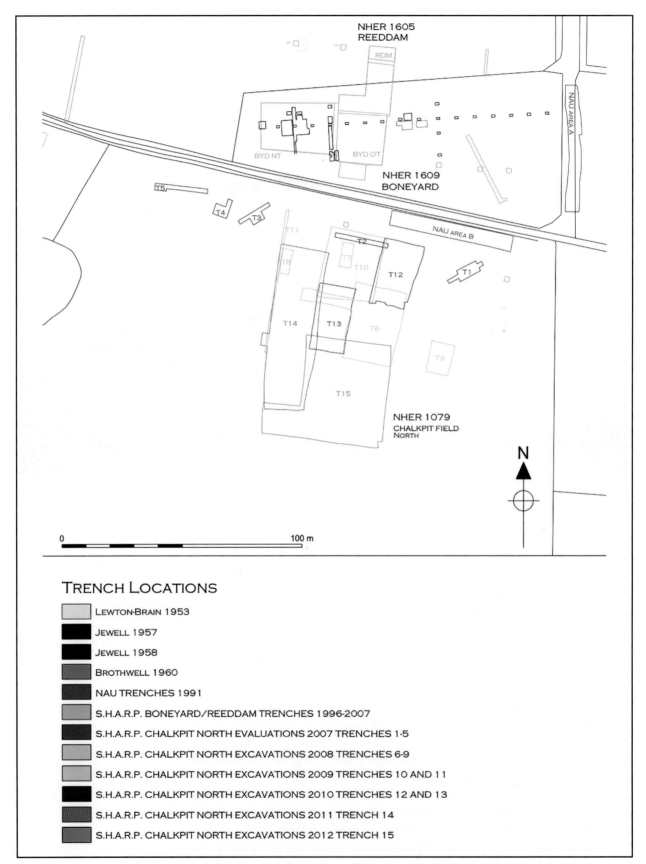

Fig. 0.5: Map showing archaeological trenches on the Boneyard-Reeddam – Lower Chalkpit site.

to those revealed on Boneyard-Reeddam. Amongst other things, we can now state with reasonable confidence that the site – for Boneyard-Reeddam and Lower Chalkpit are two parts of a single archaeological site – dates from *c*. AD 650/700 to *c*. AD 975/1025.

Plate 0.1: General view from Lower Chalkpit looking north across the Heacham Valley to the modern village of Sedgeford.

From the Late Iron Age to the High Middle Ages

A wider temporal context for the Anglo-Saxon site revealed on Boneyard-Reeddam – Lower Chalkpit is provided by a series of smaller SHARP investigations of remains from other periods. Significant Late Iron Age (Chapter 2) and Early Roman (Chapter 3) deposits have been recovered on the main site and elsewhere in the parish. We also know a fair amount about the Late Roman period (Chapter 3) and a little about the Early Anglo-Saxon period (Chapter 4). Though we currently lack the evidence for anything approaching a continuous narrative, we can at least generate some working hypotheses about the development of Sedgeford in the 700 years before the establishment of the Middle Anglo-Saxon settlement.

Rather fuller – though still far from complete – is our understanding of developments after the Boneyard-Reeddam – Lower Chalkpit settlement was abandoned, probably in the early- to mid-10th century. SHARP's analysis of the Church of St Mary the Virgin, Sedgeford's Medieval parish church

Plate 0.2: General view over Lower Chalkpit site looking north-west.

(Chapter 7), its series of excavations in West Hall Paddock and Ladywell Field (Chapter 8), and the 49 garden test-pits dug over two successive summers as part of the Sedgeford Village Survey (Chapter 9) have provided a fairly solid narrative framework for Late Anglo-Saxon and Medieval Sedgeford.

Work in progress

This report is the first fruit of work by many hundreds of students and volunteers between 1996 and the present-day. During that time, we have put up to 75 people on site each day during our regular six-week summer season, often with additional work by a dozen or so for a week or two at Easter, not to mention uncounted thousands of hours of out-of-season post-excavation work every year.

The monograph reflects the democratic and the dialectical character of the project. In the first place, it is a concise summary and synthesis – driven by interpretation, written in plain English, designed to be accessible and readable – of work contributed by dozens of SHARP's 'organic experts'. (Specialists who want more of the data and analysis on which it is based will increasingly be able to find these at our developing on-line archive at www.sharp.org.uk.)

In the second place, it makes no claim to be either complete or comprehensive, representing work in progress, providing only provisional conclusions. Research continues, and we hope will continue for many years to come, and as new information is recovered, our ideas about Sedgeford's past are bound to change. Where we are fairly confident about our working hypotheses, these are presented without equivocation. Where there is uncertainty or disagreement within the team, alternatives are offered, usually in the form of questions.

A third characteristic of the monograph is that we have attempted to place our findings in the context of what we think was happening in the wider world. Too many archaeological reports comprise a dull litany of superfluous detail that seems to have no significance outside the excavation trench. The collection of data for its own sake – pure empiricism – is a hollow endeavour.

All archaeological investigations involve sampling a greater whole. We take our sample because we seek knowledge of the whole. Scientific procedure therefore requires us to use limited data to create general hypotheses. To characterise the hard data of Harris matrices, pot typologies and osteological measurement as 'science' while treating discussion of context and meaning as mere 'speculation' is to misunderstand the nature of science. The testing of hypotheses against evidence is the very essence of it. Material without meaning is wasted effort.

Taking as our starting point an understanding that the past is different from the present, we nonetheless believe that it is at least to some degree discoverable through archaeological and historical enquiry. Consequently, at

Plate 0.3: General view across Heacham Valley.

8

each stage in the story, we aim to tell the reader how we think discoveries at Sedgeford can help us understand the wider Celtic, Romano-British, Anglo-Saxon and Medieval worlds.

We aim, in short, to tell a story, to suggest reasons why things happened as they did, and thus to make a small contribution to understanding the changing society of Britain between the Late Iron Age and the Medieval period.

Plate 0.4: General view over Heacham Valley looking south-east.

1. Landscapes and Locations

The long movement of geology

The basic underpinning of the East Anglian landscape is a geologically young 'thick flat plate of soft rocks' (Dymond 1990, 25). Movements in the Earth's crust have since tilted these rocks, raising them in the north-west corner of the region so that the plate now slopes gently south and east in the direction of the Low Countries (Fig. 1.1).

This tilting created an escarpment along the westernmost edge of Norfolk. Reaching a height of some 65m above sea level at Hunstanton in the north, the escarpment diminishes gradually as it runs south along the eastern edge of the Wash and the Fens, petering out near Hilgay (Williamson 1993, 14).

It is here in this narrow strip of land of west Norfolk that the oldest rocks of the region reveal themselves. Layers of 'various clays, sands and sandstones

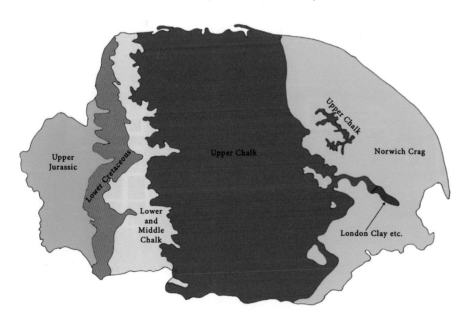

Fig. 1.1: The solid geology of Norfolk, based on *An Historical Atlas of Norfolk*.

10

Plate 1.1: The high status use of carstone in Magazine Cottage, Sedgeford – a powder magazine or armoury thought to have been built in 1640 by the prominent local Royalist Sir Hamon Le Strange, Lord of the Manor of Sedgeford, during the English Civil War.

outcrop to provide a richer and more varied texture to the local topography' (Dymond 1990, 25).

The sandstone found here is the locally important carstone, which ranges from a light honey colour to a dark ginger shade, and which is compact enough to provide Norfolk with its only true building stone (though flint, chalk, and clunch are all used, they cannot be dressed). Carstone is therefore much favoured in the vernacular architecture of north-west Norfolk (Plates 1.1 and 1.2), providing a unique flavour to local buildings (Chatwin 1961, 20).

The most important layer of the geological sandwich, though, is a 400m-thick base of Upper Cretaceous Middle Chalk, a hard, bedded, white

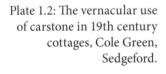

Plate 1.2: The vernacular use of carstone in 19th century cottages, Cole Green, Sedgeford.

chalk with flints and a few seams of marl (Chatwin 1961, 32).

This Middle Chalk strata outcrops in parts of the village and may have encouraged the move of the settlement focus from south of the river to its northern banks. The parish church, indeed, sits on one of these outcrops, above the floodplain, in the heart of the Medieval village.

Tom Williamson has written of Norfolk as having a generally 'muted landscape', but contrasts this to the north-western part of the county, which he presents as a more obviously rolling landscape (Williamson 1993, 11, 15). With its underlying chalk bedrock, the hills and valleys of this area form a mini downland landscape. And it is in the middle of this rolling landscape of north-west Norfolk that we find the 4,000 acres of the modern parish of Sedgeford.

Five or six kilometres inland from The Wash, Sedgeford parish is surrounded, clockwise from the north, by the parishes of Ringstead, Docking, Fring, Snettisham and Heacham. Settled in its surprisingly steep-sided valley, Sedgeford holds these rolling hills around it like a cloak of privacy – hiding, as it were, from the many tourists heading along the coast road from Kings Lynn to the seaside pleasures of Hunstanton.

The chalk bedrock is, however, overlain in many places by glacially deposited sands, gravels, loams and boulder clays. All of these deposits result from the series of glaciations that affected Norfolk during the Upper Pleistocene, the last of which was the Hunstanton Glaciation about 8000 BC. This varied surface geology gives rise to a rich variety of micro-environments offering a range of resources for the local population. It also makes excavation and interpretation a complex process.

Short movements of land and people

The surface geology obviously affects the nature of the soils in the area. Arthur Young, in his classic *General View of the Agriculture of the County of Norfolk* (1804), places this area in the Good Sands Region, which covers much of the north and west of the county. He describes the soils of Sedgeford as composed of 'sand, loamy sand, and some sandy loam on marle' (Young 1969, 158).

This first real classification of Norfolk soil types has been refined over time and now the western part of Young's Good Sands area has become more prosaically known as 'the Greensand Belt' (Dymond 1990, 29-30), or, with a greater sense of local topography, as 'the Western Escarpment' (Williamson 1993, 12).

This Western Escarpment is a complex landscape based on a series of westward flowing rivers. These rivers have cut the Escarpment into a series of blocks separated by their wide valleys, which in earlier times were frequently very marshy and often impassable. Settlements thus tend to avoid the valley bottoms as well as the exposed hilltops, sheltering on the valley flanks or in smaller tributary valleys. Villages are connected by a network of roads that follow the lines of the valleys, though avoiding the marshy bottoms.

Dymond points out that 'north-south communications along the length of the escarpment have always been far more difficult than one would expect' (1990, 30). This places a strong emphasis on the importance of traditional north-south routes, especially the Icknield Way and the Peddars Way, both of

Fig. 1.2: A reconstructed geological cross-section of the valley side to the south of Boneyard-Reeddam.

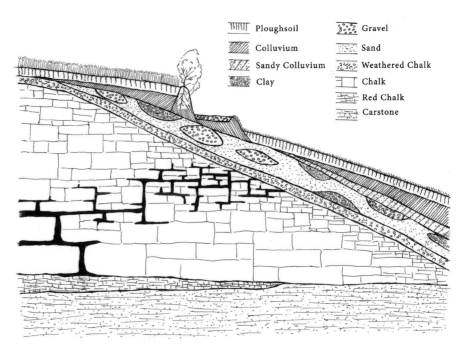

Ploughsoil
Colluvium
Sandy Colluvium
Clay
Gravel
Sand
Weathered Chalk
Chalk
Red Chalk
Carstone

which pass through the parish of Sedgeford.

Topographically, Sedgeford is dominated by the water-worn valley of the Heacham River, which once rose in the parish of Bircham Newton to flow through Fring and Sedgeford before emptying into The Wash at Heacham.

The profile of the valley in Sedgeford has changed over the course of time, both through natural and human activity. The valley bottom was wider and the sides steeper than we see today. Erosion of the hilltops and the accumulation of hill-wash in the valley bottom have flattened out the profile (Fig. 1.2).

The river is fed by many tributaries and springs, all of which would have guaranteed a source of fresh water, a very necessary resource for an agricultural population. The area, though, has suffered greatly from the over-extraction of water during the last 40 years, and this has affected the flow of the river. The dried-up courses of two tributaries can be seen feeding into the river from the north, one at the western end of the parish, and a smaller one towards its centre.

Waterways, watermills and wetlands

Water management schemes affecting both the river and its valley are not a new thing. It has been a relative constant of human interaction with the local environment since at least Late Anglo-Saxon times, when major work in the form of a dam in the Reeddam area appears to have been completed, at some point after burials ceased in the northern area of our Middle Anglo-Saxon Cemetery.

The course of the river has also been changed from the south to the north of the valley bottom. This happened sometime after the building of the dam and the move of the village focus from south of the river, where SHARP excavations have been focused, to north of the river around the present parish church. The move facilitated the creation of double moats around the two manor complexes in the core of the Medieval village.

The remains of a sophisticated Medieval water-management scheme is still evident in the Reeddam area. The *Arundinetum Dei*, literally 'the Reed-bed of God', otherwise known as 'the Great Pond', was created for the production of reeds as a cash crop and enabled the industrial-scale farming of fish both for food and for sale.

The earliest damming of the river would also have created a head of water for driving a watermill. *Domesday Book* records four mills belonging to the main manor of Sedgeford. Some, if not all, would have been watermills. Darby, in his *Domesday Geography of Eastern England*, suggests that all mills recorded in the survey were in fact watermills (as opposed to animal-powered or slave-powered ones), and it is these that are mentioned in later documentary references to Sedgeford (Darby 1952, 138).

It is likely that the Heacham River was navigable, though probably only by shallow-drafted vessels, from the coast up to the village of Fring, where the pond in the village goes by the name of 'Fring Dock' or 'Fring Harbour' (though in recent years the pond has often been dry). It appears that the river was canalised as well; certainly there are long straight stretches between Sedgeford and Fring. This canalisation of the river does not appear on the earliest estate map, however, so must post-date its creation in 1631.

To the west, the river valley meanders away towards the coast through a thin belt of lower chalk hills, such that Sedgeford cannot be seen from the sea, despite the easy access the waterway provides.

What is now the parish of Sedgeford, this naturally enclosed chalk basin, with a plentiful water supply, fertile soils in the non-marshy areas of the valley bottom, other easily workable soils, and access to a variety of resources, would surely have proved attractive to early settlers.

Routeways and seaways

It is not just the resources available that have shaped Sedgeford and its environs. Its situation within the context of the topography of north-west Norfolk has played a variety of roles in the cultural and economic life of the settlement. If water and land provide the basics for life, then the river also provides an easy east-west line of communications, whilst the important north-south land routes of the Icknield Way and Peddars Way bisect the valley in the parish. The potential was there for Sedgeford to become a transport, trade and communications nexus.

In pre-Roman times there was of course no Peddars Way, as the Roman military road has come to be known. There may, though, have been a more informal route on roughly the same alignment. Clearly though, at this time, the Icknield Way would have been the dominant route north (recent attempts to refute its very existence notwithstanding; Harrison 2003).

We can conceive of the Icknield Way as a zone of travel comprising alternative paths rather than a single trackway (Gregory 1982, 354). These are likely to reflect travellers' reactions to the varying weather and ground conditions at different times of year.

The importance of the prehistoric routeway would have been enhanced by a higher sea-level than at present, probably by around 1 to 1½ metres, bringing

Fig. 1.3: In red, the suggested Middle Anglo-Saxon coastline of west Norfolk, based on the present-day 5m OS contour line.

the sea much further inland (Davies 1996, 21). It would have been higher still by the Middle Anglo-Saxon period (Fig. 1.3), when it would have been in the region of four to five metres above today's level (Dark and Dark 1998, 22).

It is also significant that two of the few great Iron Age defended enclosures of Norfolk are positioned close to the crossings of the Thet and the Nar at the likely westernmost crossings of these rivers by the Icknield Way. As the rivers run towards The Wash they widen, and the valleys would have been marshy, making passage difficult. West of Narborough, for instance, the valley of the Nar reaches around two miles in width (Dymond 1990, 30).

The Icknield Way, then, is linked by the major crossing at Thetford, or 'the People's Ford', to Narford, 'the Ford at the Narrow Place', and in both cases the settlements give their name to the local river, technically called 'back-formations' in place-name study (Mills 2003, 456; Rye 1991, 37). Near the northern end of this routeway lies Sedgeford.

The arrival of the Roman military road now known as Peddars Way in the post-Boudican period introduced an altogether different form of land route, with its wide metalled construction. This road still leaves an obvious presence in many places in the modern landscape, amongst other things providing a boundary for several of west Norfolk's parishes.

Its longevity testifies to its presence and use in the post-Roman landscape, its name likely to be derived from a Middle English form meaning 'footpath' (Robinson 2012). There certainly appears to have been some form of trading activity still taking place along Peddars Way in the Medieval period in Sedgeford.

The road between Sedgeford and Docking originally took a different route from its modern one, climbing straight up the hill at Cole Green to head east, rather than taking the easier route up the dry valley to its north (Plate 1.3). Today there are still a few cottages forming the settlement called Littleport (Plate 1.4), or 'small market', at the junction of this route with Peddars Way (Mills 2003, 302).

Passing through Fring and the eastern edge of Sedgeford parish, once

Plate 1.3: The old road to Docking, now a metalled farm-track.

military control was firmly established, the Peddars Way would have provided a great improvement in land travel, though probably still not as easy as that by water. Peddars Way crosses the modern Norfolk/Suffolk county border at Bildeston and takes a more or less parallel course to the Icknield Way, heading for Holme-next-the-Sea and a putative ferry-port for the crossing over The Wash – though physical evidence appears to terminate on the northern edge of the village of Ringstead (Davies 2009, 155).

At Fring, however, there are strong indications of a branch road leaving Peddars Way, heading north-east in the direction of the Roman 'Saxon Shore' Fort of *Branodunum* (modern Brancaster). This would have linked the farms and villas of the Sedgeford/Fring area with *Branodunum*, and might imply that they were acting as producer sites for the Late Roman military.

The disintegration of the Late Roman economy and the confusion of the *Adventus* ('Arrival') period saw a shift in settlement pattern and agricultural strategies. But the location of Early Anglo-Saxon settlements remains elusive, and when Sedgeford's past again becomes visible through the evidence of modern excavation we are looking at a *de novo* Middle Anglo-Saxon site on the south bank of the river in the centre of the parish.

And in the case of Sedgeford, if there is a 'Middle Anglo-Saxon shuffle' (as Early Anglo-Saxon settlements relocate and agglomerate), there is also a 'Late Anglo-Saxon shift', for we find the present-day settlement on the opposite, north, bank of the river.

Naming Sedgeford

The earliest reference to the Sedgeford name is in *Domesday Book*, where the two references to the settlement come with the alternate spellings *Secesforda* and *Sexforda* (Brown 1984, 10, 20, 66, 88). The topographical element 'ford' is readily understandable for speakers of modern English. The first element of the place-name in its modern form has, however, caused some confusion.

Rye has it as being from Old English (OE) *secg* ('sedge'), and thus 'the ford where sedges grow' (1991, 17). Given a marshy valley bottom and the Medieval reed-beds, this seems a convincing explanation. However, modern place-name scholarship has the origins of the first element in a suggested Anglo-Saxon personal name *Secci* (Mills 2003, 412; Gelling and Cole 2003, 74).

Since the work of Margaret Gelling (1993), and in her later collaboration with Ann Cole (2003), it has become clear that topographic elements can form the earliest of place-names, and 'ford' is well represented in this small pre-AD 740 group (Cox 1976). This may imply that 'Sedgeford' is an early formation, especially in view of the fact that the ford in question – a crossing-point for the Icknield Way – is of more than local importance (Gelling 1978, 184-188; Gelling and Cole 2003, 71).

Three possibilities arise. There is a chance that the place-name dates from the 7th, 6th, or even 5th century AD, *Secci* perhaps being the name of an Early Anglo-Saxon pioneer-settler. Two considerations support this: the fact that the personal name *Secci* (if that is what it is) does not occur in later historical documents implies that it is early; and the 'ford' element in relation to a major crossing-point may imply the same.

On the other hand, local place-names are often lost during later landscape reorganisation. 'Secci's Ford' may, of course, have gained wider currency, but if not, then there are two other occasions when the name may have arisen. The Middle Anglo-Saxon settlement on Boneyard-Reeddam ('South Sedgeford') can be dated from *c.* AD 650/725 and appears to represent wholesale change, maybe related in some way to the division of the land into great estates, the rise of the Church, and the creation of the Kingdom of East Anglia. Perhaps it was only now that a name stuck for an increasingly important ford associated with a local lord called *Secci*.

Alternatively, the manorialisation of the landscape somewhat later, perhaps in the 10th century (and presumably following our Late Anglo-Saxon shift to 'North Sedgeford') provides another occasion when the landscape may have been renamed.

Naming Eaton

A more obviously informative place-name belongs to the subsidiary settlement of Eaton, sited along the river valley on the border with the parish of Heacham to the west, and likely at one point to have belonged to the adjoining parish (Janet Hammond, pers. comm.).

Eaton is made up of the topographical element *ea*, meaning 'water' but used in Old English as the standard word for a major river, and the habitative element *tun*, meaning 'farmstead', 'village', or 'manor' (Gelling and Cole 2003, 14). So we have 'river settlement' or 'place by the river'. Gelling and Cole suggest that *ea-tun* is functional rather than locational in meaning, adding that 'these places probably performed a special function in relation to the river, such as providing a ferry service or keeping a limited stretch of water open for the carriage of goods'.

They also aver that many *ea-tuns* are near important multiple or composite estates. Ann Cole stresses this functionality when she writes of the *tun's*

Fig. 1.4: Map showing the distribution of *eā-tūn* place-names in England and Wales (after Gelling and Cole 2003).

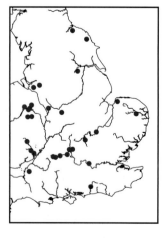

Plate 1.5: The causeway or dam across the valley at Sedgeford can clearly be seen to the right in this early photograph of the village.

responsibility for maintaining a river navigable up to its intersection with an important road (2011, 63).

It is possible that the people of Eaton provided a ferry service. But with a ford nearby in earlier periods and a route across the causeway/dam available to Late Anglo-Saxon travellers, this seems unlikely (PLate 1.6). It is more probable that Eaton acted as a transhipment and/or collection point for goods travelling to and from likely port facilities at Heacham. This would suggest a large estate in the near vicinity.

Eaton certainly maintained a distinct identity at least until the Sedgeford estate map of 1631 (Plate 1.6) was created, as the land-holding patterns depicted are quite different from those of the rest of the parish, forming a cluster of small parcels of land, in contrast to the much larger fields found elsewhere (Janet Hammond, pers. comm.). A track and plank bridge are still present today, a relic of this hamlet's access to the Church via its south porch; most parishioners entered by the north porch.

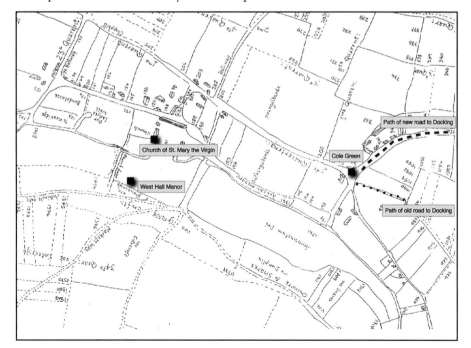

Plate 1.6: The 1631 Estate Map of Sedgeford.

Today all that is left of Eaton is the farmstead that carries its name. This deserted medieval settlement – reduced to mere humps and bumps in a field of grazing – stands testimony to the continual process of change in Sedgeford's rural landscape.

The main contributors to the writing of this chapter were:

Keith Robinson (principal author) with Dominic Andrews

References

Funnell, B., 1993, 'Solid geology', in P. Wade-Martins (ed.), *An Historical Atlas of Norfolk*, 1st edition, Norwich, Norfolk Museums Service, 12-13.

Brown, P. (ed.), 1984, *Domesday Book: Norfolk*, (2 volumes), Chichester, Phillimore.

Chatwin, C. P., 1961, *British Regional Geology: East Anglia and Adjoining Areas, London*, Institute of Geological Sciences, H.M.S.O.

Cole, A., 2011, 'Place-names as travellers' landmarks', in N. J. Higham and M. J. Ryan (eds.), *Place-names, Language and the Anglo-Saxon Landscape*, Woodbridge, Boydell, 51-68.

Cox, B., 1976, 'The place-names of the earliest English records', *English Place-Name Society Journal*, 8, 12-66.

Darby, H. C., 1952, *The Domesday Geography of Eastern England*, Cambridge, Cambridge University Press.

Dark, K. and Dark, P., 1998, *The Landscape of Roman Britain*, Stroud, Stroud Publishing.

Davies, J., 1996, 'The Iron Age and Roman Periods', in S. Margeson, B. Ayers and S. Heywood (eds.), *A Festival of Norfolk Archaeology*, Norwich, Norfolk and Norwich Archaeological Society.

Davies, J., 2009, *The Land of Boudica: Prehistoric and Roman Norfolk*, Oxford, Heritage/Norfolk Museums and Archaeological Service.

Dymond, D., 1990, *The Norfolk Landscape*, Bury St Edmunds, The Alastair Press.

Gelling, M., 1978, *Signposts to the Past: place-names and the history of England*, London, Dent.

Gelling, M., 1993, *Place-Names in the Landscape*, London, Dent.

Gelling, M. and Cole, A., 2003, *The Landscape of Place-Names*, Donington, Shaun Tyas.

Gregory, T., 1982, 'Romano-British Settlement in West Norfolk and on the Norfolk Fen Edge', in D. Miles (ed), *The Roman-British Countryside: studies in rural settlement and economy*, B.A.R. No. 103, Part II, Oxford, British Archaeological Reports, 351-376.

Harrison, S., 2003, 'The Icknield Way: some queries', in *The Archaeological Journal*, 160, 1-22.

Mills, A. D., 2003, *Oxford Dictionary of British Place-Names*, Oxford, Oxford University Press.

Robinson, B. 2012, *Peddars Way and Norfolk Coast Path*, London, Aurum Press Ltd.

Rye, J. 1991, *A Popular Guide to Norfolk Place-Names*, Dereham, The Larks Press.

Williamson, T., 1993, *The Origins of Norfolk*, Manchester, Manchester University Press.

Young, A., 1969, *General View of the Agriculture of the County of Norfolk*, New York, Augustus M Kelley, (1st edition, 1804, Board of Agriculture, London).

2. From Remote Prehistory to an Icenian Tribal Centre

Our knowledge of Sedgeford before *c.* 50 BC is still scanty. Quantities of worked flint recovered during field survey and excavation have confirmed the occasional presence of small, mobile, hunter-gatherer groups in the Mesolithic period (Box 2.1). Other types of worked flint attest later Neolithic activity and a number of round barrows, most of them ploughed-out, mark the burials of Bronze Age people (Figs. 2.1 and 2.2). One such burial was discovered by SHARP

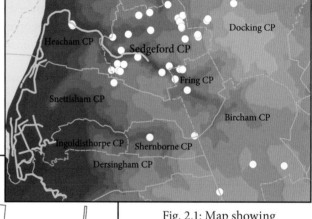

Fig. 2.1: Map showing known Late Neolithic and Bronze Age barrows and burials in Sedgeford and adjoining parishes.

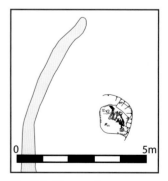

Fig. 2.2: Plan and extract (above) showing Late Neolithic/Early Bronze Age features on Boneyard-Reeddam/Lower Chalkpit site.

Box 2.1
Stone Age 'consumables'

Flint is a vital source of information for archaeologists. Not only was it an exceptional material which could be worked into a range of tools, but it survives in almost all conditions as a representation of the way people inhabited and used the changing landscape. For the periods before the introduction of pottery and metals, often the only remains to survive are flint tools and the waste material or debitage from making them.

At least 583 pieces of worked flint have been recovered from the Boneyard-Reeddam site during excavations in the 1950s and between 1996 and 2007, as well as a quantity of burnt or fire-damaged flint. Several hundred more worked flints were recovered in fieldwalking surveys.

None were recovered from sealed prehistoric contexts. Human intervention, including the digging of Anglo-Saxon burials and more recent ploughing, coupled with hill-wash bringing material from further up the slope into the valley bottom, have disturbed its distribution hugely. Nevertheless, analysis of this assemblage can tell us something about where people were collecting their raw material from, the problems they faced while working with it, and the types of implements they were making and using.

Low-grade raw material

Much of the excavated assemblage is buff flint, translucent in the thinner flakes and blades, and where present the outer 'skin' or 'cortex' is a thin chalk type. The raw material is typical of many assemblages from Norfolk, in that it has been obtained 'casually' from the surface of disturbed ground. With much of the local upper geology consisting of chalk gravels, flint would have been available in abundance and people are unlikely to have ventured more than a few hundred metres to collect it.

There is no conclusive evidence from Boneyard-Reeddam for high-quality flint of the glossy dark grey or black variety mined at sites such as Grimes Graves in the Late Neolithic period. Its use cannot be ruled out entirely, however, as it has now been observed within the assemblage from the post-2007 Lower Chalkpit excavations.

Though some of the buff flint is of reasonably good quality, much of it contains coarse inclusions, some of them quite large. These interrupt the flow when the material is being struck during knapping and often result in premature 'hinge' termination. The incidence of this problem is high.

These inclusions would, then, have made the material less predictable and more frustrating to shape. Even if the implement survived the knapping process, inclusions would have created natural weaknesses and in some instances, such as that of an Early Neolithic axe found in a hedgerow in 1999, may have caused the tools to break.

Tools and technology

Of the excavated assemblage, around 6% were finished tools, a further 5% were utilised flakes which had been employed in a task but show no more than minor evidence of further modification or 'retouching', and the remainder were unmodified flakes and cores. In the latter category are blades (defined as having a length at least twice their width and with a width greater than 12mm), bladelets (like blades but with a width of less than 12mm) and chips or spalls (small flakes with a longest dimension of less than 15mm).

A range of debitage types and implement forms are present. Given the relatively low percentage (9%) of preparation flakes (defined as having 60% or more cortex on their surfaces), many of which are small anyway, it is probable that nodules were brought onto site in a partially prepared or tested state, even though they are unlikely to have been carried over great distances. Chips or spalls make up 5% of the total;

a reasonably high figure that must in part reflect the extent of sieving during SHARP excavations. Their presence is important, insomuch as it indicates at least some in situ knapping on or around the excavated sites (Newcomer and Karlin 1987).

The majority of flakes, often long in form, are hard-hammer struck using a rounded quartzite or flint pebble. There is a notable presence of bladelets, and in these cases the use of bone or antler soft-hammers can be assumed. This is indicated by a smaller and more diffuse bulb of percussion, the characteristic 'swelling' below the point at which a human-struck flake received the impact of the hammer. Bladelets and long blade-like flakes are typical of Late Mesolithic and Early Neolithic industries.

The assemblage contains a significant number of utilised flakes. These represent a class of expedient, simple, quick to make, quick to discard tools such as might be expected when low-grade raw material was available in abundance. Again, a Late Mesolithic/Early Neolithic date is implied.

Late Mesolithic and Early Neolithic hunters c. 6,000-3,000 BC

Some of the most distinctive implements, primarily from the lower levels of the excavations, are microliths (Plate 2.1). Microliths, literally meaning 'small flints', were multi-functional and various uses have been proposed, including as reapers/sickles, harpoons, drill bits and simple cutting tools (Clark 1976; Healy *et al* 1992). Sometimes they were used on wooden shafts as arrow tips or barbs.

While microliths were produced throughout the Mesolithic and broadly define the flintworking technology of the period, their variety of forms allows them to be used for somewhat more refined dating.

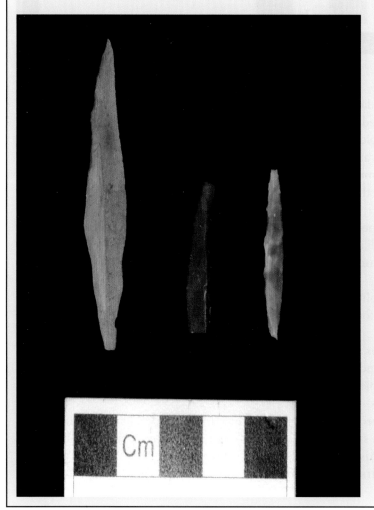

Plate 2.1: Mesolithic microliths from Boneyard-Reeddam.

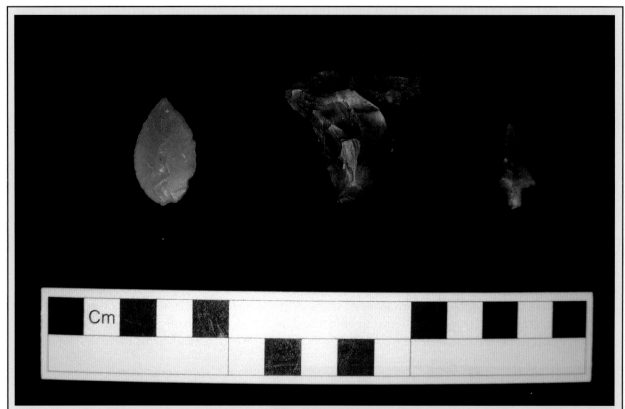

Plate 2.2: Flint arrowheads
from Boneyard-Reeddam.

The style of those found in Boneyard-Reeddam are of later Mesolithic date (Peter Robins, pers. comm.).

Prehistoric tool technology was modified in line with variations in the landscape and changes in the environment. Mesolithic people, for example, invented and used hafted flint axes and adzes. An example of an adze was recovered during the excavations. Axes were used primarily for felling trees, which had colonised the landscape as the climate warmed after the last Ice Age, whereas adzes, with the blade hafted horizontally rather than vertically, were better adapted for shaping timbers, including making log boats or dugout canoes (Butler 2005, 100).

Tools which have been skilfully sharpened by a transverse blow across the cutting edge are known as 'tranchet adzes', 'tranchet' meaning 'slice'. Flakes from this process are present in the Boneyard-Reeddam assemblage. Tranchet adzes are not uncommon finds in Norfolk, with a large number recovered from a site at Banham (Lawson 1978).

Hafted flint axes peaked during the Neolithic period with the need for greater tree clearance as people started to settle and farm the land. Axes found by SHARP are likely to represent the very start of the Neolithic period.

Arrowheads of different forms and dates are also present. The earliest is a leaf-shaped example. There are also two Neolithic chisel arrowheads and three Early Bronze Age barbed and tanged ones, including one very small but exquisitely made example. These would have been finished by pressure flaking with a bone or antler tine to remove minute flakes.

The flint assemblage from Boneyard-Reeddam is primarily of Late Mesolithic to Early Neolithic date. It allows us to populate the landscape with small groups of Late Mesolithic hunter-gatherers and implies one or more temporary hunting camps of this period. It also implies the presence, from the Early Neolithic into the Early Bronze Age, of some of the first people to clear and cultivate the land and begin to settle in more permanent communities.

Box 2.2 A Late Neolithic/Early Bronze Age crouched burial *c. 2458–2200 cal BC*

The burial

Skeleton S8001 was discovered in 2009 in Chalkpit Field, under an east-west Iron Age ditch, buried in a crouched position. It lay on its left side, orientated south-east to north-west, with the head to the south-east (Fig. 2.3 and Plate 2.3). Radiocarbon dating of the skeleton gives a date of death of 2458-2200 cal BC, i.e. in the Late Neolithic/Early Bronze Age.

Although the skeleton itself was lifted in 2009, it was not possible to excavate the whole of the grave until 2010. When fully excavated, the grave cut was roughly 1m square with rounded corners. On its northern side another cut feature, about 0.7m long by 0.25m wide, intersected the grave. Nothing was found in this feature and its purpose is unknown. One possibility is that it was a platform used during interment; another is that it contained some sort of grave marker.

The east-west ditch that cut across the grave was itself intersected by other north-south and north-east to south-west trending ditches just west of the grave. Displaced human remains were found in 2010. The five bones recovered were all missing from S8001 and were of the right size to have come from that skeleton. Moreover, the skull fragment found in 2010 fitted perfectly with the part excavated in 2009, thus proving that these remains were unquestionably part of S8001.

Clearly, when the intercutting ditch had been dug, it had come so close to the skeleton that it had skimmed off some bones from its right side. These had been carried a metre or two further west, where they remained in the bottom

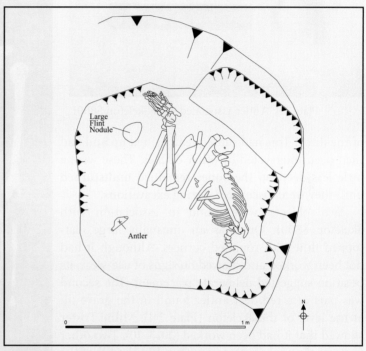
Fig. 2.3: Plan of Skeleton S8001.

Plate 2.3: The Late Neolithic/Early Bronze Age crouched burial on Lower Chalkpit during excavation.

Plate 2.4: Antler associated with Skeleton S8001.

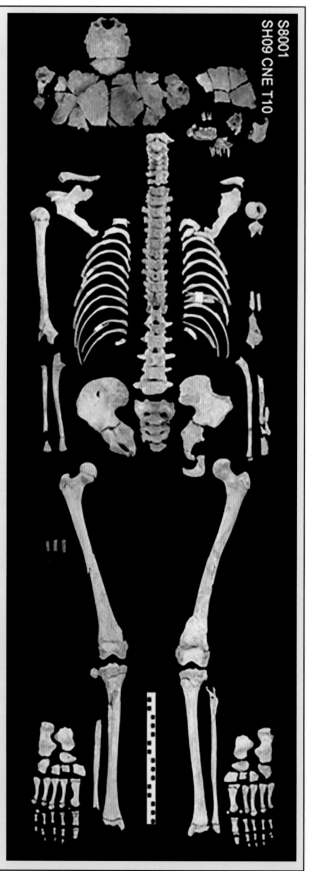

of the ditch. This had subsequently silted up and had then been intersected by other ditches. These were a little less deep, so the bones remained undisturbed until they were discovered during excavations.

Two 'objects' were found in association with Skeleton S8001. One was an unusually large, flat-topped flint with rounded corners. Although it had not been worked and showed no signs of use-wear, its position suggested deliberate placement. The second was part of a red deer antler found in the grave-fill at the level of the skeleton (Plate 2.4). Millie Foster showed that it had been worked (2013, 10). Two other parts of the same antler were found in the fill of the adjacent north-south ditch. It seems likely that they were moved in the same way as the skeleton fragments.

The skeleton

Most of Skeleton S8001 is present but the bone is generally in poor condition (Plate 2.5). The skull is very fragmentary, with most of the facial bones absent; this damage was likely caused by the cutting of the later ditch. This ditch digging could also explain the absence of most hand bones. There is surface damage and erosion of all bones, due to soil acidity.

Age at death was estimated for S8001 based on both dental and skeletal development. The wisdom teeth present are nearly fully exposed, with minimal wear on the other molar teeth, and only small amounts of plaque. Overall the teeth indicate that S8001 was about 20-21 years old when he or she died

Plate 2.5: Skeleton S8001.

(Hillson 1997, 118-147, 240-241, 259). Skeletally it is clear that S8001 was not a fully developed adult. Most of the growth plates of bones that fuse at different points in adolescence remain unfused. Overall, skeletal development indicates an age of around 15-17 years at most, depending on sex (Scheuer and Black 2000). This is younger than the age suggested by the dentition. The dental age is probably nearer the true age at death, the growth-plate fusion having been delayed by stress caused by childhood diseases or severe malnutrition, as discussed below. As a 'sub-adult', it was not possible to determine the sex or height of this skeleton.

The difference between dental and skeletal ages is most likely to be the result of disease delaying the fusion of the growth plates. During childhood, the reaction of a body subjected to major stress by, for example, periods of severe malnutrition or recurrent or extended illness, will be to defer skeletal and other development. Periods of interrupted development may sometimes be seen in the teeth as lines of enamel hypoplasia (underdevelopment) or in the bones as Harris lines. In S8001 there is possible linear enamel hypoplasia on two teeth, and radiographs of the femurs show evidence of Harris lines (Plate 2.6).

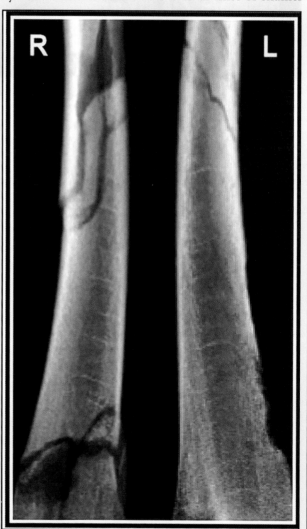

The amounts of carbon-13 and nitrogen-15 isotopes in bone provide information on a skeleton's diet. The results for S8001 match those generally found in the British Isles in this period and suggest a mixed diet consisting of both plant and animal food sources, with some protein of marine origin but most from land animals, despite Sedgeford's proximity to the coast. There is no evidence for malnutrition.

There are indications that he or she may have suffered severe illness during childhood. The right auditory meatus (ear canal) is D-shaped rather than the usual round shape, and the right mastoid process (bony prominence behind the ear) is completely eroded away (Plate 2.7). Whilst this could be the result of just in-the-ground erosion, in our opinion a more likely explanation is that this person suffered otitis media, an infection of the middle ear. If untreated, as it would have been in a pre-antibiotic era, it can become chronic or recurrent. The bacteria can enter the mastoid and cause an abscess, as seen here, and from there enter the blood causing septicaemia, or the brain causing meningitis, either of which could be life threatening (Aufderheide and Rodríguez-Martín 1998, 253).

Other pathologies present include a swelling of the outer side of the right fibula (small lower leg bone); this might be the site of a well-healed break. Both the left and right femurs (upper leg bones) show signs of inward rotation towards the middle, which would have caused a 'knock-kneed' stance.

Plate 2.6: Radiographs of Harris lines on femurs of Skeleton S8001, which could imply underdevelopment of the relatively young skeleton due to recurrent episodes of malnutrition or illness.

Squatting facets are present on the distal (ankle) ends of both tibiae (large lower leg bones); these are the result of spending a significant amount of time in a squatting position (Mays 1998, 118).

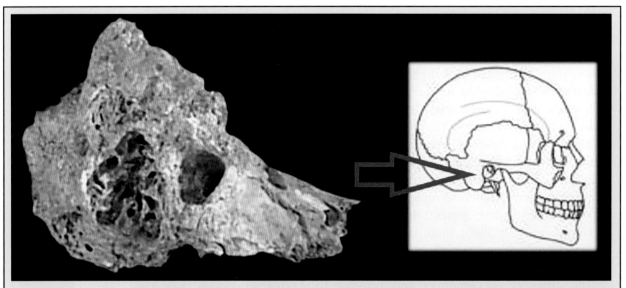

Plate 2.7: Right mastoid process and external auditory meatus (ear bone) of Skeleton S8001

The sacrum at the base of the spine is normally fused to enclose the spinal canal. In this skeleton, the sacrum was unfused (Plate 2.8). In a fully developed adult this would be evidence of spina bifida occulta. In life, some believe this to be 'clinically insignificant' (Waldron, 2009, 219). In the case of S8001 it may be just another example of the general incompleteness of development.

Plate 2.8: Unfused sacrum of Skeleton S8001.

Conclusions

Skeleton S8001 is that of a young person who lived in the Late Neolithic/Early Bronze Age. The person was about 20 years old when she or he died, and had a typical diet for the period. The most probable reason for S8001's delayed skeletal development was stress due to recurrent bouts of otitis media. This disease may even have been the cause of death.

Within SHARP's study area on Lower Chalkpit, one other crouched burial has been excavated (Box 2.3). In addition, four disarticulated human bones have been found, suggesting there were other burials in the vicinity, either lost to later disturbance or still awaiting discovery.

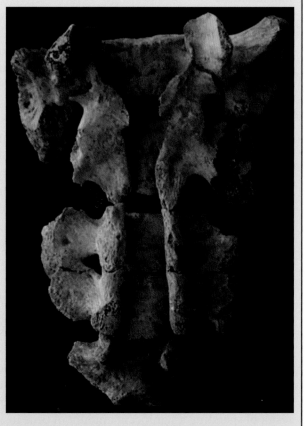

in 2009: a crouched burial of a young person, radiocarbon dated to 2458-2200 BC (Box 2.2).

At present we know almost nothing of the settlement and land-use represented by this evidence. Probably, the pattern was similar to that across Norfolk generally, with a slow growth in the number of settlements and the amount of land cleared for farming, a steady rise in population and most people working the fields but perhaps also engaged in seasonal activities that sometimes took them away from their home villages (Wymer 1994; Davies 2009 49-84).

The productivity of these communities was low: bronze was used to make weapons and ornaments, but the tools of labour were of stone, bone and wood. The Bronze Age elite of warlords and priests is represented by metalwork hoards, the long-distance movement of prestige goods, ceremonial henges and, increasingly, hillforts designed to control blocks of territory (Lawson and Wymer 1994; Davies 2009, 59-84). The gap between them and the mass of the working population was probably wide.

From the beginning of the Iron Age, in *c.* 700 BC, the pace of land clearance intensified and the countryside filled up more rapidly with farming settlements (Davies 2009, 85-92). The population was rising and putting increasing pressure on available resources. This might have produced political conflict rather than economic expansion without the technological revolution represented by the introduction of iron-working.

Iron is more demanding to work than copper (the main constituent of bronze), but ores are more plentiful and therefore cheaper and the resulting metal, especially when mixed with carbon to make a primitive form of steel, can be used to fashion axes, spades and ploughshares of exceptional hardness. Iron technology drove an agricultural revolution. 'Aristocratic' bronze had empowered a social elite. 'Democratic' iron equipped prehistoric farmers to turn forests and marshes into fields and pastures (Childe 1942, 182-183).

Even so, in our current state of knowledge, we cannot date any known settlements in Sedgeford before the Late Iron Age (100 BC-AD 60), though it is quite possible that some of those identified in field survey have their origins earlier in time, and we do have a firm Middle Iron Age radiocarbon date for the lone (and unusual) crouched burial excavated on Lower Chalkpit (Box 2.3).

Plate 2.9: General view of the Upper Chalkpit excavation in 2006. The possible Iron Age (Phase 2) round-house can be seen part-excavated in the lower right-hand corner.

Box 2.3 A Middle Iron Age crouched burial
c. 373–203 cal BC

The burial

Excavations in Chalkpit Field in 2010 revealed the grave of Skeleton S8002. The grave was 1m in diameter, almost circular, and about 0.4m deep. It had near-vertical sides and a concave base, and was cut into the natural with no disturbance from later features. The skeleton was in a very tightly crouched, prone position, oriented north-west to south-east with the head to the north-west. The head was face down, the knees curled underneath in a kneeling position and the arms folded tight to the chest, hands under the head. There were two flints, one each side of the head, which seemed to have been selected and placed to support it (Fig. 2.4 and Plate 2.10).

Near the top of the fill was a cow scapula. It had been butchered and showed no evidence of use as a tool. In the bottom of the grave was a large, flat-topped, flint nodule. Although there was no evidence of it having been worked, it was almost certainly deliberately positioned. Also recovered from the grave fill were six bead-like objects (Plate 2.12). Expert opinion from Alison Sheridan (National Museum of Scotland) was that one was a man-made

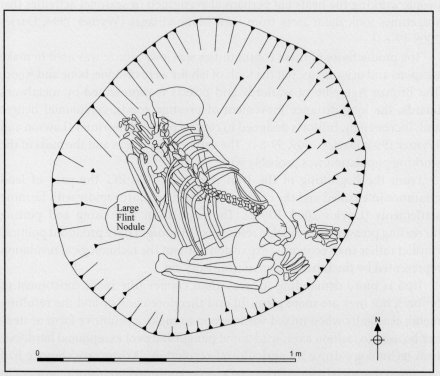

Large Flint Nodule

Fig. 2.4: Plan of Skeleton S8002.

Plate 2.10: The Middle Iron Age crouched burial on Lower Chalkpit during excavation.

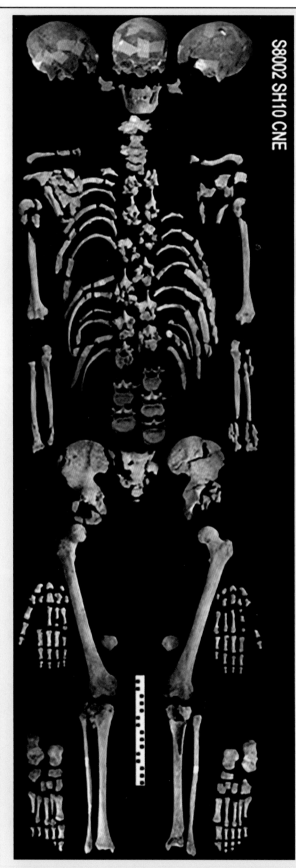

S8002 SH10 CNE

Plate 2.11: Skeleton S8002.

amber bead, another was of baked clay and the others were crinoid stems (i.e. fossils).

Nine pottery sherds were also found in the fill. One very small Anglo-Saxon sherd was found near the top of the fill and was almost certainly intrusive. The other eight were Iron Age, one of which was deep within the grave. Two sherds are well fired and came from the base of a food vessel, together weighing 24g.

Consistent with this pottery dating, a radiocarbon sample gave a date of death for S8002 of 373–203 cal BC, i.e. firmly within the Middle Iron Age.

The skeleton

The skeleton was almost entirely complete. Some bones were very fragmentary, with surface erosive changes. There is widespread prominence of muscle attachments, suggesting a physically demanding way of life.

All teeth recovered show severe wear. There is plaque on several molars, and caries in the molars and premolars on both sides. On the right, the caries form a deep, square hole between two molars on the mandible. On the left, the mandibular (lower jaw) molars were lost several years before death, with additional long-term tooth loss elsewhere. Two teeth in the maxilla (upper jaw) are broken at the level of their roots. The loss of so many teeth has led to uneven wear.

A distinct, straight groove is evident on the surfaces of the right lower molars and premolar and the upper right canine and incisor. This might have been caused by habitually pulling a thread through the teeth. The cumulative damage to the teeth could be a result of habitual use of the right-sided teeth as a third hand. The right humerus is thicker than the left and the muscle attachments are more prominent on the right side, suggesting right-handedness. This supports the postulated asymmetrical use of the mouth.

Skeleton S8002 has an estimated age at death of 45-54+ years, categorised as 'Old Adult', based on tooth wear (Brothwell 1981, 72) and changes to the pelvis (Lovejoy *et al.* 1985). S8002 was classified as a female based on the morphology of the skull and pelvis (Buikstra and Ubelaker 1994, 16-21).

She had an estimated height of 169cm, from measurements of the long bones (Trotter and Gleser

Plate 2.12: Bead-like objects from the grave of Skeleton S8002. Only the top two, one of amber (right), the other of baked clay, are in fact beads.

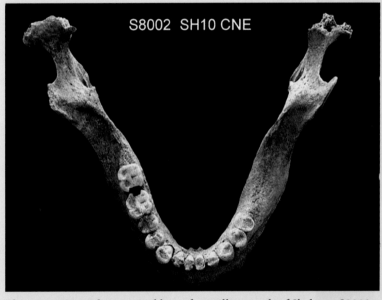

Plate 2.13: Wear, damage and loss of maxillary teeth of Skeleton S8002.

1952, 498; Brothwell 1981, 101). Average stature in Britain in the Iron Age was 162cm for females (Roberts and Cox 2003, 106). Therefore, S8002 was substantially taller than her contemporaries. Based on thickness of the shaft of the femur, her weight was estimated at 83.8kg (Ruff *et al*, 1991). This gives a Body Mass Index (BMI) of 29.3, which is overweight on current World Health Organisation recommendations.

Osteoarthritis is visible in a number of joints, including the vertebrae and hip. The distal joint of the left big toe shows an erosive form of the disease. Osteoarthritis is often related to age and a physical lifestyle, which this person seemed to have.

At the wrist, the changes could be described as osteoarthritis, but is more precisely described as the result of ulnocarpal abutment, also known as ulnar impaction syndrome (Crema *et al.* 2009). This chronic degenerative condition results from repetitive stress from impaction of the carpal bones (hand) upon the distal (wrist) end of the ulna (small lower arm bone).

There are squatting facets on the distal (ankle) ends of both tibiae (large lower leg bones) and corresponding changes at the hip joint consistent with S8002 spending a significant amount of time in a squatting position.

The amounts of carbon-13 and nitrogen-15 isotopes in bone provide information on a skeleton's diet. The results for S8002 are within the range of results from other Iron Age sites in Britain. The levels indicate a good mixed diet of both plant and animal produce, with some animal protein from marine sources, although less than might be expected considering Sedgeford's proximity to the coast.

Conclusions

Skeleton S8002 is the skeleton of an approximately 50-year-old woman who lived a hard, physical life in the Iron Age. She was approximately 169cm tall, with a robust frame. She has evidence of osteoarthritis and recurrent stresses at the wrist and changes consistent with a life spent in a squatting position. Her diet was typical for the period. Cause of death is unknown, but she reached a good age before her life ended.

A Late Iron Age farmstead
Upper Chalkpit, Phases 1 and 2
c. ?50 BC–?AD 60/61

In the summer of 2006, a team of SHARP archaeologists carried out the second of two excavations on an Iron Age and Roman site identified through a combination of fieldwalking, metal-detecting and geophysical survey. It lies at the junction of four fields on the chalk downland south of the village of Sedgeford. The excavation strategy was to sample the remains in two opposing quadrants, the north-west corner of Polar Breck Field (in 2005) and the south-west corner of Chalkpit Field (in 2006).

Fig. 2.5: Plan showing earlier Iron Age (Phase 1) features on Upper Chalkpit.

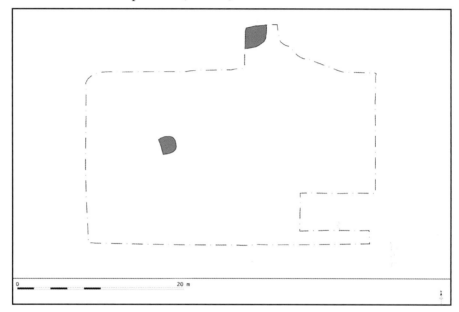

Fig. 2.6: Plan showing later Iron Age (Phase 2) features on Upper Chalkpit.

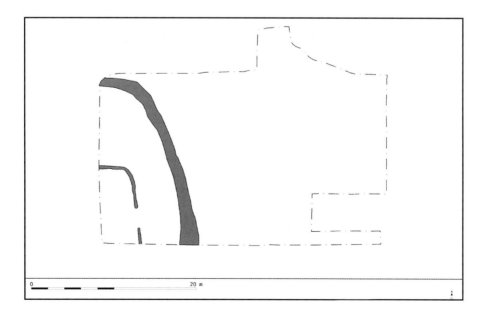

Apart from a small pit of definite Iron Age date, and a medium-sized pit of possible Iron Age date (Phase 1, Fig. 2.5), the earliest features on the site were two curving ditches (Phase 2, Fig. 2.56) on the western side of the excavation in Chalkpit Field. The larger of the two appears to have been an outer enclosure ditch, the smaller perhaps the foundation trench for a fence or even the ring-ditch/drip-gully of a structure within the enclosure. The enclosure ditch, shallow and round-bottomed, had been re-cut at least once. The inner gully was broken by a 1.5m gap, presumably an entrance-way.

It seems likely that these two features, dated by Iron Age pottery in the fills, represent the original native farmstead on the site. It was succeeded by a Romano-British farmstead, though the main evidence for this was located about 120m to the south-east, and it had a radically new layout (Phase 3), with pottery evidence pointing to a late 1st century AD start-date. What happened between Phases 2 and 3?

Some of us believe that a period of abandonment separated the Late Iron Age from the Early Romano-British farmstead. This seems implicit in the sideways shuffle, the new layout and the sharp contrast between the respective ceramic assemblages. We suspect a case of interruption rather than smooth evolution. And we can suggest an occasion and a cause.

In AD 43-84, Britain was conquered by an aggressive and ruthless imperial power. In the years around AD 60/61, a series of dramatic events centred on the Norfolk-based Iceni tribe - the Boudican Revolt - are reported by Roman historians Tacitus (*Annals*, XIV, 31; Agricola, 19) and Dio Cassius (*Roman History*, LXII, 1-2). Roman officials attempted to seize the estates of the Icenian nobility. The Iceni rose in revolt and were defeated, and both nobility and peasantry suffered heavy losses in battle and its aftermath.

Because of this, farms went untended, the harvest was not gathered and seed-corn for the following years was lacking: the result for many was starvation. At the same time, the Roman Army unleashed a storm of 'fire and sword' on rebel territory and many were killed or enslaved. This combination of battle casualties, famine and ethnic-cleansing must have left the landscape depopulated, with farms abandoned and fields overgrown. Perhaps the Late Iron Age farmstead at Sedgeford was deserted in this period.

Other explanations are possible. New homes have to be built beside old ones while the latter are still standing, otherwise the residents have nowhere to live in the interim. Rural settlements therefore have a tendency to 'drift'. And building a new home might be the occasion for a wider reorganisation of the settlement, its boundaries and its internal layout.

This seems unlikely in this case. Continuity of activity should be reflected in the finds assemblages, with, in particular, earlier pottery types present in quantity in features of the later phase. In this case, the respective 'ceramic signatures' seem quite distinct: Phase 2 looks solidly Late Iron Age, Phase 3 solidly Early Roman.

Another factor makes a break in occupation more likely: the possibility that Sedgeford formed part of an Icenian tribal centre in the Late Iron Age – something which would have made it a particular target for a vengeful Roman Army in the aftermath of the Boudican Revolt.

A Late Iron Age hilltop sanctuary?
Polar Breck
c. ?50 BC–?AD 60/61

The most spectacular evidence for the elevated status of Late Iron Age Sedgeford was the accidental discovery of a broken torc during agricultural work in 1965. Caught up in machinery on the back of a tractor, it was first mistaken for part of an old bedstead. In fact, it was an exceptionally fine piece of Late Iron Age craftwork, its intricately woven gold wires and elaborately decorated terminal forming most of a neck-ring; but it had been twisted out of shape and one of the terminals ripped off and lost.

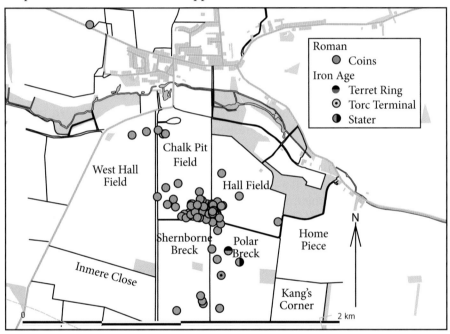

Fig. 2.7: Map showing distribution of Late Iron Age and Roman finds recovered during fieldwalking and metal-detector survey in Polar Breck, Shernborne Breck, Hall Field, Chalkpit Field and Hall Field.

During a routine field survey in Polar Breck in Easter 2004 – a combination of fieldwalking to recover potsherds and metal-detecting to recover metal artefacts – the missing terminal was found by Steve Hammond. This was confirmed by the fact that it was identical to that still attached to the original torc (held by the British Museum) and that, when the two fragments were brought together, they matched perfectly at the break (Box 2.4). Two other high-value objects were also found in the field: a gold stater and a terret ring.

Large scale machine-trenching and several weeks of excavation followed in 2005 (funded by Channel 5 for a TV documentary). These revealed a long, linear, north-south boundary in the form of a palisade trench, at least one very large pit, much evidence for burning in the pit and its vicinity, a large assemblage of Prehistoric pottery, including several examples of what appear to have been ritually deposited vessels, and a considerable quantity of crudely worked flint.

The site, a short distance south of the downland settlement discussed above, lies on the northern edge of a windy hilltop plateau, such that all features were heavily truncated by ploughing, making detailed interpretation difficult. Further work is needed. What does seem likely, however, is that the activity on

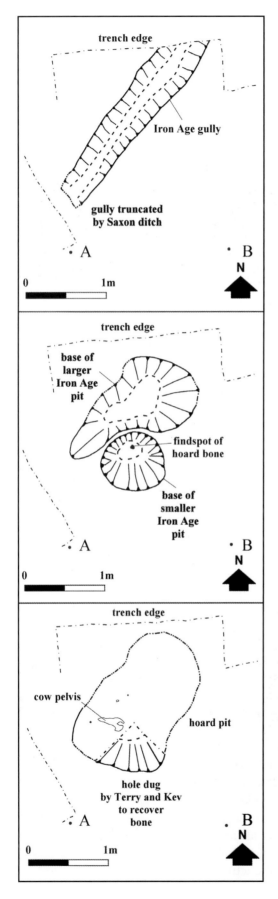

the western edge of Polar Breck forms part of a large sanctuary extending into the next field, Shernborne Breck. The latter has not yet been field-walked, but it has been metal-detected, and this has revealed a spread of Roman coins across the field boundary extending 330m east-west and 780m north-south.

A second concentration of Iron Age material has been identified immediately to the north-west, lower down the slope, extending across West Hall Field into Chalkpit Field. Two sites – numbered 33 and 34 – were recorded within this area during field surveys in the Heacham Valley carried out by local archaeologist C. H. Lewton-Brain in 1953, and comprehensive field-walking and metal-detecting in 2002 has since shown these to form part of a single spread of material extending 750m east-west and 200m north-south.

A third possible Iron Age site, on the lower slope about 1.4 km further west in Stable Breck, first recognised as a crop-mark on RAF air-photos in the 1940s, has recently been accurately plotted and reinterpreted as part of the National Mapping Programme. A complex of at least five or six rectilinear ditched enclosures, one inside another, it resembles a known type of Late Iron Age monument in Norfolk. It is especially like the most comprehensively explored of these, that at Fison Way in Thetford (Dennis and Faulkner 2005, 59-60).

The apparent similarity between the Sedgeford crop-mark monument and the excavated complex at Fison Way is such that the latter merits more detailed comment. It began as a series of separate hilltop enclosures, perhaps as early as the 4th century BC, but it was dramatically redeveloped in the 1st century AD. It then took the form of a huge square enclosure surrounded by double ditches, with a massive roundhouse inside oriented on an entranceway to the east. In its final phase, however, dated to c. AD 40-65, the main enclosure was transformed into an east-west oriented rectangle measuring 220m by 175m and containing five carefully placed structures, the central one huge and perhaps double-storey. As well as having an inner and an outer ditch, the complex was enclosed by up to nine parallel rows of timber palisade, perhaps in imitation of a sacred grove (Gregory 1991).

The Stable Breck crop-mark site in Sedgeford has yet to be explored. It may be something quite different from the multi-ditched Iron Age enclosures known elsewhere; perhaps, indeed, nothing more significant than a Medieval field-system. But it just might fit into our emerging picture of an extensive Late Iron Age ritual landscape.

Fig. 2.8: Depositing gold. Plans showing the successive phases in the development of the Iron Age pit containing the Sedgeford Hoard excavated on Boneyard-Reeddam in 2003: (top) a gully is cut and fills up; (middle) a pit is cut followed by a smaller pit containing the hoard; and (bottom) the pits merge and fill up.

Box 2.4
The Sedgeford Torc

The Sedgeford Torc (Plate 2.14) discovered on Polar Breck in 1965 was distorted and damaged when it became caught up in agricultural machinery. As well as being twisted out of shape, one of its two terminals had been torn off. The recovery of the missing terminal (Plate 2.6) by metal-detectorist Steve Hammond during a SHARP field survey in April 2004, and the subsequent reuniting of the two fragments, was an extraordinary archaeological event.

Plate 2.14: The Sedgeford Torc as found in 1965.

The Sedgeford Torc is one of the finest examples ever unearthed. Like the Snettisham 'Great Torc' from the Ken Hill 'Gold Field', the neck-ring is made from twisted gold-wire 'ropes', while the terminals take the form of hollow gold rings decorated with raised La Tène ('Early Celtic') designs. Each of the eight ropes is made from three threads of twisted wires, all of which have themselves been twisted together. The terminals were made using the 'lost-wax' casting process. The decoration comprises raised trumpet swirls and pellets against a background of 'basket weave'.

The break between neck-ring and terminal allows details of manufacture to be observed. It would seem that the terminals were cast onto the ends of the twisted ropes, these having been heated and partially melted to facilitate attachment. Also visible are metal bars passed through the collars of the terminals, apparently after casting onto the neck-ring, the purpose of which is unknown (J. D. Hill, pers. comm.).

Torcs were potent symbols of rank and wealth in Celtic society. They are sometimes referred to by ancient writers and warriors are often shown wearing them in Graeco-Roman art. Dio Cassius, in a well-known passage, tells us that Boudica always wore a large golden torc (*Roman History*, LXII, 2). The famous Dying Gaul, a masterpiece of Hellenistic art that may have been owned by Julius Caesar himself and is now on display in Rome's Capitoline Museum, depicts a fallen Celtic warrior wearing moustache, spiked-up hair and torc.

That we find such objects deposited in ritual contexts – as offerings, presumably, to Celtic deities – is confirmation of their value and meaning. Equally, where little else is known, the discovery of a torc, especially one as richly worked and decorated as that from Sedgeford, surely marks a place as sacred and special.

Plate 2.15: The missing Sedgeford Torc terminal recovered during fieldwalking and metal-detector survey in 2004.

36

Fig. 2.9: Buried gold.
Hundreds of years after it
was deposited, when the
hoard was long forgotten,
the pit in which it lay
concealed was cut into by
Anglo-Saxon grave-diggers.

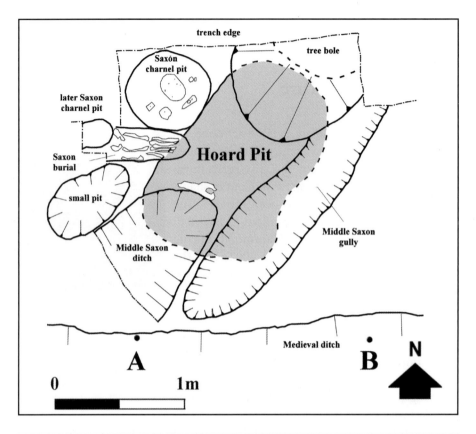

Fig. 2.10: Map showing
known Iron Age activity in
the south-central part of
Sedgeford parish.

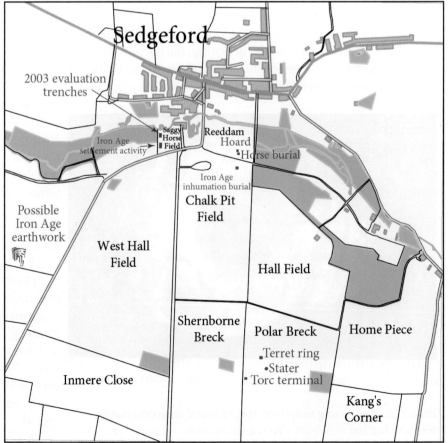

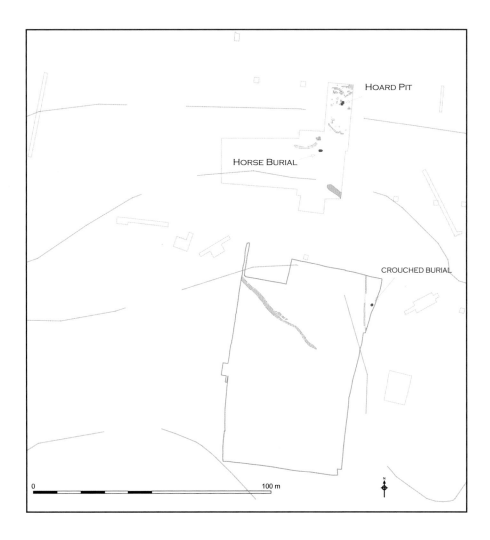

A Late Iron Age river's edge sanctuary
Boneyard-Reeddam
c. ?50 BC–?AD 60/61

The Sedgeford Hoard

Towards the end of the 2003 summer season, SHARP archaeologists Terry Baxter and Kevin Woodward made an astonishing discovery. They were doing a final metal-detector sweep before the Boneyard-Reeddam excavation was shut down and covered over for the winter. This was standard procedure to protect the site against 'nighthawks' (looters with metal-detectors who work at night). A total of eight Iron Age gold staters from a disturbed hoard had been found in previous years, so the precaution was especially necessary in this case.

What now emerged from the muddy ground between Boneyard Field and the Reeddam was the source of the coins: the intact part of the hoard, comprising 20 gold coins inside the broken knee end of a cow's upper right front leg-bone (Plates 2.17-2.19). A further 11 coins were subsequently recovered from surrounding deposits and archaeo-environmental samples, making a total of 39 in all. No doubt the original deposit was larger, with an unknown quantity recovered when

Fig. 2.12: Plan showing Iron Age (Phase 2) features and ritual deposits on Boneyard-Reeddam.

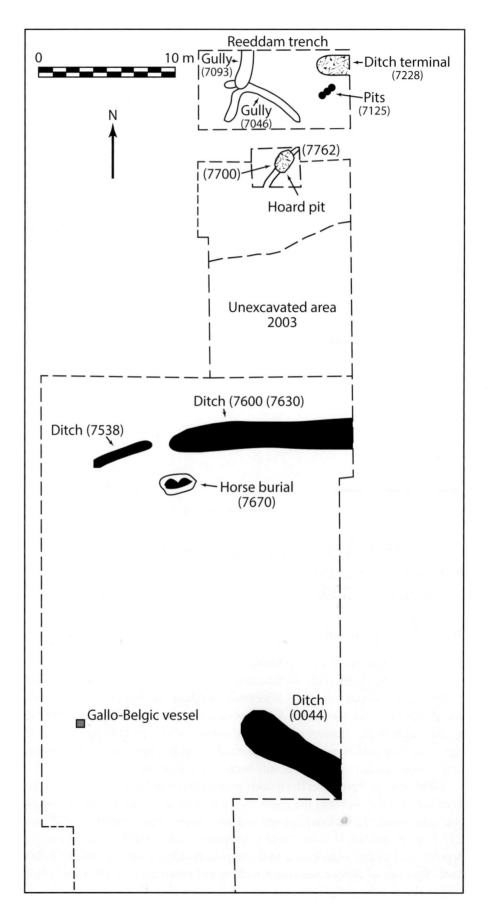

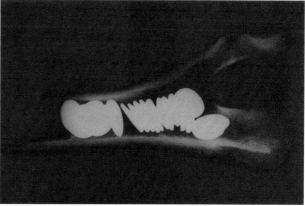

Plate 2.16: (top left) The hoard pit on Reeddam under excavation in 2003.

Plate 2.17: (top right) The Sedgeford Hoard as revealed by X-ray, courtesy of Sandringham Hospital. Twenty gold staters were stacked inside a cow bone.

Plate 2.18: (left) The Sedgeford Hoard under excavation. The staters were removed and recorded one-by-one in a day-long excavation in an improvised lab set up in Sedgeford's Old Village Hall, the SHARP headquarters.

Plate 2.19: (bottom) The Sedgeford Hoard displayed: the cow-bone container and 20 gold staters.

the hoard was disturbed, either in the Anglo-Saxon or Medieval period.

What follows is only a summary discussion of this extraordinary discovery, for it has already been fully reported in a short monograph prepared by Megan Dennis and published in 2005.

The coins were all Gallo-Belgic E staters (Box 2.5). Detailed analysis revealed a number of things about the Sedgeford assemblage. Of the seven types known, only the more common Types 1, 2 and 3 are represented. Four of the coins were die-linked with others; that is, they were struck using the same reverse-die. Several of the coins were imperfectly circular, had been struck off-centre, had striking cracks, or bore other blemishes: all evidence that either minting had been hurried or the minters unskilled – as might be expected in some sort of emergency requiring mass production of coin.

The bone container revealed no evidence that it had been specially selected or prepared in any way: it was an entirely ordinary piece of bone. Is the implication that this was a 'safety cache' – an attempt to hide treasure to keep it safe – rather than a 'ritual deposit'? Other evidence implies not.

Gareth Davies had organised an emergency excavation of the archaeological context from which the hoard was recovered as soon as it emerged. This highly skilled and meticulously recorded investigation revealed that the hoard had been placed in a small pit, but that this had been just one phase in a complex sequence of events (Fig. 2.9). This can be reconstructed as follows:

1. An Iron Age gully was cut.
2. A large Iron Age pit was cut into this gully.
3. A small pit was cut into the southern edge of the large pit.
4. A cow's leg bone filled with 39 (or more) gold staters was placed in the small pit.
5. The small pit was then backfilled and the position of the hoard marked at the top by a complete cow's pelvis.
6. The large and small pits silted up and merged, and the cow's pelvis marking the spot was covered over.
7. Another (undated) pit was cut close to the hoard pit.
8. Middle Anglo-Saxon burials, a charnel pit and a gully were cut into the hoard pit.

Box 2.5
Gaulish bullion

The coins forming the Sedgeford Hoard were all Gallo-Belgic E gold staters. Gallo-Belgic coins were first studied in the 1960s by Derek Allen, who arranged them into a series and devised the traditional nomenclature (Gallo-Belgic types A to F). All were minted in Gaul, but they also circulated in Britain, predating and then overlapping with the production of native British coins. The design of Gallo-Belgic staters was based on that of gold coins produced under Philip II of Macedon in the mid-late 4th century BC.

Gallo-Belgic Es all have the same design: the front (obverse) of the coin – which would otherwise depict a stylised head – was left blank; the back (reverse) was stamped with the image of a stylised horse.

This type is more common than any other class of Gallo-Belgic coin. They are thought to have been minted by the Ambiani tribe in northern Gaul in the early to mid 1st century BC. They may have been issued during the Gallic War of 58-51 BC, in order to pay men fighting Caesar's legions, with the Ambiani minting coins on behalf of a wider tribal confederation.

Various explanations have been proposed for their arrival in Britain: as payments to British tribal leaders for the supply of military units; as payments brought home by returning British warriors; or as portable wealth carried to Britain by Gaulish refugees fleeing the Roman conquest. That they arrived in quantity is beyond doubt: at least 22 Gallo-Belgic E hoards are known from a broad zone across south-eastern Britain (de Jersey 1996, *passim*; Dennis and Faulkner 2005, 26-31).

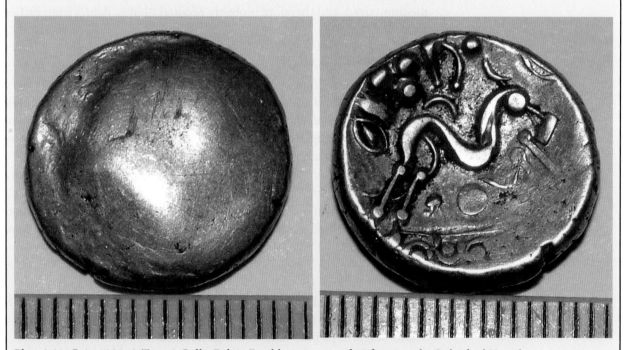

Plate 2.21: Coin 1094. A Type 2 Gallo-Belgic E gold stater, one of 39 forming the Sedgeford Hoard.

9. Tree roots grew into the hoard pit.
10. Further Anglo-Saxon burials cut into the underlying deposits.
11. A Medieval ditch was cut close to the hoard pit.

A sacred zone

The wider excavation of the Boneyard-Reeddam site provided further context (Figs. 2.11 and 2.12). A notable concentration of Iron Age features was revealed beneath the Anglo-Saxon cemetery in Reeddam – several intercutting gullies and pits and a couple of postholes. One of these gullies may have formed some sort of small circular enclosure around the hoard pit, but it is equally possible that separate phases of activity are represented. The small extent of the excavation area and the glutinous waterlogged mud, in which excavators found themselves working, obscured the archaeological features.

Interpretation hinges on the artefacts recovered both here and in other deposits nearby. These can be summarised as no fewer than seven 'Special Deposits'. Four can be dated confidently to the Iron Age; another is most likely to be of that period; the other two may be, though we cannot be certain.

Special Deposit 1

The largest gully in the vicinity of the hoard pit contained some 70 Iron Age potsherds. Of the latter, seven could be joined together to form around 25% of a single vessel, and other sherds of the same distinctive highly-friable fabric were also present. The remaining sherds were small or medium-sized, and therefore probably residual (that is, debris from earlier phases of activity).

Special Deposit 2

One of two small intercutting pits contained something similar, a very large rim sherd and a medium-sized base sherd, which, with the addition of other smaller sherds of the same high-quality fabric, appeared to form up to 15% of a single vessel. The part vessel was of 'Gallo-Belgic' type. Again, the remaining sherds looked residual.

Special Deposit 3

In an earlier test-pit dug about 20m east of the main Reeddam excavation in 1996 was a small gully containing about 15% of a 'Gallo-Belgic' type vessel.

Special Deposit 4

A heavily truncated pit in the south-western part of the Boneyard trench was found to contain 29 joining sherds forming about 35% of a complete 'Gallo-Belgic' type pot – and nothing else at all.

Special Deposit 5

A complete horse had been buried on Boneyard tightly packed into a pit measuring 1m by 1.8m across and around 0.5m deep (Plate 2.20). The legs were in a near-vertical position on the southern edge of the cut, the spine lay

Box 2.6
Posh pots

The broken part-pots found at four separate locations during the Boneyard-Reeddam excavations might once have been dismissed as routine waste disposal. This is no longer the case. Rubbish dumping – typically in the fills of ditches and pits – tends to comprise many small and medium-sized sherds mixed with animal bone and shell. To find a substantial part of a single vessel in one place looks like the deliberate and careful placing of a 'structured' or 'special' deposit.

This impression is enhanced when a vessel of special quality appears to have been chosen. The fact that a vessel is incomplete is also important: the implication may be that it has been 'killed', thus allowing it to pass from the realm of the living to that of the dead.

The wider context further supports a 'ritual' interpretation. The broken part-pots seem to stand alone, associated only with a background 'noise' of residual material, either in their own pits or at specific points in the base of a ditch. When placed alongside the hoard, the horse sacrifice and the big boundary ditches, the ritual significance of the placing of the pots seems beyond reasonable doubt.

Plate 2.22: A ritually deposited Iron Age part-pot from the Boneyard-Reeddam site as reconstructed after excavation

east-west and the head had been turned backwards into a 'looking over the shoulder' position (see Plate 2.20). A small sherd of Late Iron Age pottery was found in the pit fill, and the layer sealing the pit also contained Iron Age pottery, giving the northern horse burial a fairly secure date. (An attempt to obtain a radiocarbon date failed due to insufficient collagen in the bone.)

Special Deposit 6

A complete horse skull was also excavated nearby on Boneyard. Though no dating evidence was found in association with it, both its stratigraphic level and its proximity to the complete horse skeleton make an Iron Age date likely.

Special Deposit 7

Finally, a horse's forelimb, buried upright, was found in the same general area. The same considerations again imply an Iron Age date.

Box 2.7
Pegasus and the Kingdom of the Horse

Osteological analysis of 'Pegasus' – as the buried Iron Age horse was dubbed – showed it to have been a stallion of about eight years, in good health, standing about 13 hands high. Though only a pony by modern standards, the size of the animal was fairly typical at the time, making this sacrifice a high-value offering.

A large section of frontal bone was missing from the cranium and the position of the missing bone and associated sharp edges, fracture lines and lack of post-trauma healing make it almost certain that the injury was inflicted by a hard blow from a heavy-bladed instrument, that it was the cause of death, and that ritual sacrifice was the occasion for this.

Why a horse? Horses are depicted on the backs of all Icenian coins (Davies 2009, 115-116). Tacitus and Dio Cassius both report chariots in use during the Boudican Revolt (*Annals*, XIV, 35; *Roman History*, LXII, 8-12). Chariot fittings (for such they almost certainly were: there is no good evidence that British Celts operated as cavalry) – including bridle bits, terrets (rein rings), linch pins (to secure wheels to axles) and harness decorations – are common finds, both individually and as parts of hoards (Davies 2009, 107-108). 'Ickeny' is a Norfolk dialect word meaning 'awkward, troublesome, unmanageable' – as with a difficult horse (Robinson and Gregory 1987, 17).

The Iceni, in short, were 'the Kingdom of the Horse' (Davies 2009, 109-110). We have to assume that chariots were central to Icenian warfare, and that horses, vehicles and associated decorative metalwork (and presumably wood, wicker and leather-work) were

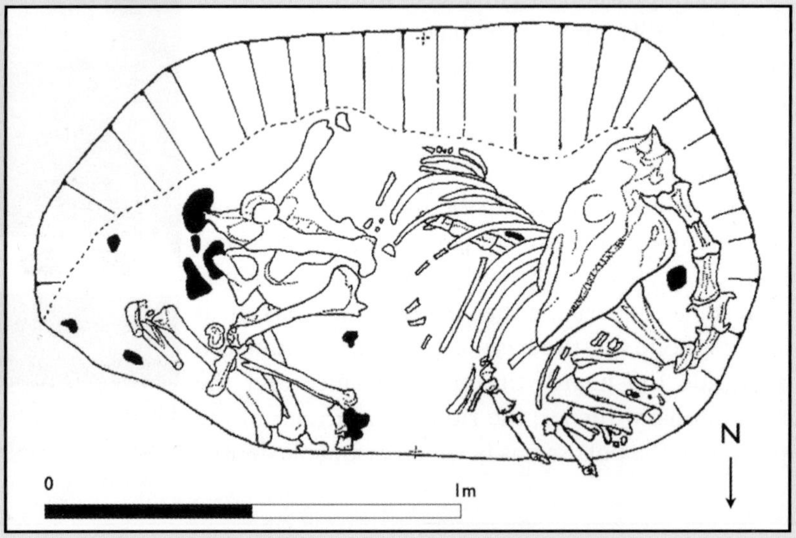

Fig. 2.13: Drawing of the horse apparently sacrificed and buried in a river's edge sanctuary on Boneyard-Reeddam in the Late Iron Age.

prestige items, indicative of aristocratic rank and status. Thus, chariot fittings became ritual offerings. And if chariot fittings, then why not the horse?

But, as John Creighton has emphasised, the horse had other meanings in the wider Celtic world. Horses appear on virtually all Celtic coins, and their central role in certain rituals is recorded in the Irish Sagas, notably at the inauguration of kings.

The new king was required to 'marry' the land to ensure the prosperity of his people. This was simple fertility magic, being a symbolic sexual union between the priest-king representing divine male power and Mother Earth. But the ritual commonly involved both horse sacrifice and ceremonies in which the identity of king and horse were merged; in one recorded case, the king would bathe in the stew made from the boiled meat of the butchered horse. Horses, then, were totemic beasts, symbols of power and agents of fertility (Creighton 2000, 286-289).

This nest of deposits sat within an Iron Age site defined by big linear ditches. A feature 1.7m wide and 0.4m deep in the north-east corner of the Reeddam trench, close to the hoard pit, was probably a ditch terminal. It contained five separate fills, the lower ones apparently slumped from the northern side, possibly indicating the former presence there of an earth bank (Fig. 2.12)

Higher up the slope was another large ditch, this one 2.5m wide and 1.2m deep, running east-west across the entire width of the excavation trench. Higher still, in the south-eastern corner of the trench, part of another huge ditch was excavated, running north-west to south-east, measuring 2m across, and probably originally dating to the Iron Age (though, with up to 14 re-cuts in places and Middle Anglo-Saxon pottery in its upper fills, it seems to have remained a feature of the landscape for many centuries).

Yet another such ditch was revealed in a long evaluation trench dug in 2000 about 30m east of the main Boneyard-Reeddam trench. Measuring 2.5m by 1.6m, this, too, had been frequently re-cut (at least eight times), had Middle Anglo-Saxon pottery in its upper U-shaped fills, but may well have had an Iron Age origin, since no potsherds were recovered from its lower V-shaped fills.

Another extent of east-west ditch, 2m wide, 0.5m deep, with Anglo-Saxon and Medieval pottery in the later fills, but only an Iron Age sherd in the lower ones, was excavated in the Reeddam 2 evaluation trench dug in 2001 and 2002. Two further evaluation trenches, dug in 2003, this time in Saggy Horse Field, also revealed Iron Age features (See Map page 36, Fig. 2.10). The trenches were too small to reveal the layout of the site, but a sequence of ditches, gullies and postholes was exposed, associated with large quantities of Iron Age pottery and an Icenian silver stater.

Mention must also be made of a somewhat mysterious site investigated by local antiquarian Holcombe Ingleby during construction of a bowling green in Sedgeford Hall Park in 1913. He reported large quantities of 'British and Roman pottery'; a published photograph does indeed show a huge assemblage (Ingleby 1922-1925, 27, 34). Unfortunately, none of it survives. In 2000, however, Sophie Cabot, Naomi Payne and other SHARP archaeologists excavated a 5m evaluation trench and other test-pits on and around the bowling green. They recovered few finds by hand but numerous small sherds of Iron Age and later pottery by sieving. They postulated that 'when Ingleby's workmen excavated the bowling green they missed these small sherds, just as we did when we excavated by hand'. Their final conclusion was that 'the quantities of pottery recovered do suggest there is an Iron Age site somewhere in the vicinity [of the bowling green]'. The implication seems to be that a Late Iron Age water's edge site extended for more than a kilometre along the south bank of the River Heacham.

Safety caches and ritual deposits

There can be little doubt that a ceremonial and ritual site is represented. The Boneyard-Reeddam site stands on the very edge of a waterway which 2,000 years ago would have flowed far more strongly than now, almost certainly with extensive areas of marshland around it: precisely the kind of natural place where Prehistoric people imagined deities to reside, such that they became the repositories of all kinds of ritual offerings.

The big ditches, probably with associated banks and perhaps palisades, would have been imposing features, designed to mark out certain spaces along the water's edge as sacred. Ritual deposition in these sacred spaces is then represented in three forms: by a hoard of at least 39 gold staters placed inside a cow bone; by the sacrifice and burial of a complete horse and possibly parts of others; and by several deposits of broken part-vessels.

This does not preclude domestic use of the site, either contemporaneously with the ritual activity or during an earlier phase of use. But clear evidence for this does not at present exist, whereas the ritual use of the site is beyond doubt.

The traditional dichotomy between (secular) 'safety caches' and (sacred) 'ritual deposits' is, in any case, misplaced. In the Graeco-Roman world, temples were also treasuries, and bullion might be 'borrowed' from the gods in time of crisis, to be paid back (with interest?) in due course. Equally, in

Fig. 2.14: Map showing known Late Iron Age sites, hoards and possible routeways in Sedgeford and surrounding parishes.

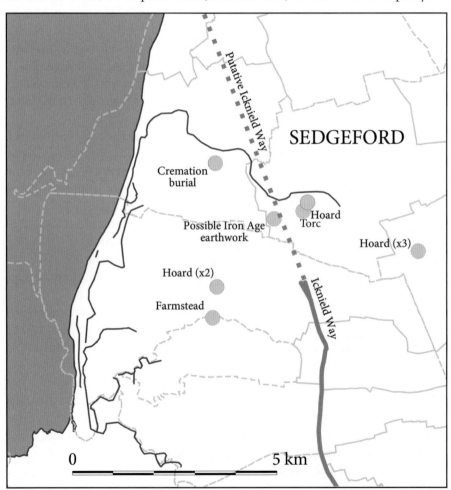

times of stress, treasure might be buried in sanctuaries both to conceal it from enemies and to secure divine favour. The concepts 'safety cache' and 'ritual deposit' are not, in the context of Prehistoric paganism, alternative categories, but complementary meanings (Hutcheson 2004, 89-98)

And what were the special 'meanings' attributed to gold torcs, silver coins and chariot fittings of polished bronze encrusted with red, blue and yellow enamel? They were many, of course, but perhaps the deepest meaning depended upon these objects' brilliance, their shininess, their resemblance to the life-giving warmth and light of the Sun. Their deposition in hilltop groves and waterside sanctuaries can then be seen as an ancient fertility rite and a magical recharging of the Earth's fecundity.

The geographical context

How do Sedgeford and Norfolk fit into the wider context of Late Iron Age Britain? Perceptions of the period tend to be dominated by what was happening in three main zones: Atlantic-coast Scotland with its characteristic brochs; Wessex with its hillforts and enclosed settlements; and South-East England with its *oppida*, rich burials, imported luxuries and early coin use. This has much to do with the archaeological visibility of major Iron Age monuments in these zones, and the result has been to distort our view of the period as a whole. There has recently been a shift towards stressing the regional diversity of Iron Age Britain.

J. D. Hill has contrasted the 'spotty' landscapes of regions like Wessex with the 'spurgy' landscapes of regions like northern East Anglia. He explains: 'A 'spotty' landscape is one made up of discrete, spatially isolated and bounded settlement entities which can be represented as neat dots on a map; a landscape full of small enclosed farmsteads with their surrounding fields, with perhaps the occasional much larger enclosed hillfort.' The contrast is with landscapes formed of sites that 'appear as spreads of material and settlement components extending over large areas: relatively large, unenclosed, agglomerations of round-houses and other structures.'

These 'spurgy' landscapes seem to comprise foci of settlement, industry and ceremony that tend to 'wander' across the area over time, implying more communal ownership of land, looser tenurial relations and perhaps less pressure on land and resources than elsewhere (Hill 1999).

This appears to be the pattern across Norfolk. There are some large-scale enclosed sites: six hillfort-type ring-works (Holkham, Warham Camp, South Creake, Bawsey, Narborough and Thetford Castle; Davies 2009, 95-100); and up to ten square enclosures (Thornham, Warham Burrows, Wighton, Alby, Bintree, Bodham, Heacham, Great Massingham, Thetford and Sedgeford; Davies 1999, 30-33; Dennis and Faulkner 2005, 59-60). Also monumental in scale are five linear dykes, four in west Norfolk (Launditch, Bichamditch, Panworth Ditch and Fossditch), one in north-west Suffolk (Black Ditches; Davies 2009, 94-95, 102).

The ring-works may have had defensive functions, but they may also have been places of gathering for the performance of collective ceremonies. The square enclosures were almost certainly of the latter kind; the type-site is the thoroughly excavated Fison Way complex at Thetford, the ceremonial function of which is beyond reasonable doubt (Gregory 1991).

But most Iron Age sites in Norfolk were not enclosed, and those that were often formed part of larger 'spurgy' sprawls of associated sites. Excavations at Harford Farm and Valley Belt on the Norwich Southern Bypass and at Park Farm on the Wymondham Bypass have revealed what appear to be ordinary domestic sites formed of widely scattered structures in a fairly open landscape (Ashwin 1999).

Of particular relevance to the interpretation of Snettisham-Sedgeford is that some of the agglomerations appear to have been especially extensive, busy and rich, yielding hoards of bullion and numerous finds of chariot fittings; except for the absence of surrounding dykes, they have *oppidum*-like characteristics. The principal examples are Caistor St Edmund, Saham Toney/ Ashill and Thetford (Davies 2009, 119-125).

The Snettisham-Sedgeford 'spurge'

The spur of chalk downland bounded by The Wash to the west, the Heacham River to the north, the hamlet of Fring to the east and the River Ingol and the village of Snettisham to the south-west seems to constitute just such a high-status agglomeration in the Late Iron Age. Lying within a broad north-west Norfolk zone where high-status Late Iron Age activity seems to have been concentrated, the Snettisham-Sedgeford agglomeration centres on Ken Hill and extends inland across the chalk massif over an area about 4 miles east-west and 3 miles north-south. This 'fan' of concentrated, high-status activity implies some sort of Icenian tribal centre.

Plate 2.23: General view of Ken Hill from the south-west. A steep-sided carstone bastion, Ken Hill would have projected into the sea in the Late Iron Age, making it an exceptionally striking landmark, especially when approaching from the sea, as represented here.

Ken Hill would have been a striking geographical feature 2,000 years ago. It is not the highest hill around: the plateau is only 40m above sea-level, whereas the ground rises to 65m in the eastern part of Sedgeford. But while the inland hills are formed of rolling chalk downland, Ken Hill is a steep-sided carstone bastion jutting into The Wash.

Its western face has been heavily quarried and thereby reconfigured as a series of terraces and giant pits; it would therefore have been a yet more impressive natural feature in the Late Iron Age. The higher sea-level at the time would have enhanced its character as a projecting headland, making it a prominent landmark on the seaward approach. Standing proud, moreover, it would also have been seen from all points of the compass on the landward side. From the hill, there are commanding views out over The Wash to Lincolnshire.

Nor is it difficult to situate Ken Hill as a central place in a regional context. The Icknield Way and the Peddar's Way run through Sedgeford towards the sea, linking the area, via the Gipping Valley, with south-eastern Suffolk and beyond. A number of small but once-navigable rivers drain westwards from the chalk downs and clay-lands of the interior into The Wash. Roads and rivers imply a crossing-point and ferry traffic. The impression is confirmed on the Lincolnshire side, where tracks also terminate at The Wash and monuments and artefacts are often similar to those of north-west Norfolk. It is likely, too, that the seaways connected ancient Icenia with the Continent, the probable source of much of the gold interred at Ken Hill (Dennis and Faulkner 2005, 64-66).

With the Fens an immense, impassable expanse of marsh and mud, the movement of people and goods was funnelled along this north-west/south-east routeway centred on The Wash. Control of the routeway would have been a source of power. Tribal potentates would have aimed at a monopoly. One can imagine Ken Hill (and is there perhaps a distant echo here of the tribal name?) as a monument to the local elite's control of territory, harbour and seaway, a control sanctified by the deities honoured in the famous 'Gold Field' sanctuary on the north-eastern slope.

For here, of course, were found the richest Iron Age hoards in Britain, comprising about 175 gold, silver and electrum torcs, 75 more or less complete, 100 represented by fragments, along with hundreds of gold coins, metal ingots, jewellery and other precious items (with rumours of much more, lost to nighthawks, including a 'bowl hoard' formed of 6,000 coins buried in a silver bowl, with a further 500 coins and ingots beneath). The treasure was buried in a series of pits, and these formed part of a 20-acre sanctuary later defined by a monumental ditch, polygonal in shape, 3m wide by 2m deep (Davies 2009, 100-105).

The treasure may originally have been displayed, like that in a Greek or Roman temple, only later being cleared to make room for more and then ritually deposited in Mother Earth. And the sanctuary is on the eastern slope, facing the rising Sun. This conjures an image: of the first rays of light at dawn striking a hundred shiny objects and bringing them dazzling to life. A more emphatic signal of the importance of the location and the elite who controlled it would be hard to imagine.

Is it too much to imagine this site, the Snettisham 'Gold Field', an ultimate place of ceremony, sacrifice and ritual deposition, as having been linked by processional ways to a series of secondary sanctuaries nearby – such as those implied on Polar Breck, Boneyard-Reeddam and perhaps many other places in the surrounding landscape?

The temporal context

What we are seeing in the archaeology appears to be a process of proto-state formation. The starting-point is the technological revolution represented by the introduction of iron.

Bronze is relatively soft and was used in the Bronze Age mainly for war-gear and ornament, not for the tools of everyday work, which continued to be fashioned from stone and wood. Iron, though harder to work, was widely available, relatively cheap and could be used to make strong, durable, sharp-edged tools. Its adoption raised the productivity of agricultural labour enormously and allowed prehistoric farmers to clear and cultivate heavier

Plate 2.24: Boudica, Queen of the Iceni, leader of the greatest recorded British revolt against Roman imperialism. Though our image of her is a cultural construct of the classical historians Tacitus and Dio Cassius – and countless later reconfigurations – she represents a process of proto-state formation which was a central feature of political development in Britain in the century before the Roman conquest.

soils like the boulder clays of Norfolk's central plateau. Settlement expanded, population increased and larger surpluses were generated.

The economic revolution – for such it was – had two major consequences for the socio-political order. First, settlement expansion meant that competition for land and resources intensified. Second, larger surpluses provided the means with which to engage in that competition. The trend, in consequence, was towards a more crowded and contested world.

Politico-military competition has its own dynamic. Once societies are competing with each other in war-making capacity, larger units have an obvious advantage. They may either overwhelm and subjugate lesser rivals, or persuade them to enter into alliances or confederations for their own protection. The logic of politico-military competition causes a progression from loosely structured local chiefdoms to more tightly organised regional kingdoms.

This process was sharply accelerated in the Late Iron Age by the impact of Roman imperialism. The Iceni – as we are perhaps entitled to call them from around 50 BC – were shaped by three successive military crises involving the Romans: the two expeditions of Julius Caesar (55 and 54 BC); the Claudian conquest and the First Icenian Revolt (AD 43-47); and the Second Icenian (or Boudican) Revolt (AD 60/61). In each case, the demands of military security would have placed exceptional pressure on tribal leaders to organise themselves into a larger polity able to unify command, pool resources and concentrate manpower.

Nor was this all. Following the defeat of the First Icenian Revolt, the Romans imposed a client king, Prasutagus, on the tribe and it is likely that the support of the imperial power – essentially in the form of subsidies and a standing threat of military intervention – enabled the new Icenian ruler to drive forwards the process of centralisation. In underpinning the power of their puppet, the Romans almost certainly strengthened the Icenian state as a whole.

The four known 'spurges' of concentrated Late Iron Age activity in Norfolk may represent the tribal centres of four cantons that were fusing into a more centralised Icenian kingdom between 50 BC and AD 60/61.

Natasha Hutcheson has noted a number of changes in the pattern of hoarding: a shift from hoards of torcs and gold coins, to hoards of gold and silver coins and then to hoards of chariot fittings; a shift from remote, natural, open locations to well-defined sanctuaries in prominent locations; and a shift from the north-western part of the county to a more even distribution but with a weighting towards the south (2004, 23-35, 89-98 *passim*).

Does this reflect the growing power of a social elite aggregated at tribal centres? Does it indicate a shift in the locus of power from the north-west to the south? Or is the implication that the dominant elite group, originally based in the north-west, was extending its power across the county and becoming more peripatetic?

A further question concerns the dating of hoards in relation to political events. The historical sources imply three major crises triggered by Roman imperial aggression. Were these the occasions when many of the hoards were buried? Perhaps. Either way, they stand testimony to a political order that was doomed by the events of AD 60/61.

Boudica's final battle was the Hastings of the Icenian aristocracy: the power of the kingdom's ruling caste of warrior-charioteers and druidic priests was broken, and their tribal centres and estates were laid waste by rampaging soldiery. Such is the impression we have. What eventually emerged from the wreckage was something radically different.

The main contributors to the writing of this chapter were:

Neil Faulkner (principal author), Megan Dennis (principal author), Katie Mckinnon, Kath Walker and Pamela J. Cross

References

Ashwin, T., 1999, 'Studying Iron Age Settlement in Norfolk', in J. Davies and T. Williamson (eds.), *Land of the Iceni: the Iron Age in northern East Anglia*, Norwich, Centre of East Anglian Studies, 100-124.

Aufderheide, A.C. and Rodríguez-Martín, C., 1998, *The Cambridge Encyclopedia of Human Palaeopathology*, Cambridge, Cambridge University Press.

Brothwell, D.R., 1981, *Digging up bones*, Ithaca, New York, Cornell University Press.

Buikstra, J.E. and Ubelaker, D.H., 1994, *Standards for data collection from human skeletal remains*, Arkansas Archaeological Survey research series No. 44, Fayetteville, Arkansas.

Butler, C., 2005, *Prehistoric Flintwork*, London, Tempus.

Childe, V.G., 1942, *What Happened in History*, London, Penguin.

Clarke, D. L., 1976, 'Mesolithic Europe: the economic basis', in G de Sieveking *et al* (eds.), *Problems in Economic and Social Archaeology*, London, Duckworth, 449-481.

Creighton, J., 2000, *Coins and Power in Late Iron Age Britain*, Cambridge, Cambridge University Press.

Crema, M.D., Marra, M.D., Guermazi, A., Roemer, F.W., Bohndorf, K. and Jomaah,

N., 2009, 'MDCT arthrography features of ulnocarpal impaction syndrome', in *American Journal of Roentgenology* I 193, 5.

Davies, J., 2009, *The Land of Boudica: prehistoric and Roman Norfolk*, Oxford, Heritage/Norfolk Museums and Archaeology Service.

de Jersey, P., 1996, *Celtic Coinage in Britain*, Princes Risborough, Shire.

Dennis, M. and Faulkner, N., 2005, *The Sedgeford Hoard*, Stroud, Tempus.

Foster, C., 2013, 'Is it all in the mound! An archaeological, antiquarian, osteological and palaeodietary assessment of an Early Bronze Age individual burial at Sedgeford, Norfolk', unpub. BA dissertation, University of Reading.

Gregory, T., 1991, *Excavations in Thetford, 1980-1982, Fison Way, Volume 1*, East Anglian Archaeology Report 53, Gressenhall, Norfolk Museums Service.

Healy, F., Heaton, M. and Lobb, S. J., 1992, 'Excavations of a Mesolithic site at Thatcham, Berkshire', in *Proceedings of the Prehistoric Society*, 58, 41-76.

Hill, J. D., 1999, 'Settlement, Landscape and Regionality: Norfolk and Suffolk in the pre-Roman Iron Age of Britain and beyond', in J. Davies and T. Williamson (eds.), *Land of the Iceni: the Iron Age in northern East Anglia*, Norwich, Centre of East Anglian Studies, 185-207.

Hillson, S., 1997, *Dental Anthropology*, Cambridge, Cambridge University Press.

Hutcheson, N., 2004, *Later Iron Age Norfolk: metalwork, landscape and society*, B.A.R. British Series 361, Oxford, British Archaeological Reports.

Ingleby, H., 1922-1925, *The Charm of a Village: an account of Sedgeford with its history and its carnivals*, London, Clement Ingleby.

Jay, M. and Richards, M., 2007, 'British Iron Age diet: stable isotopes and other evidence', in *Proceedings of the Prehistoric Society*, 73, 169-190.

Lawson, A.J., 1978, 'The investigation of a Mesolithic and later site at Banham', in *East Anglian Archaeology*, 8, 9-18.

Lawson, A. and Wymer, J., 1994, 'The Bronze Age', in P. Wade-Martins (ed.), *An Historical Atlas of Norfolk*, 2nd edition, Norwich, Norfolk Museums Service, 30-31.

Lovejoy, C.O., Meindl, R.S., Pryzbeck,T.R. and Mensforth, R.P., 1985, 'Chronological metamorphosis of the auricular surface of the ilium: a new method for determination of age at death', in *American Journal of Physical Anthropology*, 68, 47-56.

Mays, S., 1998, *The Archaeology of Human Bones*, London, Routledge.

Newcomer, M. H. and Karlin, C., 1987, 'Flint chips from Pincevent', in G. de Sieveking and M. H. Newcomer (eds.), *The human uses of flint and chert: papers from the fourth international flint symposium*, Cambridge, Cambridge University Press, 33-36.

Payne, N., 2000, 'The bowling green evaluation', in R. Hoggett (ed.), *SHARP Interim Report 2000*.

Roberts, C. and Cox, M., 2003, *Health and disease in Britain from prehistory to the present day*, Sutton Publishing, Stroud, Gloucestershire.

Robinson, B. and Gregory, T., 1987, *Celtic Fire and Roman Rule*, North Walsham, Poppyland.

Ruff, C.B., Scott, W.W. and Liu, A.Y.C., 1991, 'Articular and diaphyseal remodelling of the proximal femur with changes in body mass in adults', in *American Journal of Physical Anthropology*, 86, 397-413.

Scheuer, L. and Black, S., 2000, *Developmental Juvenile Osteology*, London, Academic Press.

Svyatko, S., n.d., 'Information about stable carbon and nitrogen analysis', at www.chrono.qub.ac.uk/Resources/MassSpec/Svetlana/.

Trotter, M. and Gleser, G.C., 1952, 'Estimation of stature from long bones of American whites and negroes', in *American Journal of Physical Anthropology*, 10, 463-514.

Waldron, T., 2009, *Palaeopathology*, Cambridge, Cambridge University Press.

Wymer, J., 1994, 'The Neolithic Period', in P. Wade-Martins (ed.), *An Historical Atlas of Norfolk*, 2nd edition, Norwich, Norfolk Museums Service, 26-27.

3. An Early Roman Farmstead, a Late Roman Villa Estate and a Body in an Oven

An Early Roman farmstead
Lower Polar Breck, Phase 3
c. AD 100–250/275

The first part of our story ended abruptly and violently with the destruction of the Kingdom of the Iceni. Some of us believe we have the mark of these events imprinted on the landscape at Sedgeford. The downland farmstead on Upper Chalkpit investigated in 2006 seems to have been abandoned at the end of the Iron Age, only to be succeeded by a Romano-British farmstead somewhat later in a slightly different location and with a radically new layout.

The Iron Age farmstead was represented by inner and outer curvilinear gullies revealed in the Upper Chalkpit Trench excavated in 2006. The successor Romano-British farmstead was located in the Lower Polar Breck Trench (Plate 3.1) excavated immediately to the south-east in 2005. This is, of course, a single site straddling the intersection of four large fields. It was originally located in fieldwalking and metal-detector survey, and then confirmed and elucidated by geophysical survey (Fig. 3.1).

The Lower Polar Breck Trench (Fig. 3.2) revealed a roughly east-west aligned ditch extending from the south-western corner of the trench and terminating in its eastern half. After a gap in the line of about 6m, a second ditch continued on the same alignment to the eastern edge of the trench; the latter, presumably, was contemporary with the first and part of the same landscape remodelling, and the gap was perhaps some sort of entranceway. A third ditch, smaller and aligned approximately north-south, extended at right-angles from the first. Though heavily truncated, sufficient evidence survived to imply a co-axial layout of enclosures.

The eastern extent of the main boundary ditch was recut at least once (Phase 3b). The pottery assemblage implies a long period of activity, with the fills having fabrics and forms ranging in date from the late 1st to at least the mid 3rd century. The quantity and character of the pottery implies domestic occupation – there were 182 sherds, with a good proportion of early finewares, including a necked jar.

Phases 1 and 2 on this site are discussed in Chapter 2.

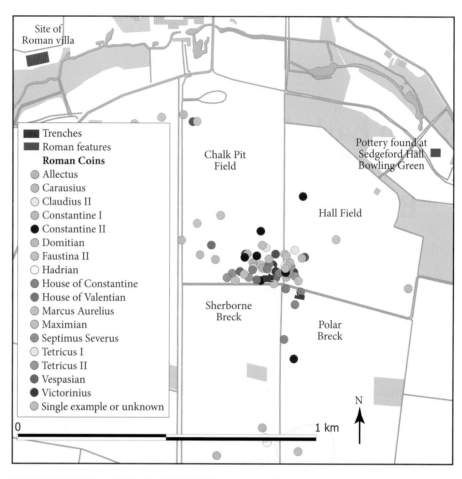

Fig. 3.1: Plan showing Roman finds from fieldwalking and metal-detector survey and excavation trenches on the Upper Chalkpit-Lower Polar Breck site. Roman coins are identified by period when more than one example has been found.

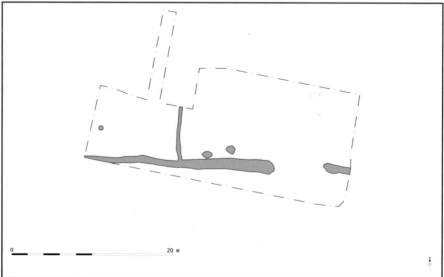

Fig. 3.2: Plan showing Early Roman farmstead (Phase 3) on Lower Polar Breck.

Much of the pottery, though, was relatively late and the ditch yielded a late coin, a radiate or nummus of late 3rd or 4th century date. This material probably represents the later infilling of the ditch. Much of the early pottery, on the other hand, has the appearance of primary material, so we can assume that the ditch was most likely dug in the late 1st or early 2nd century AD.

What happened between Phases 2 (the Late Iron Age farmstead) and 3

Plate 3.1: General view of Early Roman farmstead on Lower Polar Breck under excavation looking south-west.

(the Early Roman farmstead)? It seems likely that a period of abandonment separated the two farmsteads. This appears implicit in the sideways shuffle of the settlement, the radically new layout and the sharp contrast between the ceramic assemblages recovered from the enclosure ditch in Upper Chalkpit and the boundary ditches in Lower Polar Breck. Our working hypothesis is an interruption of activity and a hiatus of some duration. We have argued above that the grim aftermath of the Boudican Revolt would provide an appropriate historical context.

Then, maybe two or three generations later, as the population recovered, the farm was reoccupied, perhaps by descendants of the original occupants. They may have remodelled the landscape because little trace remained of former land divisions. Or because they had different ideas about how best to organise the farm. Or even to distance themselves symbolically from a tainted, haunted, taboo-laden past.

We do not know. What we can say is that, if the 'Boudican hypothesis' is correct, that is, if the break between Phases 2 and 3 can be associated with the upheaval of AD 60/61, then what we are seeing archaeologically is a contested landscape. The abandonment of the Late Iron Age farmstead and the later imposition of a Romano-British farmstead at one remove and on a new alignment may be archaeological testimony to the struggle for control of Norfolk between Icenian nobility and Roman imperial state in the middle of the 1st century AD.

A Late Roman villa estate?
Upper Chalkpit-Lower Polar Breck, Phase 4
c. AD 250/275–275/300

At some point, probably in the mid to late 3rd century AD, a straight east-west ditch was dug across Upper Chalkpit Trench (Fig. 3.3, top). The original dimensions have been lost to later recutting, though as reconstituted it measured approximately 1.65m wide by 0.70m deep (after plough truncation). Too little of the original fills survived later recutting to provide dating evidence, but the ditch can be compared with a new layout on a similar alignment in Lower Polar Breck Trench (Fig. 3.3, bottom).

Here, two substantial ditches were set at right angles to each other, one running approximately north-south (cutting the Phase 3 east-west ditch), the other east-west, with a narrow gap between them. Both ditches were comparable in size and shape to that in Upper Chalkpit. All three ditches were at some point re-cut at least once on the same alignments (Phases 4b).

The two Lower Polar Breck ditches framed an area in the north-west corner of the trench which was surfaced with rammed chalk and flint pressed into natural clay. Since no structural evidence was found, it seems likely that this was an external yard, though the implication may be that buildings were close by. This seems confirmed by the artefacts. Some 392 sherds were recovered from the two Phase 4 ditches and the cobbled yard in Lower Polar Breck (compared with only 47 from the Phase 4 ditch in Upper Chalkpit). There were also a fragment of vessel glass, a bone pin and a bronze coin of Carausius dated AD 290-293.

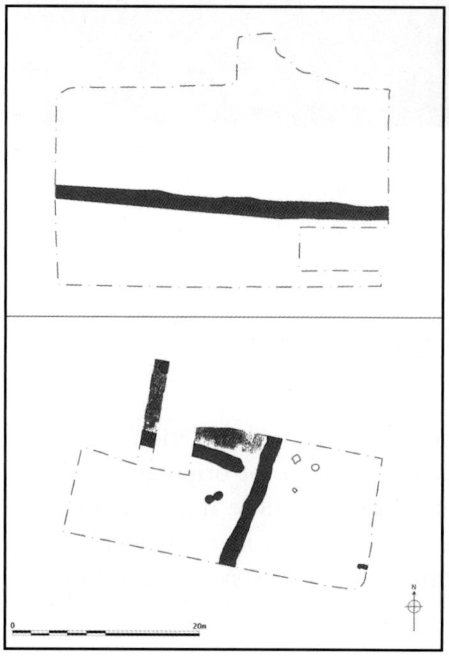

The shared co-axial alignment and similar size and shape of these three ditches make it very likely that they belong to a single reorganisation of the landscape. This is supported by their common Late Roman ceramic date. How might this event be explained?

The Phase 4 ditches are larger

Fig. 3.3: Plan showing Late Roman landscape reorganisation (Phase 4) on Upper Chalkpit-Lower Polar Breck site. Top: Upper Chalkpit. Bottom: Lower Polar Breck

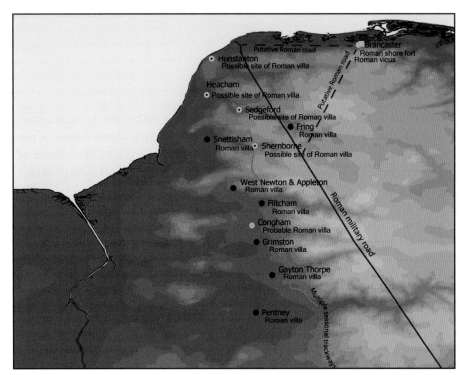

Fig. 3.4: Map showing the line of villas, probably Late Roman in date, running along the Greensand ridge of north-west Norfolk.

and more extensive than those of Phase 3 (or, for that matter, of Phase 2), implying a greater investment of effort in remodelling the landscape, perhaps transcending in scale what might be expected of a single farmstead. Our working hypothesis is, therefore, that there may be a relationship between the Phase 4 reorganisation and the probable establishment of a Late Roman villa a short distance away.

A Late Roman military-supply economy?

Much of the British landscape seems to have been reorganised into villa estates in the Late Roman period (Fig. 3.4). There is one probable villa in Sedgeford. Others are known or suspected in the neighbouring parishes of Heacham, Snettisham and Fring and along the Greensand ridge of north-west Norfolk, following the line of the Icknield Way (Gregory 1982). Michael de Bootman, in a systematic trawl through the local HER (Historic Environment Record), has recently shown that about 90 definite or possible villas are known across Norfolk as a whole. Where dating evidence is available, these villas usually turn out to be relatively late foundations (Michael de Bootman, pers. comm.; John Smallwood, pers. comm.).

Sedgeford Villa – if such it be – seems to fit the pattern. According to a report on a field reconnaissance at the site in 1944, 'areas of flint, brick, flue- and roof-tile rubble associated with 3rd and 4th century pottery' extended across about an acre of arable ground, while 'a scatter of pink concrete, brick, fine-tile and tesserae indicate several structures' (Norfolk HER 1603). This probable villa, located on gently rising ground just south of the River Heacham, lies only about 1.5km from the Romano-British settlement under discussion here.

The appearance of these Late Roman villas in north-west Norfolk and the implicit reorganisation of the entire landscape into villa estates, is broadly

Box 3.1
Mutton, beef and the military-supply economy

Our analysis of 861 animal bone fragments from the Upper Chalkpit-Lower Polar Breck excavations has revealed a marked increase in the relative proportion of cattle compared with sheep between the 2nd and 4th centuries. Age-at-death analysis of the cattle mandibles has revealed a complete absence of animals older than 36 months. This shows that the primary butchery of older animals was being carried out elsewhere.

The Sedgeford pattern contrasts with that at the Roman Saxon Shore fort at nearby Brancaster, where animals of all ages are represented, but where the majority were either sub-adult or mature. Fragmentation and butchery analysis of the Brancaster assemblage also points to animals arriving 'on the hoof' for on-site butchery.

The implication is that Sedgeford was a producer site whereas Brancaster was a consumer site. Brancaster Fort lies about seven miles north-east of Sedgeford, and it is notable that a secondary road, which branches off the Peddars Way at Fring, would have provided a direct link between the two places in the Roman period. The fort was probably founded in the mid 3rd century AD, a date that matches well with that for both the development of villa estates generally in north-west Norfolk, and for the proposed transition from farmstead to villa estate at Sedgeford.

The analysis shows that the emphasis shifted back to sheep husbandry in the later 4th century, at the very time when Roman military garrisons were being run down across Britain. This strengthens the hypothesis that Sedgeford was networked into a wider military-supply economy during the 4th century, with specialised beef production and droveways to the local fort.

The Sedgeford agricultural settlement was participating in two distinct economies simultaneously, and the balance of production oscillated between the two over time. The first involved beef production for the local Roman military site and perhaps for the wider market. This was down to its excellent transport links, as well as its situation close to production centres for salt (the main preservative). The second was a more rudimentary subsistence economy based on sheep, which would have provided the local population with meat, milk and wool.

Fig. 3.5: Graph showing the rising proportion of cattle compared with sheep at the Upper Chalkpit-Lower Polar Breck site (by Minimum Number of Individuals).

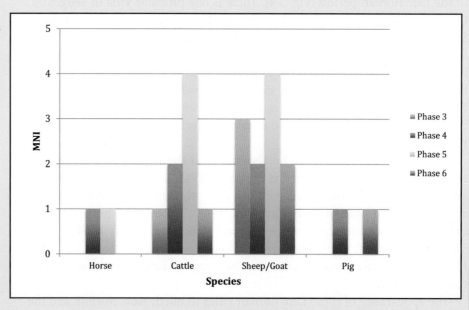

contemporary with Phase 4 on our Upper Chalkpit-Lower Polar Breck downland settlement site.

The Late Roman 'rise of the villas' appears at odds with the contemporary 'decline of the towns' (Faulkner 2000, 121-149). To whom were the villas supplying produce if urban markets were shrinking? The answer seems to be the army. In addition to much historical evidence for the growing militarisation of the Late Empire, many new forts were built and many old ones refurbished in the 3rd and 4th centuries. Sedgeford, quite apart from its proximity to the sea, and therefore its convenience for the export of agricultural produce to the Roman Army on Hadrian's Wall and on the Rhine, was well placed to supply the new local fort at Brancaster.

Social change is implicit in the construction of villas and major landscape reorganisation. Villas represent control over land and labour by a class of gentry and a greater concentration of wealth at the top of rural society. It is tempting to link the villas – and the perhaps associated abandonment or transformation of Romano-British farmsteads – with the numerous references to *coloni* across much of the empire in Late Roman sources (Jones 1964, *passim*). The *coloni* were peasants who had been reduced to serfdom, becoming tied to a particular estate, making it easier for both landlords and tax-collectors to ratchet up the rate of exploitation.

The reorganisation of the landscape in Phase 4 was probably linked to the development of a villa estate and new ways of working the land, and we can assume that this would have meant winners and losers. Subsequent developments seem to confirm this. For the site was soon transformed even more radically, from what had once been a Romano-British farmstead into a Late Roman agricultural processing plant.

A Late Roman Agricultural Processing Plant
Upper Chalkpit, Phase 5
c. AD 275/300-300/350

At some point, the Late Roman villa-estate layout was modified when a new north-south ditch was cut in the southern part of the Upper Chalkpit Trench. This joined with the large east-west ditch, which was recut along its western extent, forming a new right-angled enclosure; the eastern extent of the east-west ditch then seems to have gone out of use (Phase 5, Fig. 3.6). The new right-angled ditch was recut at least twice (Phases 5b and 5c).

This may be the occasion when two other changes occurred, though either or both could equally well belong to an earlier or later phase, since there are no direct stratigraphic relationships. A north-south linear gully was cut, approximately defining an enclosed space in the north-central area of Upper Chalkpit. This gully was slight – a maximum of 0.40m wide and 0.12m deep – and the most likely interpretation is that it represents a former fence-line.

If so, it may have been bounding a working area where a grain-drying oven was located in the north-central area of the trench. There appear to have been two successive oven-and-flue systems. The first was a long flue, 12m or more in length, comprising a single channel measuring up to 0.90m wide by 0.50m deep which then subdivided into two parallel channels measuring up

Fig. 3.6: Plan showing the Late Roman agricultural processing plant (Phase 5) on Upper Chalkpit.

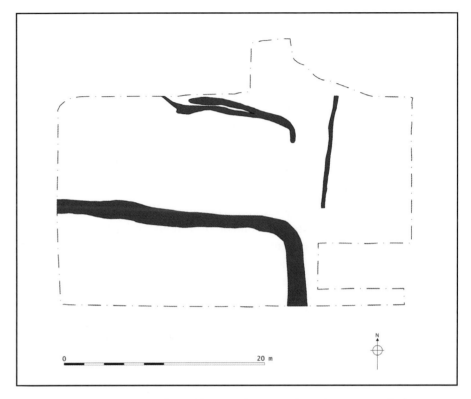

to 0.45m wide by 0.40m deep (the southern one) and 0.60m wide by 0.30m deep (the northern one).

The flues were filled with mid-brown and light orangey-brown silt and sand, but in the southern one there was also abundant evidence of burning in the form of charcoal-rich black and red staining. There seems little doubt that the flue system represents the remains of a grain-drying oven or malting floor, though it was not possible to reconstruct its form from the limited evidence recovered.

Grain-drying ovens are common discoveries on Romano-British rural sites. They vary greatly in design and quality. The trend appears to be for ovens to become increasingly sophisticated in design and engineering in the Late Roman period. This is likely to reflect the growth of villa estates, industrial-scale production and the military-supply economy in Late Antiquity.

They are often found in association with large quantities of charred grain, and the traditional assumption has been that they were corn-driers, used to dry grain prior to export or long-term storage, much as farmers use large hot-air fans for the same purpose today. Alternative uses have, however, been proposed, notably in malting/brewing, or even, in some contexts, water heating. Perhaps they were multi-purpose.

All features attributed to Phase 5 – the boundary ditch, the fence-line and the double-flue system – have been securely dated by pottery to the Late Roman period. In addition, the sheer quantity of pottery and animal bone deposited, coupled with the discovery of a spindle-whorl, a glass bead, a pair of tweezers, a possible finger-ring and an iron artefact of some kind, imply domestic occupation on the site. Perhaps estate-workers were accommodated in the immediate vicinity of the processing plant.

An Improved Oven
Upper Chalkpit, Phase 6
c. AD 300/350-350/375

At some point, probably in the early-mid 4th century AD, the layout of the site was modified again. A new north-south ditch was cut to the west of the processing plant. This met the original east-west ditch, which was re-cut along its western extent, forming a right-angled enclosure in the north-west corner of the trench; the rest of the ditch system then seems to have gone out of use, though the fence-line may have remained.

The processing plant seems to have been rebuilt wholesale, with a new crop- or grain-drying oven and a substantial four-post structure (Fig. 3.7). The oven had a complex form. The central furnace was rectangular, oriented north-south and measured approximately 0.60m east-west, 1.30m north-south and up to 0.20m deep (but had been plough-truncated).

The oven had been cut into the subsoil and the walls lined with clay approximately 0.30m thick. Three openings on the western side fed hot air into the flue system (Plate 3.3). A central flue, of variable width of approximately

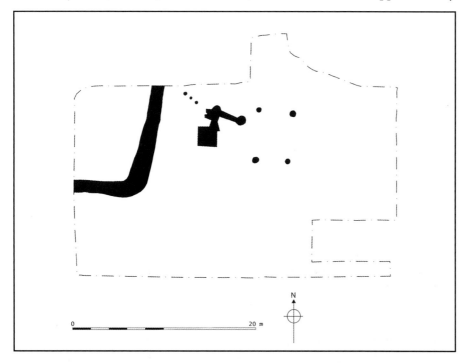

Fig. 3.7: Plan showing the second grain-drying/malting oven (Phase 6) on Upper Chalkpit.

0.30-0.50m and up to 0.40m deep, carried hot air around three sides of the furnace. The third, eastern arm of this central flue, approximately 3.25m long externally, carried the air beyond the central furnace on the northern side into an outer flue (Plate 3.2). The walls of both furnace and central flue were near vertical and flat-bottomed.

The outer flue, arranged approximately at right angles to the eastern arm of the central flue, measured almost 4m in length and was half a metre deep. It comprised a round chamber up to a metre across at the western end, a straight channel half a metre wide and another round chamber up to a metre across

62

Plate 3.2: The second
Late Roman grain-
drying/malting oven under
excavation looking east.

at the eastern end. The walls of the structure were near vertical and the base
flat-bottomed.

In two places, clear evidence of modification was found. First, the northern
extent of the eastern arm of the central flue had been narrowed, apparently
by packing the original channel and then cutting a new one, reducing the
width from about 0.50m to 0.35m. The purpose, presumably, was to increase
efficiency: a narrower flue must have induced a faster and hotter flow of air.
Second, in the western extent of the outer flue, a re-cutting of the channel was
seen in section and while this event was not fully understood, it seems likely
that it was linked with the modification observed in the central flue.

Plate 3.3: The second
Late Roman grain-
drying/malting oven after
excavation .

The whole complex contained abundant evidence of extreme heat, with reddened and blackened fills, deposits of charcoal and burnt grain and fire-hardening and discoloration of the clay walls. Its identification as a grain-drying or malting oven seems beyond doubt.

The oven appears to have been designed to carry hot air to a raised granary defined by four posts. Though heavily truncated, it was clear that the postholes had supported substantial timber structures, the best preserved measuring 0.70m across and 0.60m deep. The structure implied by the arrangement of posts would have measured 4.3m east-west by 5.9m north-south.

Another structure, represented by a line of three closely-placed postholes just over a metre north-west of the oven, was of indeterminate form and purpose. It probably belongs to this phase, since it clearly cuts and therefore post-dates the Phase 5 double-flue system.

We assume that the purpose and effect of the distinctive design of the oven was to prevent direct contact between sparks from the furnace and the granary. The precise method by which the hot air was transferred from the end of the secondary flue to the grain could not be reconstructed.

The body in the oven
Upper Chalkpit, Phase 7
c. ?AD 350/375

Industrial activity probably ceased on the site at some point in the mid to late 4th century AD. The pottery assemblage includes some material likely to be of this date (Alice Lyons, pers. comm.). The latest coin from the site dates to the 350s AD, and the latest from its environs to perhaps the 380s AD, but these later issues are swamped by much larger quantities of late 3rd and early-mid 4th century coins.

Before the site was permanently abandoned, however, the furnace was fired one last time. On this occasion the purpose was to cremate a human body. Lying on a layer of soft black ash and charcoal mixed with burnt grain were the fragmentary burnt remains of what turned out to be a complete skeleton (Plate 3.5). The body respected part of the clay wall and roof of the oven superstructure, which had already collapsed, showing that it was partially ruinous when fired for the last time.

The remains were dug in four successive horizontal layers, or 'spits' (Plate 3.8), and each bone fragment was three-dimensionally recorded and then separately bagged and labelled. This allowed subsequent osteological reconstruction of the orientation of the body in the oven, showing that the head had been pushed up against the southern edge, the body had been lying on its right side and the legs had been bent, presumably in order to fit the body inside the chamber (Plate 3.6). The body had been raked after the fire had de-fleshed the bones; a bone fragment from the lower arm was found by the feet.

It was possible to establish that the deceased had been an adult man, approximately 40 years old, with some signs of ante-mortem tooth loss. There was no evidence of trauma on the bones, but these of course survived only in a very fragmentary and fire-damaged condition.

A radiocarbon determination of the age of the body came out at AD 225-

64

Fig. 3.8: Plan showing the position of the burnt bone recovered from spits 1 and 2 in the oven (Phase 7).

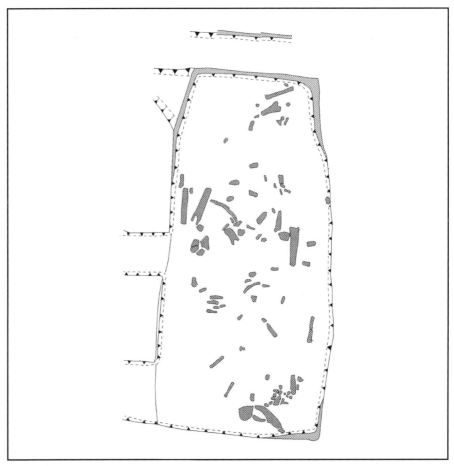

383 (cal. 95%). This means that there is a 95% probability that the body was burnt between these two dates. The evidence of pottery, coins and stratigraphy argues that it was in fact done towards the end of this period. The cremation

Plate 3.4: The body in the oven under excavation by Zannah Baldry.

appears to have been the final event on the site – performed when the oven was already crumbling, having gone out of use perhaps shortly after mid-century, the latest coin being an issue of Magnentius (AD 350-353).

Cremation was not common in the Late Roman period, inhumation having become well established as the normal rite. Although there is evidence that cremation persisted, especially in rural areas, the discovery of an in-situ cremation is extremely rare for this period. The body in the oven is therefore a four-fold anomaly: it is Late Roman in date; it was found in a grain-drying or malting oven; the remains appear to have been left in situ rather than buried; and they did not form part of a cemetery.

Plate 3.5: The body in the oven as revealed by excavation looking south. Note the skull fragments pushed up against the further edge of the oven.

What does this body represent? The SHARP Team is divided and uncertain. There seem to be two main possibilities. One is that the body in the oven represents an unusual cremation burial, since strange and random burials are a feature of Romano-British rural archaeology. The form suggested is an ad-hoc version of what is more formally known as a 'bustum burial'. This is a type of cremation in which a pit is constructed beneath the pyre. The cremated bones then fall into the pit and are buried rather than being collected for re-deposition elsewhere, as is done in most other types of cremation. Grave-goods may or may not be present. Although the treatment of the body in the Sedgeford case might appear to have been less than respectful, the evidence may represent nothing more than the raking essential for the complete burning of the body in an enclosed space. Mention should be made of a 3rd century AD burial in the fill of the stokehole of a pottery kiln at neighbouring Snettisham; not a cremation, but a parallel of sorts nonetheless (Lyons 2004, 24).

This brings us to the second possibility: that this was an attempt to dispose of the body of someone who had been murdered. The circumstantial evidence can be summarised as follows. Isolated burials do occur, but they are the exception not the rule; the vast majority of clearly defined Roman burials, whether cremations or inhumations, are in some sort of association with other bodies in a cemetery, however small. The Sedgeford case was not a proper bustum, there being no pit to receive the bones and no proper burial per se. The placing and raking of the body do appear to have been somewhat 'rough and ready'.

What circumstances might have given rise to 'illegitimate' deposits of human remains in the archaeological record for Late Roman Britain? In the

Plate 3.6: The body in the
oven reconstructed.

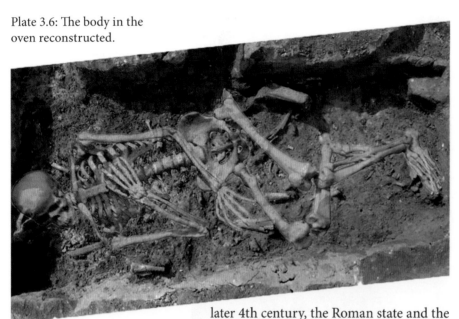

later 4th century, the Roman state and the
Romanised elite lost control over much of
the British countryside. The archaeological evidence seems incontrovertible
in that occupation in forts, towns and villas declined after *c.* AD 350, if not
earlier, and ceased entirely in the years immediately after AD 400. The world
of soldiers, tax-collectors and landlords appears to have fallen apart.

This must have been an era of contested authority and contested landscapes,
as old structures of power were successfully challenged and overturned.
This may have taken different forms. One possibility is that implicit in
various references to *bagaudae* in the western provinces of the Late Roman
Empire: that is, rural social bandits whose resistance to the authority of the
state and the landlords occasionally swelled into full-scale peasant revolt
and the establishment of 'liberated zones' (Thompson 1952, 1977; Faulkner
forthcoming). Another is that of a more generic breakdown of 'law and order',
a resurgence of tribal conflict and the reconfiguration of Britannia as a classic
'failed state' (Laycock 2008).

The Sedgeford body in the oven is certainly not unique. Rod Mackey
excavated another at Welton Wold in East Yorkshire in the 1970s. He reports:
'A sudden dramatic event appears to have ended all occupation at Welton in the
early 5th century. A vivid indication of what may have happened came from
the crop-drier in the sunken-floored building, where the body of a woman
had been pushed, feet-first, into the flue while the fire was still burning. It
would appear that this building, along with the corridor house and one of the
aisled barns, was destroyed by fire ...'

Mackey makes this further point: 'Those who seek to 'pacify' this period
often point to the lack of evidence for violence in the archaeological record,
but they overlook the fact that virtually all the contemporary living-floors and
land surfaces in rural areas have been destroyed by ploughing. Such evidence
might only survive in sunken-floored buildings, as it did in the one at Welton'
(Mackey 2007; pers. comm.).

The rise and fall of the villa estates

Roman Britain was an arena of struggle. The island was conquered by an aggressive and exploitative imperial superpower in the years AD 43-84. In places the indigenous aristocracy mounted an embittered defence of their territory. Often, when they did so, they tapped deep pools of hostility to the occupation forces among the common people of the countryside.

Some such mix powered the Norfolk-centred Boudican Revolt of AD 60/61. When it was defeated, the territory of the Iceni was ravaged by 'fire and sword'. Then a new order was constructed: an imperial regime of landlords, tax-collectors and soldiers in place of the traditional tribal society of the Late Iron Age.

The Roman Empire was a system of robbery with violence whose purpose was to enrich and empower the empire-builders. The mass of people, agricultural producers of one sort or another, paid for empire (the army) and 'civilisation' (the consumption of the elite in towns and villas) in the form of tax, rent, debt and labour service. In essence, the Empire was a system for extracting surplus from the labour of the provincial peasantry and using it to sustain an infrastructure of power.

To maintain control over land and labour, Roman policy was to underpin the wealth and power of local elites and turn them into a class of loyal 'Romanised' gentry. In return for security of property and position, these Romano-British landowners, organised into local ruling bodies, typically town councils, were expected to collect taxes and maintain order. This process was almost certainly gravely impaired in Norfolk by the consequences of the Boudican Revolt. A large proportion of the native aristocracy had been driven into revolt and was presumably destroyed in the fighting and its aftermath. A proportion of the native peasantry must also have been destroyed, and the land therefore, to a significant degree, left depopulated and uncultivated in the years immediately following AD 60/61. This may explain why the imprint of Romanised civilisation seems weaker in Norfolk than in other parts of south-eastern Britain. By the Late Roman period, however, much of the county, not least the north-western part of it, had filled up with villas. A Romanised landowning elite had presumably established itself.

The landowning class – ranging from super-rich imperial 'grandees' to minor local 'gentry' – seem to have used their economic power, their social networks and their political connections to increase their wealth. Late Roman sources imply that much of the Western Imperial peasantry had been reduced to serf status by the 4th century AD. Archaeology records a steady rise in the size and grandeur of villas, reaching a peak, in Britain at least, in the late 3rd and early 4th century AD (Faulkner 2000, 71-74).

Roman Britain, in short, was a class society in which the few (those who lived in grand houses in town and country) grew rich through the exploitation of the many. So instead of thinking of changes in settlement layout and land management simply in terms of functional efficiency – the usual approach – we should pose the question 'who benefits?'.

Change is rarely uncontested, because, more often than not, what is efficient for one turns out to be exploitation for another. Roman Britain, with its huge social chasms and its crude and sometimes brutal mechanisms of surplus appropriation, must have been riddled with latent conflict. The countryside would have been a contested landscape – a place where independent farmsteads were absorbed into villa estates, where tenant farmers became serfs and where, because of this, the breakdown of 'law and order' in remote rural areas must have been rapid once the coercive apparatus of the Roman imperial state had ceased to function.

The main contributors to the writing of this chapter were:

Neil Faulkner (principal author), Matt Hobson (principal author), Lorraine Horsley and Mark Blagg-Newsome

References

Faulkner, N., 2000, *The Decline and Fall of Roman Britain*, Stroud, Tempus.

Faulkner, N., forthcoming, 'Gildas: the red monk of the first peasants' revolt', in Roman Society publication of the AD 410: End of Roman Britain conference.

Gregory, T., 1982, 'Romano-British settlement in West Norfolk and on the Norfolk Fen Edge', in The Romano-British Countryside: studies in rural settlement and economy, B.A.R. No. 103, Part II, Oxford, 351-376.

Jones, A.H.M., 1964, *The Later Roman Empire, 284-602: a social, economic and administrative survey*, Oxford, Blackwell.

Laycock, S., 2008, *Britannia, the failed state: tribal conflicts and the end of Roman Britain*, Stroud, Tempus.

Lyons, A., 2004, *Romano-British Industrial Activity at Snettisham*, Norfolk EAA Occasional Paper 18, Norfolk Museums & Archaeology Services.

Mackey, R., 2007, 'Welton and other eastern Yorkshire villas – evidence for change in the 4th century and beyond', in R.M. and D.E. Friendship-Taylor, *From Villa to Village*, Upper Nene Archaeological Society, Fascicule 7.

Thompson, E.A., 1952, 'Peasant revolts in Late Roman Gaul and Spain', in *Past and Present*, 2, 11-23.

Thompson, E.A., 1977, 'Britain, AD 406-410', in *Britannia*, 8, 303-318.

4. The Coming of the Anglo-Saxons

Roman authority in Britain degraded rapidly from the AD 380s onwards and had terminated completely by AD 410. During the late 4th and early 5th century AD, the former province (and later diocese) of Britannia experienced economic, social, political and cultural transformation on an extraordinary scale. Romanised occupation of forts, towns and villas ended. Inflows of Roman coin dropped to a tiny trickle. Mass production of wheel-thrown pottery ceased. Long-distance trade and communication became rare. As far as we can tell, most people lived in isolated communities, engaged in subsistence agriculture, with minimal links to the wider world.

Written sources for this period are close to non-existent. It is certainly a 'dark age' in terms of historical knowledge. Such narrative sources as we have are much later in date, and their accounts of 5th century events are a mix of orally transmitted legends and 'invented' genealogies and stories designed to legitimise the power of Middle Anglo-Saxon rulers. We think, in particular, of the work of the Venerable Bede.

Bede's *Historia Ecclesiastica Gentis Anglorum*, or 'Ecclesiastical History of the English People' (AD 731), talks of widespread 'migrations' of Angles, Saxons and Jutes into England, leaving Angulus (southern Denmark) uninhabited (Book 1, Chapter 15). Historians once used this as evidence for a widespread post-Roman *adventus* ('entry') by Germanic invaders, spearheaded by the Saxon warlords Hengest and Horsa, who supposedly arrived on the shores of Kent in *c.* AD 449.

This was naive and simplistic. It failed to take proper account of the context within which Bede worked, the character of the source material available to him and the political purpose of his writing. The scholar Eric John tells us that the story of Jutes, Angles and Saxons comes from a Kentish source contemporary with Bede and 'has been cobbled clumsily into Bede's text' (John 1996, 4-5).

Indeed, in a later section of the *Historia Ecclesiastica*, Bede writes that 'there were very many peoples in Germany... from whom the Angles and Saxons, who now live in Britain, derive their origin... these people are the Frisians, Rugians, Danes, Huns, Old Saxons and Boruhtware (Bructeri)' (Book 5, Chapter 9) – a much wider gene pool to draw from than is suggested by the earlier list. Archaeology, for all its limitations, seems a surer guide to a proper understanding of the period.

In Norfolk, there is a complete absence of documentation for the 5th

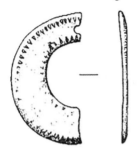

and 6th centuries AD. The scant archaeological evidence tends to support the wider national picture of sharp discontinuities between the 4th and 5th centuries AD. Roman coins post-dating AD 378 are relatively rare (Davies 2009, 233). Period XVb (AD 378-388) coins accounted for only 2% of the total at Brancaster Saxon Shore Fort, while Period XVI (AD 388-402) was represented by a single coin in an identifiable assemblage of 725 (Sparey Green and Gregory 1985). There is no good reason for believing that Roman activity continued on any Norfolk site after *c*. AD 400.

The archaeological evidence from Sedgeford parish fits this pattern well. The Roman agricultural processing site on Upper Chalkpit-Lower Polar Breck seems to have been abandoned by the AD 380s at the latest. Thereafter, until *c*. AD 650/700, evidence for human settlement remains elusive.

Early Anglo-Saxon settlers?

A single pot base (NHER 1603) and a brooch fragment (NHER 37252) of Early Anglo-Saxon date were found on the site of a presumed (but unexcavated) Roman villa north of the river. Although a spatial relationship between Early Anglo-Saxon settlements and Roman buildings in west Norfolk is well-known (Gregory 1982) these finds cannot, by themselves, confirm an Early Anglo-Saxon settlement.

A similar situation is found at the southern edge of the parish, where possible Early Anglo-Saxon pottery sherds and a girdle hanger were recovered during the excavation of ditches on the Roman agricultural processing site at Upper Chalkpit-Lower Polar Breck.

A single decorated sherd of Early Anglo-Saxon pottery recovered during test-pitting at Cole Green in the modern village (see chapter 9) might represent settlement or a cemetery nearby.

In the environs of the Middle Anglo-Saxon settlement on Lower Chalkpit, on the other hand, there is little or nothing in the way of 5th to early 7th century AD artefactual evidence, making it almost certain that this settlement is a *de novo* foundation of mid-late 7th century AD at the earliest.

And yet, as we saw in Chapter 1, several fragments of landscape evidence

Plate 4.1: A piece of Early Anglo-Saxon pot discovered during the course of the Sedgeford Village Survey.

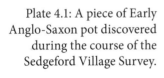

do imply Early Anglo-Settlement in Sedgeford. But what was the character of this community, and what was the nature of the human settlement and land use implied? It is the evidence of burials of 5th to 7th century AD date – even without any modern excavation – that throws the most light on these questions.

Early Anglo-Saxon cemeteries?

During the 19th and early 20th century, a number of cremation urns were recovered in the parish, two of which survive in the Norwich Castle Museum, along with an illustration of a third (and the possibility that two others may also, at some point, have been deposited here).

It is difficult to match these to the somewhat contradictory accounts of what has, at various points, come to light. Our evidence takes the form of brief reports supplied by Holcombe Ingleby, the owner of Sedgeford Hall in the early 20th century, Rainbird Clarke, a leading East Anglian archaeologist in the interwar period, and the official records of Norwich Castle Museum and the Norfolk Historic Environment Record. Let us consider each object in turn.

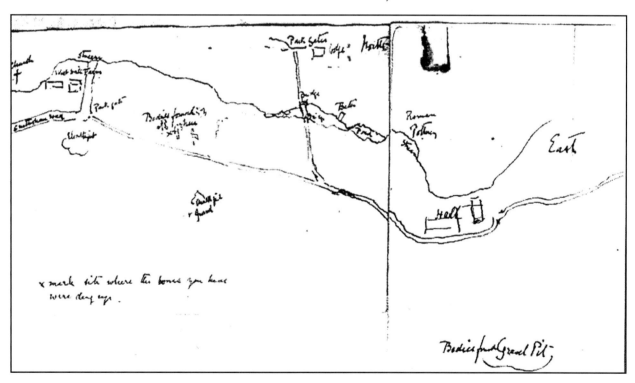

Urn 1 is a decorated cremation urn found in 1826 in a gravel quarry 'north of the river'. It may have contained burnt bone (now lost), and it may have come from the vicinity of the deserted Medieval settlement at Eaton.

Urn 2 is a plain cremation urn found in the 19th century but only acquisitioned by Norwich Castle Museum in 1974. This may be the urn that Holcombe Ingleby says was found 'on the west side of the valley' – though Clarke specifically says that this urn was curated at Sedgeford Hall and subsequently lost without trace.

Fig. 4.2: A map drawn in 1913 by Harriett Ingleby showing possible burial location.

Fig. 4.3: Map of possible Early Anglo-Saxon cemetery sites in Sedgeford.

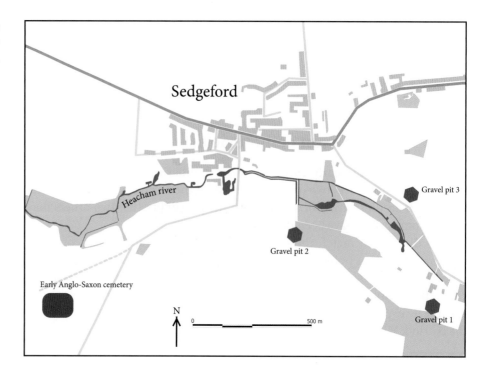

Urn 3 was another plain urn except for bands around the shoulder, but it does not survive and is represented only by a grainy photograph. Since the photograph appears in a publication by Holcombe Ingleby, it may be that this is in fact the vessel found 'on the west side of the valley' that Clarke reports at Sedgeford Hall and later lost. On the other hand, Clarke reports two urns at the Norwich Castle Museum in 1939, and the implication may be that the second is indeed Urn 3, since Urn 2 was acquisitioned only in 1974.

How many cemeteries are represented? We do not know. The records are again scanty and confusing.

When Urn 1 was discovered in 1826, it was, it seems, only one of many. Holcombe Ingleby later reports: 'A labourer, carting gravel from a pit, found, on the falling of some gravel from the side of the pit, a line of urns standing mouth upwards, and without any covers: all but this one are probably destroyed.'

Where was this gravel pit? Local tradition has it that that Urn 1 was found in a pit in Hall Wood a short distance south of Sedgeford Hall (Pit 1).

Pit 1

This pit is shown on a sketch map (see Fig. 4.2) drawn by Harriett Ingleby (the wife of Holcombe Ingleby). It has the words 'Bodies found' next to the words 'Gravel Pit' in this location. (This map was supplied to the Royal College of Surgeons when some human remains from Sedgeford were sent to them by Holcombe Ingleby sometime between 1913 and 1922. It is held in their archive.) Limited evaluation pits were dug in this gravel pit in 2000, but nothing was found and the area is not suitable for geophysical survey.

At least one other chalk and gravel pit is known further west in Hall Wood (Pit 2).

Pit 2

This is also shown on the sketch-map drawn by Harriett Ingleby. She did not suggest, however, that either human remains or cremation urns had been found here. The site has not been investigated.

Holcombe Ingleby specifically stated that Urn 1 was found on the northern side of the river, and this is how its provenance is recorded at the Norwich Castle Museum. One possibility is a pit cut into a gravel terrace above the Sedgeford-Fring road (Pit 3).

Pit 3

The pit is now very overgrown and has been used for waste dumping. It has not been investigated.

Holcombe Ingleby himself excavated a group of inhumations from another site marked on Harriet's sketch map. In a location which is clearly the field now known as Boneyard there are the words 'Bodies found here' and an 'X'; at the bottom of the sketch is written 'X mark site where the bones you have were dug up'. Some of the remains were sent to the Royal College of Surgeons Museum in London, and were later transferred to the Natural History Museum. There is no reason to doubt that these are the remains of Middle Anglo-Saxons from the Boneyard-Reeddam cemetery investigated by SHARP between 1996 and 2007 (see the next two chapters); in other words, they were not Early Anglo-Saxons.

Plate 4.2: Sedgeford Urn 1.

Plate 4.3 Sedgeford Urn 2.

Plate 4.4: Sedgeford Urn 3
.

All of these sites are on the eastern side of the parish. Yet Holcombe Ingleby was unequivocal about a discovery on the western side, and the Norfolk Historic Environment Record reports both an urn from the 'west side of the valley' and another 'found at Eaton'. It is highly likely that one or both came from the Early Anglo-Saxon cemetery now known to exist in the western part of the parish on the site of a probable ploughed-out barrow, where an Early Anglo-Saxon spearhead was found in 1952 (NHER 1473).

Plate 4.5: Sedgeford Urn 1 with lid in place.

0 cm   20 cm

More than 180 artefacts have been recovered from this site by metal-detector survey, dating from the late 5th to the early 7th century AD. The objects include many brooches, wrist clasps and girdle hangers, a strap fitting, a ring, a gilt shield mount, a sword, tweezers and a bucket, which might represent an accessory vessel. A fragment of decorated silver sheet is a high-status find. Human bone is also present, implying disturbed inhumation burials. Towards the eastern extent of the site, however, finds of melted copper-alloy artefacts, pottery fragments, burnt human remains and a burnt antler indicate the additional presence of cremation burials.

Many finds come from a discrete, roughly circular area of dark soil, 90m in diameter, towards the north-eastern extent of the site, presumed to be the location of a ploughed-out prehistoric barrow. The site also overlooks the probable Roman villa on the northern slope of the Heacham River valley. The implication is deliberate placing of the cemetery to achieve symbolic 'appropriation' of the landscape by a new culture-group.

It is clear that both cremation and inhumation was practised in Sedgeford between the 5th and 7th centuries, apparently at the same locations. Yet establishing the location, let alone the relative chronology, of most of the cemeteries is at present impossible. It is notable, however, that the Early Anglo-Saxon material appears to be located at a distance from the main Middle Anglo-Saxon site, which is positioned almost centrally between presumed Early Anglo-Saxon cemeteries. Comparison may be made with Bloodmoor Hill, Carlton Colville, Suffolk, where metal detector finds of 5th and 6th century AD artefacts have been recovered about 500m south-west of a settlement and cemetery of the 6th to 8th centuries AD (possibly representing an estate centre) (Lucy *et al* 2009, 8-11).

Elite displacement or folk movement?

Much of the evidence reviewed here is overtly Germanic in character – from the art styles of metal objects to the pagan practice of cremation and burial in urns. What should we make of it?

That the two centuries from AD 400 to 600 saw a degree of migration – whether through invasion or invitation – of people from north-west Europe and Scandinavia into England is clear. Indeed, some 5th century cremation urns found at Markshall in Norfolk appear to have been made by the same potter as urns found in Wehden in Lower Saxony, perhaps implying direct migration to the former from the latter by a specific group of Saxons (Myres and Green 1973).

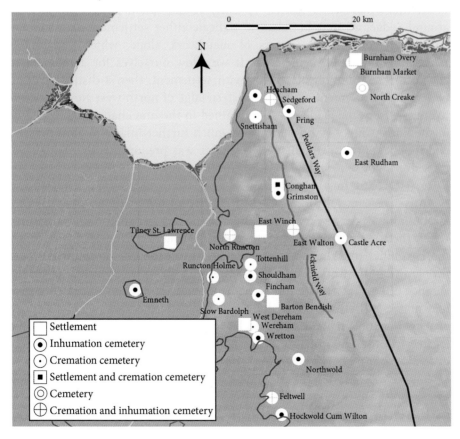

Fig. 4.4: Map showing distribution of Early Anglo-Saxon sites in north-west Norfolk. The red line indicates a possible coastline for the east of the Wash, based on the five metre contour.

This may not imply a mass movement of people; indeed, this traditional interpretation of the Anglo-Saxon *adventus* is now widely challenged. The common assumption today is that a relatively small number of warriors – a military elite – imposed themselves on the south-eastern parts of the island and, by some means, caused the local British population to adopt a new culture – the culture we see represented in artefacts, burial practice and language. This may be what the Sedgeford evidence indicates.

At this stage, however, thinking of Sedgeford – a parish – as a coherent entity may not be helpful. It is unlikely that the parochial system would have formed until Anglo-Saxon England had moved away from the purely local and rural to evolve more centralised political authority. Because of this, to provide a better interpretation of the settlement evidence in Sedgeford parish, it may be useful to look at the surrounding area (Fig. 4.5). What sort of broader pattern can we see?

At Snettisham, Early Anglo-Saxon pottery, animal bone and undated metalworking debris was recovered near a Roman villa during the 1950s (NHER 1531/1529). These finds might represent the main settlement which the Sedgeford cemeteries served, though there was also a large Early Anglo-Saxon cemetery to the north of Snettisham. There may also have been a settlement at Heacham on the coastal fringe, where a possible Middle Anglo-Saxon site of exchange, adjacent to an Early Anglo-Saxon cemetery, is indicated by metalwork finds north and east of the present settlement (NHER 16297, 37217). Fieldwalking finds of Early Anglo-Saxon pottery from Docking, which was to become the centre of a Late Anglo-Saxon hundred, may also indicate a settlement as opposed to a cemetery (NHER 34174).

At this wider scale, scatters of Early Anglo-Saxon pottery in parishes around Sedgeford may be taken to indicate either settlement or cremation burials, in contrast to scatters of metalwork alone, which presumably represent inhumation cemeteries. If we allow ourselves for a moment to equate the distribution of pottery with settlement, then a distinct pattern of dispersed settlement along the western edge of north-west Norfolk seems to emerge from the evidence. As explained in the first chapter, the coastline in the Early Anglo-Saxon period was much further inland than at present, and it appears that settlement at this time was predominantly, though not exclusively, concentrated along the coastal edges and at the mouths of the Rivers Heacham, Ingol and Hun.

In contrast, metalwork scatters indicative of inhumation cemeteries are located away from the main settlement areas further inland and along the rivers; there seem to be notable examples at Fring and Ringstead. This raises the possibility that there was a deliberate delineation between areas where people lived and worked and areas where the dead were buried. If so, the absence of Early Anglo-Saxon settlement evidence within Sedgeford parish may not be entirely unexpected. Though the pattern across much of the rest of Anglo-Saxon England seems to be for settlements and cemeteries to be located in close proximity, typically within half a kilometre of each other, a different pattern may be emerging for north-west Norfolk.

It is possible, of course, that we have a residual Romano-British population whose presence is revealed only through their adoption of Anglo-Saxon burial practice, their settlements remaining, here as across most of Britain, archaeologically invisible. Equally, we may simply have failed as yet to locate an Early Anglo-Saxon settlement focus.

Whether or not there was deliberate separation between a zone of the living and a zone of the dead, the general evidence raises one final – and crucial – question that leads us into the next chapter of the book: the much debated issue of settlement nucleation.

Although we at present lack hard evidence for Early Anglo-Saxon settlement in the Sedgeford environs, our working hypothesis has to be that the general pattern was similar to that for Anglo-Saxon England more widely, namely that settlements were small and scattered and that, internally, they had the form of a 'loose' or 'informal' cluster. Both Mucking in Essex and West Stow in Suffolk provide type-sites. Mucking featured loose clusters of timber halls and ancillary buildings that shifted position perhaps every 25 or 30 years, with little evidence for bounded enclosures. This form of settlement may have been made possible by lack of pressure upon, or restriction in the use of, the available land (Hamerow 1993, *passim*; Hamerow 2002, 94-95; Turner 2003, 51). West Stow may have been less mobile, with replacement structures constructed in close proximity to earlier ones, but it too comprised timber halls and ancillary buildings within a settlement space that seems to have lacked clearly defined plot boundaries, at least until the final phase of occupation (Welch 1992, 21-28). This 'looseness' may reflect the relatively egalitarian and free organisation of Early Anglo-Saxon society, as revealed in the archaeology of both the Early English settlements and their Continental antecedents (Hamerow 1991).

In contrast, the subsequent Middle Anglo-Saxon settlement and cemetery on the Boneyard-Reeddam and Lower Chalkpit site, the subject of the next chapter, appears to be the first post-Roman nucleated settlement in Sedgeford parish. By 'nucleated' we mean a multi-functional settlement focus where, for whatever reason and by whatever authority, individuals and communities are brought together in the same location for a sustained period (though the use of a term such as 'village', with all its implied High Medieval infrastructure of church and manor, may be inappropriate at this early date).

Although, as more settlements are investigated, the evolutionary model of simple 'dispersed' to complex 'nucleated' settlement is breaking down, it is certain that the 7th and 8th centuries AD do indeed see the emergence of new settlement types like that at Sedgeford. Why was this happening?

A key characteristic of Middle Anglo-Saxon nucleated sites is the introduction of boundary features (such as ditches around individual plots). These seem to reflect the imposition of new forms of social relationship and new notions of private ownership of space (Reynolds 2003). The most likely explanation for this is the emergence of elite groups, whether secular, ecclesiastical, or both, who had taken control of the landscape, its resources and its people, and who were reorganising these to facilitate resource exploitation and to improve surplus accumulation. Boundaries may have anthropological significance, as when sanctuaries are enclosed to separate sacred and profane space. But they may also have sociological significance, as when they enclose the commons, demarcate private property and give testimony to new social relations.

The main contributors to the writing of this chapter were:

Gareth Davies (principal author) with Keith Robinson, Nicci Neilson, Brenda Stibbons.

References

Davies, J., 2009, *The Land of Boudica: Prehistoric and Roman Norfolk*, Oxford, Heritage/Norfolk Museums and Archaeology Service.

Gregory, T., 1982, 'Romano-British settlement in West Norfolk and on the Norfolk Fen Edge', in *The Romano-British Countryside: studies in rural settlement and economy*, B.A.R. No. 103, Part II, Oxford, 351-376.

Hamerow, H.F., 1991, 'Settlement mobility and the "Middle Saxon Shift": rural settlements and settlement patterns in Anglo-Saxon England', in *Anglo-Saxon England*, 20, 1-17.

Hamerow, H.F., 1993, *Mucking, Volume 2, The Anglo-Saxon Settlement*, London, English Heritage.

Hamerow, H.F., 2002, *Early Medieval Settlements: the archaeology of rural communities in north-west Europe, 400-900*, Oxford, Oxford University Press.

Ingleby, H., 1922-1925, *The Charm of a Village: an account of Sedgeford with its history and its carnivals*, London, Clement Ingleby.

John, E., 1996, *Reassessing Anglo-Saxon England*, Manchester, Manchester University Press.

Lucy, S., Dickens, A. and Tipper, J., 2009, *The Anglo-Saxon Settlement and Cemetery at Bloodmoor Hill, Carlton Colville, Suffolk*, East Anglian Archaeology No. 131, Cambridge, Cambridge Archaeological Unit with ALGAO East.

McClure, J. and Collins, R. (eds), 1999, *Bede: the Ecclesiastical History of the English People*, Oxford, Oxford University Press.

Myres, J.N.L. and Green, B., 1973, *The Anglo-Saxon Cemeteries of Caistor-by-Norwich and Markshall*, Norfolk, Society of Antiquaries of London, Research Committee Report No. 30, London, Society of Antiquaries London.

Reynolds, A., 2003 'Boundaries and settlements in later sixth to eleventh century England', in D. Griffiths, *et al* (eds.), *Boundaries in Early Medieval Britain*, Anglo-Saxon Studies in Archaeology and History, No. 12, Oxford, Oxford University School of Archaeology, 98-136.

Sparey Green, C. and Gregory, T., 1985, 'Surface finds: the coins', in J. Hinchliffe with C. Sparey Green (eds.), *Excavations at Brancaster*, 1974 and 1977, East Anglian Archaeology Report No. 23, Gressenhall, Norfolk Archaeological Unit, 190-194.

Turner, S., 2003, 'Boundaries and religion: the demarcation of early Christian settlements in Britain', in D. Griffiths *et al* (eds.), *Boundaries in Early Medieval Britain, Anglo-Saxon Studies in Archaeology and History*, No. 12, Oxford, Oxford University School of Archaeology, 50-57.

Welch, M., 1992, *Anglo-Saxon England*, London, Batsford.

5. A Middle Anglo-Saxon Settlement

Introduction

SHARP's excavations on the Boneyard-Reeddam site, begun in 1996 and completed in 2007, followed several previous phases of archaeological investigation in the immediate area. In 1953 a local amateur, C. Lewton-Brain, had investigated an earthwork visible in the Reeddam, which he interpreted as a hut platform. The small triangular field immediately south of Reeddam had come to be known locally as 'the Boneyard' due to the ploughing up of human bone. The name was substantiated when the threat of deep ploughing led to two seasons of excavation by the Ministry of Public Buildings and Works under the direction of Peter Jewell in the years 1957-1958.

Jewell's work was aimed at determining the general character and extent of the site. It therefore began with extensive test-pitting, followed by the excavation of several larger areas. He excavated 'some thirty' skeletons as well as focusing on an area of settlement towards the western limit of the cemetery. Two years later, Don Brothwell conducted a further excavation and recovered a larger sample of human remains. Finally, in 1991, an archaeological watching brief undertaken by the Norfolk Archaeological Unit on the cutting of an Anglian Water sewage pipe along the southern and eastern limits of Boneyard Field recorded the remains of a bread oven, crop-drier, or kiln of some other kind of probable Middle Anglo-Saxon date (Bates 1991).

The excavations of Jewell and Brothwell were never published, and the only record of Lewton-Brain's investigations was a series of letters he wrote to the then-curator of Norwich Castle Museum, R. Rainbird Clarke. A major aim of the SHARP team from the beginning was therefore to make information on the Anglo-Saxon cemetery more widely available, as well as conducting further large-scale excavations to build a fuller picture of the site, its character and its chronology.

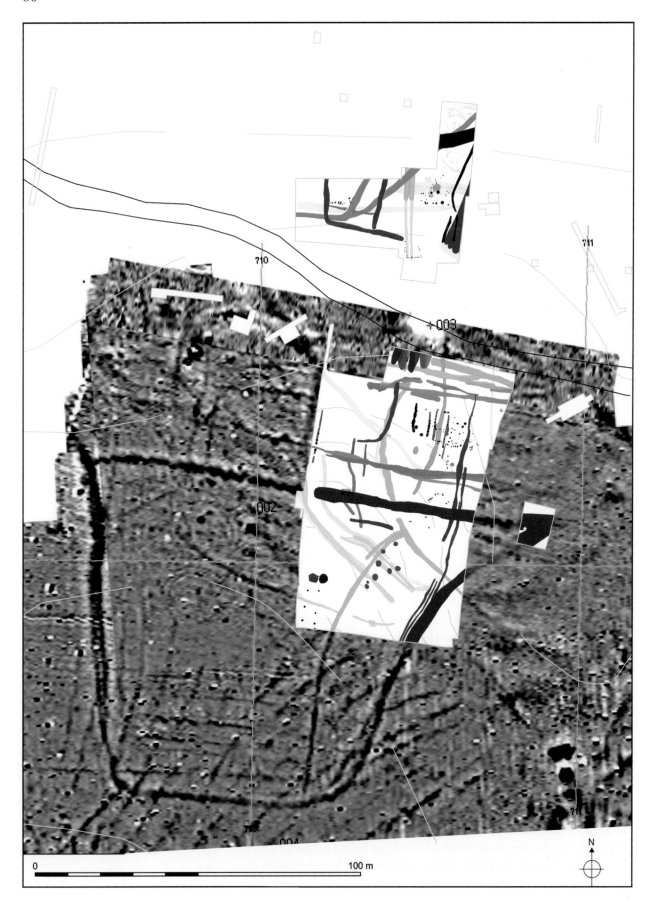

0   100 m

N

As the Boneyard-Reeddam excavations concluded in the summer of 2007, evaluation work commenced on the northern part of Chalkpit Field, which lies on the opposite side of the trackway immediately south of Boneyard and Reeddam. The field is named after a disused chalk-pit in its north-western corner. The archaeological site has been dubbed 'Chalkpit North' or 'Lower Chalkpit'; the latter designation is used throughout this volume.

The River Heacham currently runs about 200m north of Lower Chalkpit, though it was almost certainly closer to the site in Anglo-Saxon times, with the river valley as a whole probably forming an extensive marshland. The valley rises relatively steeply from the Reeddam, through Boneyard, and onwards up Chalkpit Field towards, at its southern end, a gently sloping downland plateau of approximately 60m or so at the highest points.

The eastern edge of Lower Chalkpit rises from a well defined north-south glacial gully. The western edge has been quarried for chalk. The geology comprises Cretaceous Middle Chalk overlain by very mixed glacial and alluvial sand, gravel and crushed chalk. On the higher parts of the site, which ranges from approximately 26m to 34m above sea-level, plough truncation has destroyed all evidence except for the bases of features cut into the chalk bedrock.

Fieldwalking in 1996-1997 and 2002 recovered a significant quantity of Ipswich and Thetford-type Wares in an area extending about 100m south of the northern end of Chalkpit Field. The surface scatter appeared to peter out towards both the north-east and north-west corners of the field.

In April 2007 a magnetometry survey was undertaken over a rectangular area measuring 200m east-west by 120m north-south. The survey grid was aligned with the northern field boundary and extended across the area of the pottery scatter. The survey revealed a number of north-south and east-west linear 'anomalies' likely to represent the remains of boundary ditches, along with various discrete 'anomalies' suggestive of pits or kilns/ovens. Particularly striking was what appeared to be a huge D-shaped enclosure surrounded by a wide, deep ditch truly monumental in scale.

The layout of the anomalies strongly suggested the ditched fields and trackways, rectangular plot boundaries and associated domestic features of a well-organised community, very likely of Middle to Late Anglo-Saxon date. The density of the features and the cross-cutting of different alignments implied more than one phase of use.

The Lower Chalkpit excavations are ongoing. More of the site is due to be revealed in future seasons. Full post-excavation analysis of existing assemblages of animal bones and small finds is yet to be done. However, stratigraphic analysis of the sequence of cuts and deposits excavated between 2007 and 2012, assisted by pottery analysis which has kept pace with the excavations, is already complete. What follows, therefore, is a single story: that of an evolving Anglo-Saxon settlement and cemetery of c. AD 650/700-925/950, based upon two major zones of open-area research excavation, that in Lower Chalkpit and that in Boneyard-Reeddam. There seems little doubt, moreover, that this was the primary settlement in the Sedgeford area at this date. Extensive fieldwalking, especially in the southern part of the parish, and the work of the Sedgeford Village Survey on the northern side of the river (as reported in Chapter 9), revealed no evidence of Middle Anglo-Saxon settlement elsewhere.

Fig. 5.1, opposite: Plan showing all major archaeological features revealed on the main excavations on Boneyard-Reeddam and Lower Chalkpit between 1996 and 2012, superimposed on a magnetometry survey. A plan showing all excavations on the Boneyard-Reeddam and Lower Chalkpit site is on page 4.

82

Plate 5.1: View across the Boneyard excavation in 1996 looking north-west.

Plate 5.2: View of the Reeddam excavation in 1997 looking north-east.

Plate 5.3: View across New Trench on Boneyard in 2002 looking north.

Plate 5.4: View across Old Trench on Boneyard in 2002 looking north-east. Note the baulk on the left-hand side separating Old from New Trench.

Plate 5.5: View of the Old Trench excavation in 2006 looking east, showing the waterlogged conditions and dark soil staining at the bottom of the slope.

Plate 5.6: View of the New Trench excavation in 2006 looking south, showing the dry, sandy soil conditions at the top of the slope.

Plate 5.7: View of the Lower Chalkpit excavations in 2009 looking north-west.

Plate 5.8: View of the Lower Chalkpit excavations in 2011 looking north-west, showing plough-marks across the chalk bedrock indicative of severe truncation of archaeological features.

The Boneyard-Reeddam and Lower Chalkpit excavations

SHARP's programme of excavation on Boneyard Field began in the dry summer of 1996, with the opening of a 20m x 15m area between the then-backfilled trenches excavated by Jewell and Brothwell between 1957 and 1960. Additionally, four test-pits and an evaluation trench were opened in the Reeddam, rendered more accessible then by the relatively low water-level that year.

The following excavation season saw the commencement of a 10m x 5m area excavation in the Reeddam, directly north of the main trench, and linked to it by a 3m-wide connecting trench, later expanded to the full 10m width over the course of the following seasons.

Two evaluation trenches, the first of these excavated in 2000 to the east of the main excavation area, and the second in 2001-2002 to the west (a 35m x 1.5m trench aligned north-south known as 'Reeddam 2'), were positioned to confirm that the main focus of the cemetery did indeed lie between them.

By 2001 we had decided that Jewell's former trenches could best be located in relation to SHARP's excavations by a further large area excavation within which they would be fully incorporated. The entire former area of SHARP's excavation now became known as 'Old Trench', with the large area opened in 2001 being referred to as 'New Trench'. The narrow baulk between these two areas was eventually removed, and they are therefore discussed here as a whole. This is the Boneyard-Reeddam excavation of 1996-2007.

In the year the Boneyard-Reeddam excavations ended, five evaluation trenches (1-5) were dug on Lower Chalkpit in response to earlier fieldwalking and geophysical evidence. These confirmed the quality of the archaeology and provided the basis for digging a series of open-area excavation trenches in the succeeding years. Trench 6 was the main excavation in 2008, but was supplemented by the smaller Trenches 7, 8 and 9. Trench 10 was dug in 2009 and a long, narrow, naturally formed rain-gully was cleaned and recorded (Trench 11). Trenches 12 and 13 were dug in 2010, Trench 14 in 2011 and Trench 15 in 2012. (Trenches 16 and 17 were excavated in 2013, but results from these excavations are not included in this publication).

The overall sample is large. The Boneyard-Reeddam excavations measured 50m by 40m at their greatest extent and approximately 1,200m² in total, the Lower Chalkpit excavations 90m by 60m and 5,400m² overall. Taking account of various other smaller interventions over the years, more than 7,000m² of the Middle Anglo-Saxon settlement and associated cemetery have been seen in excavation. Many questions remain; but there is much that can now be reported.

An Anglo-Saxon rural settlement
Phase 3 c. AD 650/700-725

After Late Iron Age activity ceased on Boneyard-Reeddam (Phase 2a), perhaps with some sort of 'closure' ceremony at the sacred site in the 60s AD (see Chapter 2), the land seems to have been given over to agricultural use. The only major Roman feature was a substantial east-west ditch (Phase 2b), presumably some sort of land boundary associated with the development of a new agricultural regime, most likely in the late 1st or early 2nd century AD at the earliest. Then activity ceased entirely, or at least such as might give rise to archaeological features.

This period of inactivity, perhaps from AD 200 to AD 650/700, is represented physically by the accumulation of a thick layer of hillwash over the central and northern portions of the trench, sealing the Late Iron Age and Roman features beneath.

Phases 1 and 2 on this site are discussed in Chapter 2.

The site is located on quite a steep north-facing slope, with hillwash deposits far thicker at the foot of the slope. At the southern extent of the excavation area, however, the same process of erosion and deposition from top to bottom has meant not only the absence of this layer, but also severe truncation and much poorer preservation of archaeological features. The ploughing out of Anglo-Saxon graves on the upper part of the slope during the 20th century – thus 'the Boneyard' – is an obvious indication of the problem. For the most part, this post-Roman hillwash layer is a mid-brown sandy silt, although at the foot of the slope it has been leached to a mid-grey colour due to waterlogging.

The first phase of post-Roman activity is represented by two parallel north-south aligned ditches, which were cut into the hillwash layer on the middle slope, and into natural glacial sand at the top. These two ditches formed a single boundary running the entire length of the trench. What did this boundary delineate?

A strong possibility is that it was an early cemetery boundary. A secondary possibility is that Structure C (Fig. 5.4) was also contemporary with it. Neither cemetery nor structure have been shown on the Phase 3 plan, however, as we cannot be sure. What is certainly true is that the boundary was partially reinstated in Phase 4, by which time there can be no real doubt that both the cemetery and probably Structure C were in use. Our problem here is that there were no direct stratigraphic relationships between ditches, burials and postholes, so the different features represented are, in a sense, 'floating'.

Our assumption is that the double-ditched boundary on Boneyard-Reeddam was broadly contemporary with what appears to be a ditched trackway on a north-west to south-east alignment on Lower Chalkpit (Fig. 5.2). The uniform width, the distinctive kink towards the north-eastern end, the slight character of the ditches and the similarity of the respective fills, all point to the two ditches having formed two sides of some sort of track or droveway. This ditched trackway, moreover, may have doubled as a boundary around a settled area to its north-west.

The ditches were re-cut at least three times, suggesting that the trackway and boundary were in use for some time. One intriguing find from the fill of one of the ditches was an articulated dog skeleton, partly cut away by a ditch of later date. The only other features that appear to have been contemporary are a couple of random extents of ditch and a pit, from which no useful conclusions can be drawn.

The features of this phase are dated by local, handmade, grass-tempered pottery. Though this type of pottery was produced throughout the Early Anglo-Saxon period and well into the Middle Anglo-Saxon period, a tighter date is made possible by two other considerations. The first is the total absence of Ipswich Ware, which is abundant in later deposits across the site, making it almost certain that this phase predates the first arrival of Ipswich Ware at Sedgeford, probably around AD 720/725. The second is the absence of any apparent break in activity between Phases 3 and 4, making it unlikely that much time elapsed between them; since Phase 4 is dated by Ipswich Ware, we can therefore safely assume that Phase 3 represents late 7th or early 8th century activity.

Though the evidence is ephemeral and fragmentary, there is enough to say that the Middle Anglo-Saxon nucleated settlement and associated cemetery in

Fig. 5.2: Plan of Phase 3 of the Middle Anglo-Saxon settlement and cemetery on Boneyard-Reeddam/Lower Chalkpit.

0   100 m

N

the centre of Sedgeford had its origins in the years around AD 700 at the latest. We can further speculate that some kind of centralised authority – whether secular or ecclesiastical – may already have been imposing a formal layout to demarcate space on Boneyard-Reeddam. We may in that case also note the apparent contrast between the linear regularity of the possible western cemetery boundary and the curvilinear and ephemeral character of the supposed settlement boundary further up the slope (Figs. 5.3 and 5.4).

An Anglo-Saxon rural settlement
Phase 4 c. AD 725-?775/825

Irrespective of whether or not the cemetery was first used in Phase 3, there seems little doubt that it was in use by Phase 4, when the linear, north-south, double-ditched boundary was re-cut, but only along its northern extent. While the burials respect this reinstated boundary, along with a rectangular area immediately east of it, several others cut the fills of its earlier southern extension. Perhaps the implication is that a small cemetery eventually outgrew its original limits and spread across an earlier boundary. Again, the circumstantial evidence might be pointing towards an origin for the cemetery during Phase 3.

The layout of the graves makes it almost certain that Structure C (Figs. 5.3 and 5.4) was contemporary with the cemetery. The posthole arrangement implies a small structure of at least 5m by 3m, aligned east-west and therefore at right-angles to the western cemetery boundary. There may also have been associated east-west beam-slots or drip gullies, but the evidence was highly ephemeral and uncertain. Several refuse pits containing animal bones and oyster shells were found in its general vicinity.

The north-south boundary ditches terminated roughly in line with the southern side of Structure C, adding to the impression that we have a group of features – burials, building and boundary – that were contemporary and related to one another in some way. Was Structure C some sort of timber chapel? Many of the fills contained quantities of Ipswich Ware, pushing this phase beyond *c.* AD 720/725.

Broadly contemporary with Structure C – and dated by a mix of grass-tempered pottery and some Ipswich Ware – was a substantial curvilinear boundary ditch on Lower Chalkpit. It seems very likely that this was enclosing a settlement to the east. The boundary was formed of two extents of curving ditch separated by an entranceway. The ditch shows evidence of having been re-cut, suggesting active maintenance of the boundary.

The northern end of the ditch contained an articulated calf skeleton with a deposit of unprocessed mussel-shells on top (Plate 5.9). This looks like a 'structured deposit' and evidence for some sort of ceremonial marking of the boundary at another entranceway.

Opposite and close to the more southerly entrance was Structure A (Figs. 5.3 and 5.4). Measuring just under 5m by 5m, Structure A stands on a north-east to south-west alignment and is formed of 20 postholes forming a rough rectangle on three sides, the rest having been lost due to the later cutting of a ditch. It is likely to have been a residential 'hall'. Close dating is impossible, but the building's alignment, its truncation by a later ditch and the proximity of the entranceway through the boundary ditch, all imply that it belongs to Phase 4.

Plate 5.9: Photo of the articulated calf skeleton – and probable ritual deposit – in the boundary ditch of the Middle Anglo-Saxon settlement of Phase 4.

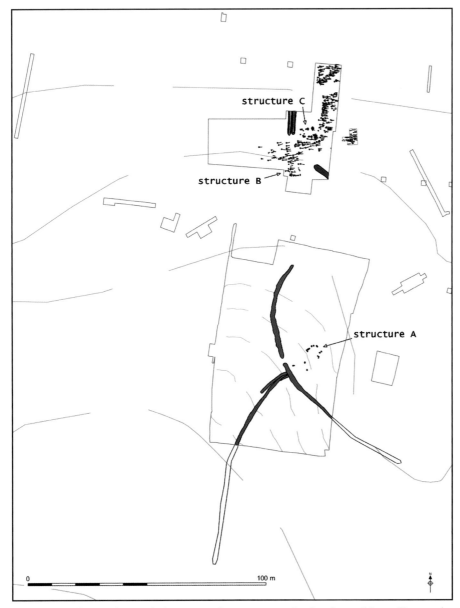

Fig. 5.3: Plan of Phase 4 of the Middle Anglo-Saxon settlement and cemetery on Boneyard-Reeddam/Lower Chalkpit.

There is less to be said about another curving ditch, aligned broadly north-east to south-west, which joins the other close to its entranceway. Clearly these two features were contemporary and therefore part of a single system of land division. Re-cutting again provides evidence for relative longevity. We are left guessing as to its purpose.

The contrast between the rectilinear form of the cemetery layout on Boneyard-Reeddam and the curvilinear form of the settlement layout on Lower Chalkpit must again be stressed. We cannot be certain, but the temptation is to speculate that the Church was imposing a regular order on the cemetery – 'the realm of the dead' – at a time when lordship, whether ecclesiastical or secular, was not sufficiently developed to be able to impose a comparable order on the associated settlement – 'the realm of the living'. This is perhaps the imprint of a world in transition – from the relative looseness of Early Anglo-Saxon society to the more regulated, top-down social order of later centuries.

Box 5.1
Middle Anglo-Saxon buildings in Sedgeford

Phase 4 (c. AD 725–?775/825)

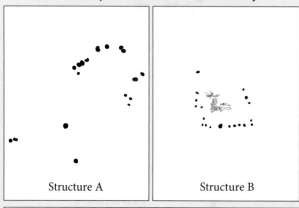

Structure A

Structure B

Structure C

Phase 5a (c. AD ?775/825–?800/875)

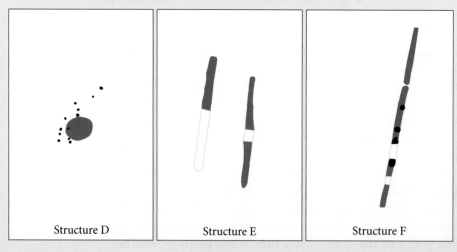

Structure D

Structure E

Structure F

0   20 M

Fig. 5.4: Individual plans of the Middle-Late Anglo-Saxon structures found on Boneyard-Reeddam and Lower
Chalkpit. All are drawn to the same scale and orientation. They show the building methods used.
Posthole structures: A, B, C, G, J and K.
Post-in-trench structures F, H and I
Beamslot structure E.

Phase 5b (c. AD ?800/875-850/925)

Structure G

Phase 6 (c. AD 850/925-?900/950)

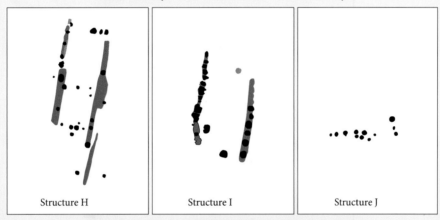

Structure H   Structure I   Structure J

Phase 7 (c. AD ?900/950-?975/1025)

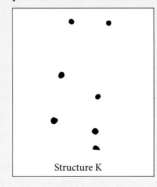

Structure K

An Anglo-Saxon cemetery
Phases ?3, 4 and 5 c. AD 650/725–850/875

SHARP excavated 291 discrete Anglo-Saxon burials on the Boneyard-Reeddam site between 1996 and 2007 and 126 others were excavated in 1957, 1958 and 1960. Our current best guess is that this probably represents between a quarter and a half of the total cemetery population, a rough estimate based on the density of the sample investigated and our current best guess about the approximate limits of the cemetery on the basis of excavation evidence.

The burials appear to follow a broadly Christian rite. They were laid out on their backs with their heads approximately to the west and feet roughly to the east. The Boneyard-Reeddam burials do not seem to contain grave-goods. This essentially pagan practice was disappearing during the 7th century AD, when many 'Final Phase' Early Anglo-Saxon cemeteries received burials without

Fig. 5.5: Plan of the Middle Anglo-Saxon cemetery on Boneyard-Reeddam (Phases 3, 4 and 5).

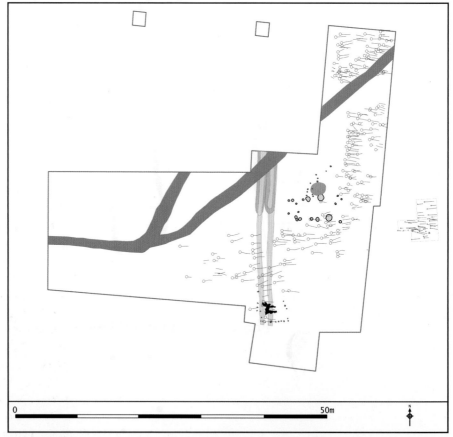

grave-goods; the Boneyard-Reeddam cemetery can be regarded as a firmly Christian-style cemetery post-dating the transitional period represented by the 'Final Phase'. There are, however, a couple of oddities.

The first is the burial of a horse, radiocarbon-dated between the late 7th and the early 9th century AD. The horse may have been buried with a woman, or the latter burial may have been one of a number cutting into that of the horse; there is disagreement within the Team (see Box 5.2). The second is represented by a small pit containing an Ipswich Ware pitcher, two iron

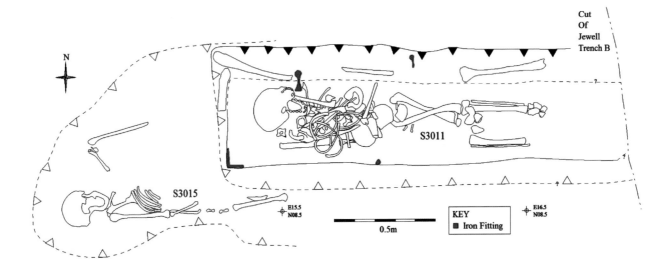

knives and a quantity of smithing slag (Plate 5.10). This may or may not have been associated with cremated human bone: none was found, but the deposit lay just beneath the ploughsoil and had been heavily disturbed.

These two examples may indicate the survival of different burial practices at the beginning of the cemetery's life or even somewhat later. The radiocarbon date for the horse skeleton is similar to that for two Boneyard-Reeddam human skeletons – AD 670-820 compared with AD 662-869 and AD 713-884 – and the Ipswich Ware pitcher implies a date of AD 720/725 at the earliest. Whether early or later, these two burials were unquestionably abnormal. The rest of the excavated burials all fall into one of two types: coffined and un-coffined.

Fig. 5.6: Plan of Skeleton S3011 showing that it was buried in a coffin. The coffin fittings are shown in red and soil staining from the wood was clearly defined on the south and west sides. The grave cut for S3011 disturbed bones from a previous burial, S3015, which were then placed around the coffin.

Coffin burials

The less common rite employed wooden coffins. The main evidence for these has been in the form of large, heavily corroded iron coffin-fittings and nails.

Plate 5.10: A broken Ipswich Ware pitcher associated with the two iron knives found in a pit on Boneyard in 1996.

Eighty coffin fittings were recovered from the Boneyard-Reeddam excavations, although not all of these were found within grave-cuts. In a very few cases, the decayed wood of the coffin had also left stains in the soil surrounding the body. The best example is shown in Fig. 5.6.

The surviving evidence indicates that the normal shape for a Sedgeford coffin was a simple rectangular box. The planks which formed the box were held together at right angles to one another by L-shaped iron brackets, a form of construction known from other Anglo-Saxon burial sites (e.g. Heighway and Bryant 1999, 209). In at least three cases the iron brackets were hinged, turning a simple coffin into a chest burial (Kjølbye-Biddle 1995, 490). Such burial practice is characteristic of the Middle Anglo-Saxon period, particularly in northern England (Craig-Atkins 2012, 317).

This merits further comment. In many traditional societies, chests for storing household valuables are important high-status domestic artefacts, denoting the prosperity and well-being of the family. The burial of a body in a chest – whether a reused household item or a purpose-built funerary artefact similar in form – would have corresponding significance. The deceased would be passing from life to death (or rather, to the afterlife) contained within a symbolic representation of the household. Perhaps, in this sense, Middle Anglo-Saxon burials contained grave-goods after all – ones reconfigured to conform to the now dominant Christian rite. If chest burial is indeed a sign of high status at Sedgeford, it is particularly interesting that our best preserved example contained the skeleton of a boy only about 10 years old.

Another common feature of coffined burial is that, as Fig. 5.6 shows, the bones in the thoracic (chest) area become jumbled up. This can occur because the putrefaction of the body occurs more quickly than the decay of the coffin. As there is empty space available, the bloating which is part of the putrefaction can jumble these bones during a sudden release of the built-up pressure. The disarray of the bones that results can be an indication of a coffined burial even where no coffin-fittings or wood-stains remain.

Shroud, dressed or naked burials

The more common rite in the Boneyard-Reeddam cemetery was uncoffined burial. In these cases the body appears to have been more 'constricted' and the bones are usually in something closer to their normal anatomical positions.

This may be evidence that the body was wrapped in a shroud. On the other hand, the effect of the mass of soil pressing directly on the decaying body may well have been more important than the wrapping. A dressed or naked body placed directly in the soil with arms and legs neatly positioned would, when skeletonised, be hard to differentiate from a shrouded burial without a coffin. Either way, the assumption is that in Western Europe generally the years around AD 700 marked a turning-point in burial custom, after which corpses were inhumed in a shroud or buried naked (Samson 1999, 132). Of England specifically the assumption is that by the 8th century AD clothed burial had virtually disappeared and that burial in a shroud was the 'almost universal style' (Taylor 2001, 174).

The replacement of dressed burial with a shroud and the elimination of deliberately placed grave-goods have long been interpreted as essential elements in the Christian burial practices adopted soon after the religion became established in England. More recent studies of Middle and Late Anglo-Saxon cemeteries have shown, however, that as late as the 10th and 11th centuries AD, even though funerary arrangements may have come increasingly under the direct control of the Church, 'there was still opportunity for localised and individual traditions and beliefs to be expressed through the medium of burial'. The evidence for this can be summarised as 'the variation within and between cemeteries' and the 'artefacts found within graves' (Hadley and Buckberry 2007, 140). In addition to the horse and pitcher 'burials' mentioned above, another which may reflect the continuation of individual traditions at Sedgeford is the 'shell burial' described in Box 5.3.

At Sedgeford the interpretation of artefacts found within the grave fills is complicated by several factors. Of these, the great density of burial and the multiple intercutting of graves is perhaps the most significant. In the northern part of the site, at the bottom of the slope where the hillwash is deepest, there were as many as five phases of burial, sometimes one on top of the other, but more often with later burials cutting into and through earlier ones.

A common practice of the gravediggers after disturbing bones from earlier graves was to then place the resulting disarticulated bone, or charnel, around the edges of the grave-cut for the individual they were currently burying. This can be seen clearly in Fig. 5.6. In some instances the charnel found within a grave-cut could be re-united with a partially articulated skeleton excavated from the immediate vicinity that had been visibly disturbed during the cutting of the later grave. A great deal of disarticulated human bone was also recovered from the upper layers of hillwash, derived no doubt from bodies eroding out or ploughed out further up the slope.

This discussion is relevant to the matter of grave-goods. The fact that most graves were cut into layers of post-Roman hillwash made them difficult to identify, especially at the bottom of the slope, where the leached soil was a uniform mid-grey. This, combined with the intercutting and disturbance of burials, made it very hard to associate occasional artefacts with particular skeletons.

In the Reeddam, where the soil was at its darkest, the excavators, in distinguishing the sequence of burial and identifying later truncating features, were often forced to rely on observing the presence or absence of parts of the articulated skeleton rather than differences in the soil. Some of the later ditches, for example, might be clearly visible further up the slope, but would be identifiable only as linear anomalies of disarticulated bone in the Reeddam. Only with the earliest burials, which were cut into orange and yellow glacial sand beneath the layers of hillwash, was stratigraphic definition of cuts relatively straightforward.

An Anglo-Saxon grid-plan settlement
Phase 5 AD ?775/825–850/925

A radical change is implicit in Phase 5. Part of the cemetery seems to have gone out of use, if not immediately (in Phase 5a), then a short while after (Phase 5b). This is signalled by the digging of a north-east to south-west aligned ditch

Box 5.2
An Anglo-Saxon noblewoman?

In 1997 the skeletons of a young woman and two children were excavated in the Middle Anglo-Saxon cemetery on Boneyard-Reeddam. The woman appeared to have her head upon the hip of the partial remains of a horse, whose fore-body had been disturbed by the subsequent burial of one of the children. The woman and children were buried extended (not 'crouched'), supine (on their backs) and aligned west-east, as was the norm in the cemetery as a whole.

The horse, a young male of about 14 hands, was placed on its left side, aligned north-south and extending northward. The later burial of a child to the north may have precipitated the removal of the fore part of the horse and/or the plough, which also damaged the human skeletons, may have disrupted and scattered portions of the horse skeleton. A cervical vertebra can be seen in the excavation photo above right of the child's head, and a rib bone was in the next burial beyond.

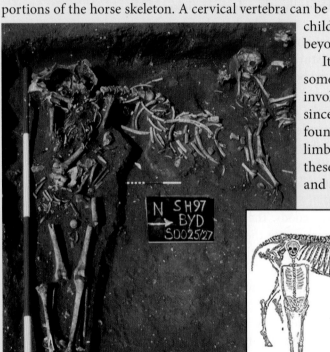

It is also possible the horse skull was removed at some point for reburial or other ritual use. Rituals involving horse skulls have been practised at least since the Bronze Age. A separate horse skull was found east of this burial and a complete horse fore-limb further north. Unfortunately, the dating of these deposits is unknown. They may be Iron Age and are referred to in Chapter 2 as Special Deposits 6 and 7. They may, on the other hand, be Middle Anglo-Saxon and thus loosely associated with the horse skeleton under discussion here.

Intriguingly, the woman, the horse and a small set of nearby burials appear to be around or within a structure (Structure B, Figs. 5.3 and 5.4), at the edge of which is the horse skull and the Ipswich Ware pitcher buried with two iron knives and some smithing slag. The postholes suggest some kind of shrine or funerary structure associated with this set of burials.

The excavators interpreted the remains as possibly those of a 'Danish lady buried with her horse'. After a complete horse of probable Iron Age date was discovered to the north (see Chapter 2), an alternative interpretation was proposed, namely that the original southern horse was also

Plate 5.11: Photo showing the burial of a woman and a horse and the two intercutting child burials.

Iron Age and that the (Anglo-Saxon) woman had been buried in such a way as to preserve the early horse bone in the grave.

In 2008, however, bio-archaeologist Pam Cross undertook a detailed study of the site's horse remains and associated human burials which included radiocarbon-dating of the two horses and the woman. Due to collagen degradation of the bone of the northern horse, only the southern one returned a date: AD 670-820 (cal. 95% probability) (Cross, 2009, 26-27, A10-11). This date is consistent with previous dates obtained from human-bone samples from the cemetery. The southern horse was, it seems, buried during the use-life of the Middle Anglo-Saxon cemetery on Boneyard-Reeddam.

It remains possible that the burial of horse and woman represent two separate events. The hind-legs of the horse were missing, as if cut away during the digging of the grave-cut for the woman. On the other hand, these might have been removed ritually, or they may have been lost to some unidentified later disturbance. The woman's head was certainly resting on the horse's pelvis. Given the date for the horse, the balance of probability seems to favour contemporary burial.

Human-horse burials are not common either in Britain or on the Continent, but they do occur. These are usually interpreted as elite warrior burials (the majority are male) – there are examples at Sutton Hoo, Great Chesterford (which also has some juvenile burials nearby) and Lakenheath (all admittedly of somewhat earlier date). There are also some female-horse burials from Scandinavia (Cross 2009, 68-75).

Given the lack of completely comparable burials and the discomfort of other specialists regarding a woman-horse burial in what is considered to be a Christian-period Anglo-Saxon cemetery, Pam Cross carried out a very careful review of the burial, applying forensic and osteological methods in relation to both skeletons and excavation records. The conclusion remained that the woman and the horse were buried together or within a very short period of each other.

The key points are as follows; the spine and pelvic bones of the horse remained in anatomical position, whereas, if skeletised at the time of the woman's burial, they would have been disturbed without very careful excavation. In addition, one of the woman's neck vertebrae was found within the pelvic cavity, which strongly suggests that they decomposed together and that therefore both were fleshed when the woman's head was initially placed on the horse.

This then raises the question why a woman was buried with a horse in a Christian-era cemetery. According to Bede, many areas had to be repeatedly Christianised, implying strong survival and occasional resurgence of paganism. This was particularly true in the east, which was highly interactive with the various non-Christian cultures of north-western Europe. Much of this area, including Norfolk, later became part of the pagan Danelaw in the late 9th century.

In any case, our modern, post-Reformation interpretation of what constitutes 'Christian' practice may not align with the reality of diverse regional practices in the Anglo-Saxon and Medieval periods. Sedgeford's Christian status may have been 'transitional' for a sustained period, combining elements of traditional paganism with elements of what was, in effect, a new state religion being imposed from on high (Cross 2009, 8-20; 2011, 208). Other scholars have also noted that even in 10th and 11th century England 'local communities seem to have been permitted a fair degree of latitude in determining the form of burial and commemoration deemed appropriate for their family and friends' (Hadley and Buckberry 2007, 147). Nonetheless, the Boneyard woman-horse burial is exceptional even with the sort of variation in burial forms discussed by Hadley and Buckberry. To date, only three burials involving women and horses have been found in Britain: two Romano-British burials in the north and one Viking burial of a man, a horse and a woman (the latter interpreted as a sacrifice/attendant to the male).

No other burials with the Sedgeford body placement have as yet been found, but human-horse burials exhibit a great variety of form, and while they have a general similarity, they are often highly personal. Needless to say, burial with a horse must imply exceptionally elevated status. It should therefore occasion no surprise that such burials are rare and that they tend to be individualised.

98

Box 5.3
Shell burial

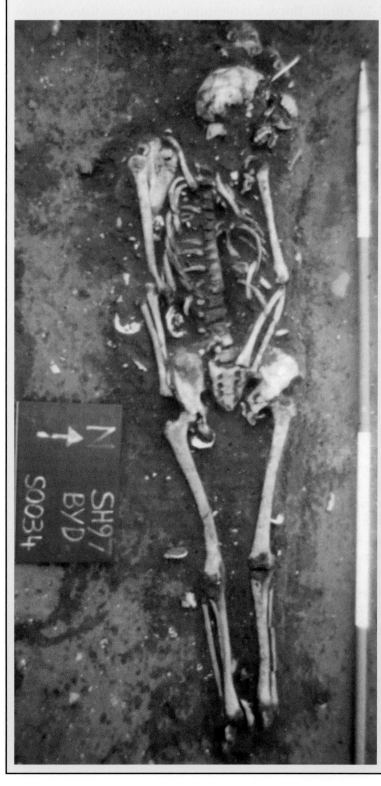

Although shells are common finds on Boneyard-Reeddam, those associated with Skeleton S0034 were different, both in number and placement. This particular burial was covered with a scattered but deliberately placed layer of oyster shells. It was the only one of its kind.

According to the bulk finds record, at least 137 shells were present. Plate 5.13 shows some of the shells in-situ and Plate 5.12 shows the skeleton that was buried beneath them (the bones in the top right corner of Plate 5.13 are from the adjacent burial).

Skeleton S0034 displayed a number of distinctive characteristics. Pelvic features suggest that the person was male, but some of those on the skull were less definite. This might be because he died at a young age – about 18-25 years – since some of the sexually dimorphic characteristics on the cranium only become fully apparent at a late stage of development. He was also small for a man at around 165cm (5ft 5in).

On the upper part of the left arm, close to the shoulder, there is an elliptical lesion. It is located where the tendon from the latissimus dorsi – the broadest muscle in the back – inserts into the upper arm (see Fig. 5.7). The lesion indicates inflammation of the muscle attachment resulting from damage to the insertion.

The most likely cause of such inflammation is over-exertion of the muscle. As the lesion has rounded edges, it is likely that S0034 continued to use the muscle, thus preventing complete healing. There is no corresponding

Plate 5.12: Skeleton S0034 – the body beneath the shells.

lesion on the right side, indicating that the injury was sustained in an action performed with an emphasis on his left arm.

Elsewhere the skeleton displays a seeming slight scoliosis (curvature) towards the left in the lumbar (lower back) area and unusually large back parts of the lower ribs on the left side. The latissimus dorsi originates along the entire lower half of the spine and the lower three ribs, areas that appear to display compensatory pathology in this individual.

Overall, this suggests that in life S0034 habitually performed some sort of pull-down action on the left side of his body that strongly used the latissimus dorsi. An imaginative speculation that links the skeleton and the shells is that he might have been a fisherman who punted or paddled his boat along the Heacham River, bringing oysters from the coast to Sedgeford. However, as many have observed, drawing such precise and exclusive interpretations from the evidence is dangerous (see e.g. Waldron 2007, 117). Long-term punting might be compatible with the skeletal changes seen, but there is no proof that this actually happened.

Nevertheless, this unusual burial, with its covering of shells, supports the contention that in Middle to Late Anglo-Saxon England 'the decline in the use of grave goods did not lead to uniformity of burial practices but instead the expression of individuality through other aspects of the burial rite' (Buckberry and Cherryson 2010, ix).

Plate 5.13: The shell burial (S0034) on Boneyard-Reeddam.
Fig. 5.7: Position and attachment points of latissimus dorsi.

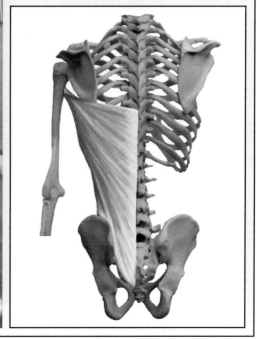

system, the eastern branch of which cut through many burials in the north-eastern part of the site.

It is possible, of course, that the entire cemetery now went out of use, but this seems unlikely for several reasons. First, the eastern arm of the new ditch system appears to respect the sweep of burials rising, crescent-like, up the slope of Boneyard Old Trench and into the south-eastern part of New Trench.

Second, Structure D (Fig. 5.4 and 5.8) seems to belong to this phase and to have existed at the same time as the cemetery, since it occupies the rectangular plot where Structure C previously stood. The burials are still ranged on two sides of it, yet it seems to be on a new alignment approximating to that of the eastern arm. The evidence is limited: a modest pit reminiscent of an 'SFB' (a sunken-featured building or *grübenhaus* characteristic of Anglo-Saxon

Fig. 5.8: Plan of Phase 5a of the Middle Anglo-Saxon settlement and cemetery on Boneyard-Reeddam/Lower Chalkpit with the trackway as shown on the 1631 Estate map superimposed..

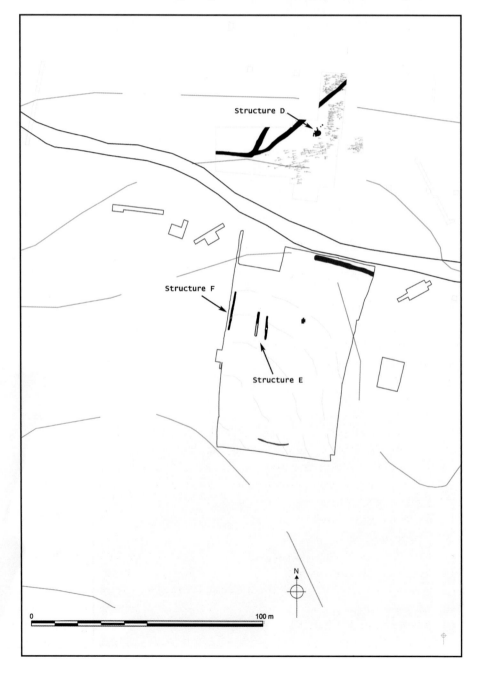

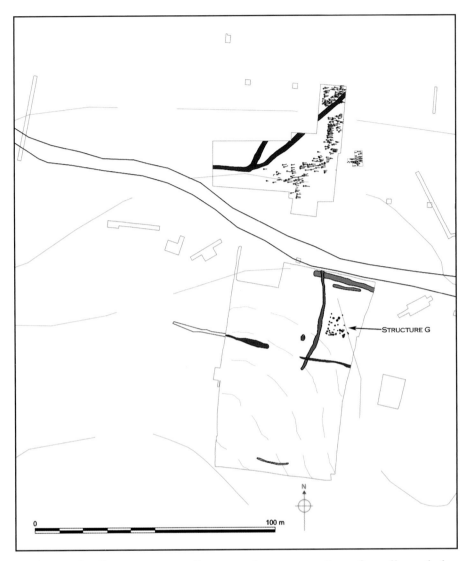

STRUCTURE G

Fig. 5.9: Plan of Phase 5b of the Middle Anglo-Saxon settlement and cemetery on Boneyard-Reeddam/Lower Chalkpit.

0   100 m

settlements), albeit a very small one, and a scraggy line of small postholes extending 6m. But it was definitely 'a something'; and it does seem to be contemporary with the new boundary ditch to one side and the cemetery on the other.

On the other hand, the new boundary ditch contained a considerable quantity of smithing slag in its upper fills, which were also quite dark and rich in charcoal. This may imply that part of the site at least was changing in function, and the redefinition of space may have been related to this.

That this boundary was maintained for some considerable period is indicated by the fact that it was re-cut. Our best indication of its date is the fact that Thetford-type Ware was recovered only in small quantities from the uppermost fills – so the digging of the ditch system pre-dates its arrival on the site.

The changes were more radical still on Lower Chalkpit. Here the established form of the settlement, as defined by long but slight curvilinear boundaries, was transformed by the imposition of a new rectangular grid oriented north-south and east-west. Its earliest manifestation seems to have been two halls, Structures E and F (Figs. 5.4 and 5.8), which were only recognised after excavation. These were on the same alignment as new rectilinear boundaries, yet were cut by the earliest of these, so we can only assume that they relate to the earliest phase of the gridding, the boundaries of which were not seen (Phase 5a).

Structure E was of beam-slot construction and measured approximately 10m by 5m. Structure F was bigger and more substantially built, its eastern wall extending 16m and being of post-in-trench construction; the western wall was beyond the limit of excavation.

The revised layout becomes much clearer in Phase 5b. By the time the rectangular grid in Lower Chalkpit was laid out, grass-tempered pottery had gone out of use, so we can date the new-look settlement to the later 8th century AD at the earliest. A typical plot was defined by frequently re-cut boundary ditches (and presumably lost banks), perhaps measuring35m by 25m, and presumably incorporating a main residence (a hall), various outbuildings and subsidiary structures, backyard and garden areas, storage pits, water troughs and suchlike.

Severe plough-truncation across most of the site meant that little, however, of this likely range of activity was represented by archaeological traces. The outlines of possible halls are sometimes discernable, but much else has been reduced to random survivals of more deeply cut features, the function of which cannot be identified. That they were 'halls' is our interpretation, not a fact.

Structure G (Fig. 5.4 and 5.9) is a case in point. Standing neatly within Phase 5 plot boundaries and aligned north-south, it comprises a mass of 26 postholes, some of which undoubtedly represent structural timbers, but many others of which cannot be ascribed any clear function. Just beyond the south-eastern corner of the building, moreover, lies a group of small postholes or stakeholes that must relate to some subsidiary structure. Structure G seems to measure a little in excess of 8m by 4m. It may have been a direct replacement of Structure A from Phase 4, these being on the same alignment, but this is pure speculation.

One final comment is that the new rectilinear layout seems to have left a permanent imprint on the landscape. The modern trackway that separates Boneyard-Reeddam and Lower Chalkpit is on the same east-west alignment as the Middle Anglo-Saxon boundaries. Since it appears on the 1631 estate map of Sedgeford, it is highly likely that it is a survival of the 8th century AD.

The bounding of space – specifically, the rectilinear bounding of individual plots within a gridded settlement – implies changes in political authority and the social order. Andrew Reynolds has recently discussed this at length in a major paper on Anglo-Saxon boundaries, and John Blair is completing a comprehensive survey of Anglo-Saxon settlement layouts as revealed in the under-researched 'grey literature' generated by commercial rescue-archaeology (Reynolds 2003; Blair 2013; John Blair, pers. comm.). Their work is highly relevant here.

Reynolds sees the development of boundaries within settlements from the later 6th century AD, especially in the 7th and 8th centuries, as a reflection of a changing social order increasingly preoccupied with defining individual responsibilities. This in turn, he suggests, should be viewed in the context of 'the growth and consolidation of the early English kingdoms, whose increasing geographical extent, at the expense of each other, required new forms of social organisation'.

Box 5.4
Anglo-Saxon dress pins

Headed copper-alloy dress pins are the most likely artefacts to have been buried in direct association with the body, as they may have functioned as shroud pins. Thirty examples were recovered during the 1996-2007 Boneyard-Reeddam excavations in addition to the three found during Jewell's work in the late 1950s. There is also a single pin from the evaluation of Lower Chalkpit in 2007. In two instances dress pins were found in association with bodies, suggesting that such pins were occasionally used as shroud pins; their most common use, however, was undoubtedly to secure the clothes of the living.

Twenty-one pins are complete or near complete with just the very tips missing, seven are incomplete and six are shaft fragments only. All are typically Middle Anglo-Saxon, and parallels can be found in the large assemblages from Brandon (Suffolk), Flixborough (Lincolnshire) and Hamwic (Hampshire) (Tester *et al* forthcoming, figs 8.4-8.7; Evans and Loveluck 2009, 32-69; Hinton 1996, 14-37).

Many of the Boneyard pins have thickened shafts and/or collars below the head, which are characteristic of pins of this date. Heads range from globular (13) and bi-conical (3) through facetted (13) and spiral-headed (2). The complete and near-complete examples range in length from 48 to 99mm.

One of the two pins found with Skeleton S0034 is bent just below the swelling in its shaft to form a 45° angle. Both of the pins found with this skeleton (a male of around 20 years) appear to have been deliberately placed within the grave, presumably to secure a shroud at the head and pelvis. One of the two pins was assigned the context number of the layer through which the grave was cut, but, as was common on Boneyard-Reeddam, the grave-cut was not discernible, so it may well have originally lain within the grave itself. It is also possible that the two pins were placed in different graves, the incomplete example perhaps having been disturbed during the digging of an adjacent grave and ending up in its fill.

Another dress pin was found on the pelvis of a female who died aged about 45-55 years, and again this example appears to have been in association with the skeleton rather than in its fill by chance. This pin was not bent.

It seems likely that some of the other pins, particularly those with no modification to the shaft, washed down the hill from the settlement, perhaps with an occasional chance loss in the cemetery. In addition to the three pins from grave fills discussed above, four others were unstratified and two more were from cleaning layers (so are essentially also without context), five were from modern topsoil, ploughsoil, or hillwash layers, six were from earlier post-cemetery hillwash layers, three were from Middle or Late Anglo-Saxon cut features, two were from layers described as Middle or Late Anglo-Saxon occupation spreads and four were from pre-cemetery hillwash layers.

Three of the four 'pre-cemetery' finds have intact heads, but each is of different form (one spiral-headed, one globular and one facetted) and each has parallels among those from later layers. Riddler suggests that copper-alloy pins like these do not occur before c. AD 720 at the earliest (2012, 143). The implication would seem to be that the cemetery did not exist prior to this date, but this need not follow, partly because small, heavy finds can often move down the soil matrix (i.e. they become 'intrusive') and partly because the cemetery was extensive and some parts may have been in use decades before others.

With the exception of a few dress pins perhaps used to gather the shroud, we believe that the great majority of the small finds from the Boneyard-Reeddam excavation, including many personal items, were not intentionally included in burials. Indeed, many of the finds from the excavations are fragmentary, making it likely that most were discarded items or chance losses washing down the hill from the adjacent settlement and occasionally finding their way into grave fills. However, in a tiny number of cases the presence in a grave of the odd small item may indicate that the person was clothed when they were buried – representing a modest deviation from the increasingly dominant Christian rite of undressed burial.

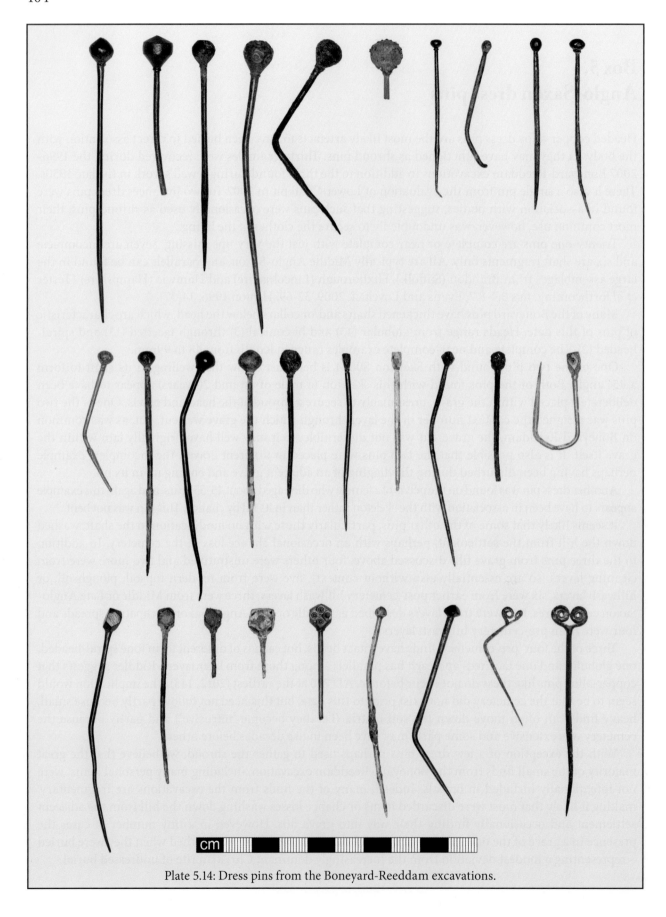

Plate 5.14: Dress pins from the Boneyard-Reeddam excavations.

Box 5.5
Anglo-Saxon combs

A considerable number of fragmentary bone and antler combs have been recovered on Boneyard-Reeddam. These are common finds on Anglo-Saxon settlement sites. The tooth and end segments of composite combs were enclosed by two antler or bone connecting-plates and held together with rivets, usually of iron. Composite combs can have teeth on one side only, or on both sides. They are typologically datable, but the ascribed date ranges are broad (e.g. Ashby 2007; 2011).

Because it is so fragmentary, the Sedgeford comb is not easy to categorise and date, but it has been possible to class the majority of the fragments as being from single-sided, double-sided, or handled combs (the latter one-piece or two-piece). There are a further 14 fragments too small to be closely identified; these are not discussed in detail here.

A minimum of ten single-sided combs are represented. The decoration varies from simple and rudimentary to more elaborate and skilfully executed. Of the three combs that have both connecting-plates, two are decorated only on one side (the 'display' side) and one is simply decorated on both.

The decorative elements include groups of straight and chevron parallel lines, rings-and-dots, closed or open cross-hatching and single transverse zigzagged lines formed of V-shapes ('fret pattern') alternating with groups of transverse lines. The latter pattern appears on three of the single-sided combs and also on one of the handled combs.

Although the material is too fragmentary to be sure, most of the single-sided combs are probably Ashby's Type 2b, 'bowed' (also sometimes referred to as 'hogbacked' or 'winged' combs), which date from the 7th and 8th centuries AD.

Most of the decoration appears on connecting-plates, but one of the tooth segments is also decorated with double ring-and-dot motifs. This and another tooth segment which is double riveted are both pieces of doubled-connecting-plate combs (I. Riddler, pers. comm.). These have two connecting-plates on each side, with a space in between, and are extensively decorated on connecting-plates, tooth segments and end segments. The type is fairly unusual, although there are 16 fragments from Ipswich (Riddler *et al* forthcoming). It is not found in the Late Anglo-Saxon period.

There are fragments of three or possibly four double-sided combs, including two with tooth and connecting-plate fragments from the same comb, a piece of connecting-plate and a tooth segment. The tooth segment was from the same context as one of the composite fragments and could have belonged to the same comb. All of these combs are likely to be variants of Ashby's Type 12 (S. Ashby, pers. comm.), which was in use from the 6th to 9th centuries AD, but is especially common in 8th and 9th century AD deposits (Riddler and Trzaska-Nartowski 2011, 133).

The most complete double-sided comb is finely decorated with lines of ring-and-dot divided by narrow incised lines. The other decorated example has groups of four transverse parallel incised lines on the surviving connecting-plate. On all the double-sided comb fragments the teeth are differentiated, that is, they are narrower on one side. This is not seen very often in the Middle Anglo-Saxon period, but was more common in Early Anglo-Saxon times (I. Riddler, pers. comm.). It is possible that the Sedgeford double-sided comb fragments are of earlier Middle Anglo-Saxon date.

There are parts of six asymmetric handled combs from Boneyard-Reeddam. This type of comb has a handle extending to one side of a single row of teeth (Ashby's Type 3) and dates from the 8th to 11th centuries AD (Ashby 2007, 2). There are two broad forms of handled combs, one with two-piece riveted connecting-plates and the other which has a slot cut into a one-piece handle, into which the teeth are inserted (Riddler 1990, 9). Three of the Sedgeford handled combs are of the former type, with just a fragment of the 'connecting-plate' surviving in each case. Decoration includes fret pattern and bands of

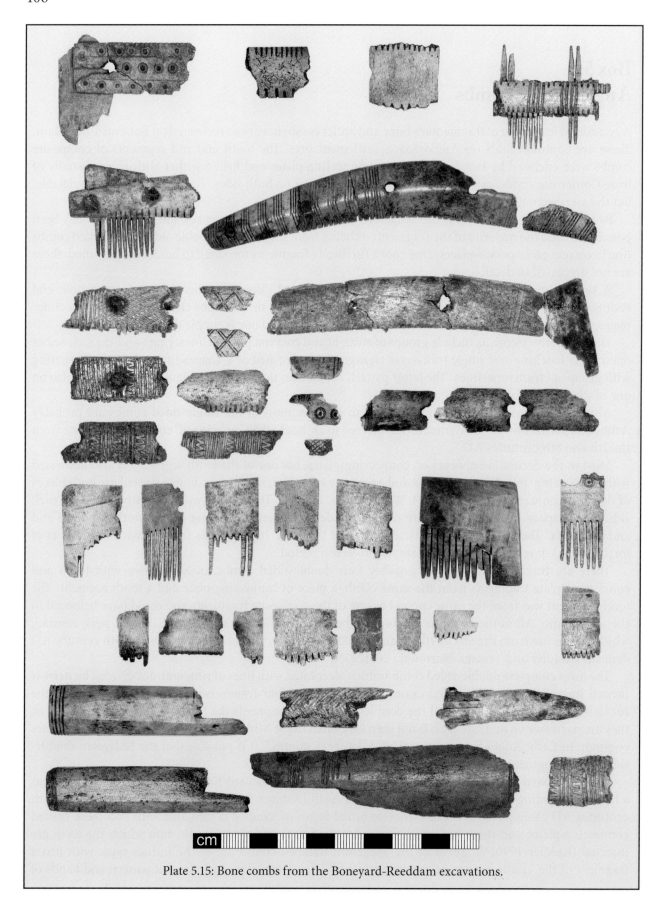

Plate 5.15: Bone combs from the Boneyard-Reeddam excavations.

transverse lines, parallel chevrons and simple groups of incised transverse lines.

The other three handles are of the one-piece type. Two are similar, with octagonal cross-sections and simple decoration in the form of a border of narrow incised lines at the end. The other is very worn, but appears to be totally undecorated. Handled combs with little decoration fall into a distinctive Middle Anglo-Saxon group, of which there are a number of examples from Ipswich (Riddler *et al* forthcoming).

Single-piece comb handles are the norm to the south of the River Humber (Riddler 1990, 9), so it is interesting that there is an equal number of both types at Sedgeford, which is some distance further south (Riddler 1990, 9). There is another example of this type from East Anglia, from North Elmham in Norfolk (Wade-Martins 1980, fig. 259.5).

Many of the comb fragments come from post-cemetery hillwash layers, so it is likely that they were not grave goods but chance losses from the settlement, eroding out from further up the slope and being washed down the hill. There are several finds, however, that are of a more secure nature.

One of the comb handles is from a Middle Anglo-Saxon pit, while several other fragments are from occupation layers that were assigned a Middle Anglo-Saxon date. A fragment of single-sided tooth segment was found in a Middle Anglo-Saxon ditch thought to be contemporary with the cemetery, and an incomplete single-sided comb came from a Middle to Late Anglo-Saxon post-cemetery ditch. Four small fragments, all from combs of indeterminate form, were found in a post-cemetery ditch which cut into burials.

Three comb fragments appear to be from pre-cemetery hillwash, although the degree of truncation of this layer makes their stratigraphic integrity insecure. Two of these formed part of one or two double-sided combs. The other item is the undecorated bone handle which is likely to be of 8th century AD date (I. Riddler, pers. comm.). This was from either a pre-cemetery hillwash or possibly an unrecognised upper fill of a large east-west Early Roman ditch that was still silting up in Anglo-Saxon times; it may also be the case that the artefact was intrusive.

The Sedgeford assemblage is a fairly unremarkable group of Anglo-Saxon combs, indicative of normal domestic occupation and in keeping with the rest of the finds assemblage. The only unusual pieces are the two fragments from doubled connecting-plate combs, and the three examples of two-piece comb handles, the latter representing a small group outside the expected distribution for such objects. The entire comb assemblage is likely to date to the 7th and 8th centuries AD and perhaps somewhat into the 9th, though by the 9th century bone was already being replaced by antler as the preferred material for manufacture (I. Riddler, pers. comm.)

Plate 5.16: An incomplete decorative bone comb found in Lower Chalkpit.

Blair has not only found consistent evidence for rectangular grid-planning over a large swathe of Middle and Late Anglo-Saxon England, but also clear indications of the repeated use of multiples of a standardised measure, the short perch of approximately 4.6m. The implication is that some centralised authority was at work, and Blair speculates that Church surveyors may have been marking out the landscape in late 8th or early 9th century England much as Roman *agrimensores* surely were in 2nd century Britannia.

An Anglo-Saxon grid-plan settlement
Phase 6 c. AD 850/925–?900/950

At some point in the late 9th or early 10th century AD, a substantial structure was built immediately adjacent to the cemetery on its western side. The Phase 5 ditch system, which had either silted up or been backfilled, was replaced by a narrow, vertically-sided footing trench, backfilled with large amounts of fired clay.

The form of this trench makes it almost certain that it once contained substantial wooden posts (had it been open the sides would have eroded into a V- or U-shape), and the presence of fired clay implies that the original structure involved wattle-and-daub walls which later burnt down. Immediately north of the western extent of the footing trench, and on the same alignment, was a series of postholes forming two sides of a building measuring at least 7m by 2m (Structure J, Fig. 5.4 and 5.11). This alignment seemed to terminate opposite a break (and presumed entranceway) in the footing trench.

What is not clear is whether the footing trench supported a palisaded boundary enclosing a relatively small building or was itself part of a much larger structure, with the postholes to the north forming an internal aisle or partition. The possible wattle-and-daub wall may imply the latter. On the other hand, the resulting structure would have been very large indeed, since it extended some 17m east-west and at least 11m north-south.

The cemetery may or may not have fallen out of use at this time. Since there were no direct stratigraphic relationships between the Phase 6 features in New Trench and any burials, it is impossible to say. At the very least, however, the cemetery area continued to be respected, for nowhere did the footing trench cut through any burials, and no other obvious settlement features encroached on them at this time either.

Once again, only a very rough estimate of date can be arrived at from the fact that Ipswich Ware and Thetford-type Ware pottery sherds were found in roughly equal quantities in the fill of the footing trench. The implication is that this trench was cut around the time that Thetford-type Ware was displacing Ipswich Ware as the dominant ceramic in local use.

The Phase 6 footing trench and posthole alignment on Boneyard New Trench are on the same alignment as the trackway shown on the 1631 Estate Map and the east-west boundaries of the rectilinear plots on Lower Chalkpit. We seem to be witness to a single planned settlement layout extending across a zone of at least 100m in either direction.

In this period, defined chronologically by the even mix of Ipswich and Thetford pottery, the Lower Chalkpit plots seem to have been re-established

Fig. 5.10: Plan of Phase 6 of the Middle Anglo-Saxon settlement and cemetery on Boneyard-Reeddam/Lower Chalkpit.

STRUCTURE J

STRUCTURE I ← STRUCTURE H

0   100 m

N

on the same alignments but on slightly different lines. The chances are that we have recovered evidence for only a handful of occasions when ditches were dredged, re-cut or excavated anew among many hundreds of such occasions in the life-history of the settlement. Our own experience has shown that a single heavy storm can flood a trench with mud; it seems likely that re-cutting boundary ditches was a regular procedure for the inhabitants of Middle Anglo-Saxon Sedgeford. It should not surprise us that boundaries in this dynamic micro-landscape seem to 'drift' over time.

Phase 6, then, is characterised by substantially reworked rectilinear boundaries on Lower Chalkpit, with up to six re-cuts evident in places. The northernmost east-west boundary excavated also produced evidence for at least two phases of palisade trenching. This seems to mirror that revealed on Boneyard New Trench, and we can perhaps conjure a picture of more impressive settlement boundaries running along either side of the main east-west trackway through the settlement – the trackway separating the two halves of the site which still survives.

South of this boundary, the plot contained two substantial halls (and possible traces of another). Structure H (Fig. 5.4 and 5.11) was up to 11m long and 4m wide and was of post-in-trench construction on the long sides and posthole construction on the short, and was sub-divided by an internal partition. Immediately south-east of it was another length of trench and a couple of floating postholes; we do not know what kind of structure is represented.

The remains of Structure I (Fig. 5.4 and 5.11) lay alongside those of

Box 5.6
Anglo-Saxon beads

Eight glass beads, two of amber and one of carstone were found in the Boneyard-Reeddam excavations. One of the glass beads, however, is an incomplete Oldbury type of Late Iron Age date. This was recovered from topsoil out in the Reeddam. A few beads of this type were apparently reused during Anglo-Saxon times and this may have been the case for the Sedgeford example (Guido 1978, 54).

Three of the other beads (two of glass and the carstone example) were from grave fills, but none is recorded as being in close association with a skeleton. One of the burials was of an older woman. The other skeleton was truncated by a ditch, so its sex is unknown. It seems most likely that these beads came from pre- or early cemetery deposits which were disturbed during grave-digging. Alternatively, they might indicate that these corpses were dressed when they were buried.

The carstone bead is crude and undecorated and difficult to date or interpret further. The two glass beads are very similar in form, colour and decoration. Their overall shape is globular and they are made from dark greenish glass adorned with simple white and red millefiore motifs. The type is unusual and most likely imported. There is a parallel from a cemetery to the south of Hamburg in Germany dating from the 8th or 9th century AD (Birte Brugmann, pers. comm.)

A blue glass bead could either be Iron Age or Anglo-Saxon typologically, but was found in a Middle Anglo-Saxon cemetery layer, so is likely to be of this date. The remaining glass beads are from post-cemetery hillwash layers. They include an incomplete thin annular example in transparent light turquoise, an irregular globular bead in opaque dark blue with lighter striations, an opaque white and bright turquoise fragment, possibly originally globular and decorated with two wavy lines and an incomplete short cylinder in opaque black or very dark green with two yellow marvered lines. There is a broad parallel for the latter at Brandon (Tester *et al* forthcoming, no. 2060, plate 8.1).

One of the amber beads was unstratified and the other was in a Middle Anglo-Saxon layer. The latter is large (its maximum length is 25mm) and irregularly shaped. There are several similar beads from Grave 25 at Petersfinger in Wiltshire (Brugmann 2004, plate 75).

Plate 5.17: Nicci Neilson with a newly-found bead.

Plate 5.18: Beads from the Boneyard-Reeddam excavations.

Box 5.7
Anglo-Saxon brooches and buckles

Brooches

Three or four coiled one-piece or safety-pin brooches of Middle Anglo-Saxon date were recovered on the Boneyard-Reeddam excavations, and a further example came from the 2007 evaluation on Lower Chalkpit. The two larger brooches are decorated with rings-and-dots, as is the possible brooch fragment, but the smallest brooch lacks any obvious decoration.

Excavations at Flixborough on Humberside have produced eight copper-alloy safety-pin brooches, as well as one of silver and 22 of iron, which are thought to date from the 8th and possibly into the 9th centuries AD (Evans and Loveluck 2009, 1-3). There are also five from Brandon in Suffolk, which are likely to be late 7th or 8th century AD (Tester *et al* forthcoming, no. 5007, fig. 8.1). A dozen further examples of this brooch type have been recorded on the Portable Antiquities Scheme database from as far afield as Gloucestershire, Nottinghamshire and Kent.

The more complete Sedgeford brooches were found in a Late Anglo-Saxon ditch fill, a Middle to Late Anglo-Saxon hillwash layer and a post-cemetery hillwash. The possible brooch fragment was found in the fill of the grave of a probable female aged 25-35. As usual with the densely packed and heavily disturbed Boneyard-Reeddam cemetery, it is impossible to say whether or not this was a deliberately deposited grave-good, but it is possible that its presence indicates that this woman was dressed when buried.

Buckles and strap-ends

Parts of two (or possibly three) Anglo-Saxon copper-alloy buckles were also found, one of which is extremely simple and not closely datable typologically. It consists of a flattened rod of copper-alloy wire which has been bent into a small oval frame, with the addition of a basic pin. This was from a cleaning context at the start of the 2006 season, but by this stage of the project we were well into the Anglo-Saxon layers and the pottery from the context indicated a 9th-10th century AD date.

Another possible buckle frame had been made in the same way but would have formed a more rectangular shape. This was from a post-cemetery hillwash layer of 13th century or later date. Again, this is so simple it cannot be dated typologically, but it could be Anglo-Saxon.

The other buckle component is a flat, broadly triangular plate that terminates in a circular section with a central rivet-hole. Three broadly similar although more complete buckles are known from elsewhere, two from Faversham in Kent, the other from near Cambridge; these have triangular plates with rounded terminals and three-domed attachment rivets (MacGregor and Bolick 1993, 195-196, nos. 34.12, 34.13 and 34.15).

Marzinzik gives buckles with triangular plates (her Class II.23) a fairly tight date range between the late 6th and late 7th centuries AD (2003, 49-50). The Sedgeford buckle-plate was unstratified, but it seems safe to assume that it belonged to one of the first inhabitants of the new settlement, with its presumed start-date in the years before AD 700.

A single copper-alloy strap-end is an example of Thomas's Class A, Type 2, and dates from the 9th century AD (Thomas 2003, 2-3). It is fairly short and squat, with one split end and what appears to be the remains of a blob of solder on the reverse. The front is decorated with incised lines which form a symmetrical loosely zoomorphic pattern. It is of a type more usually found in the north of England (G. Thomas, pers. comm.). This was from a context described as a cemetery layer which had a pottery date of 9th to 10th century AD.

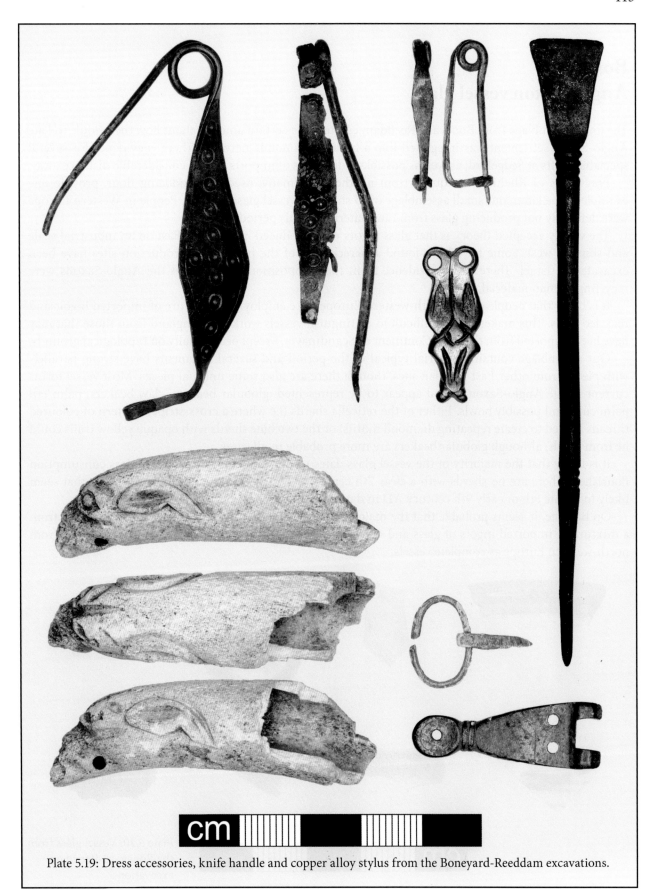

Plate 5.19: Dress accessories, knife handle and copper alloy stylus from the Boneyard-Reeddam excavations.

Box 5.8
Anglo-Saxon vessel glass

The finds assemblage from Boneyard-Reeddam can tell us a certain amount about how the Middle to Late Anglo-Saxon settlement was integrated into a broader economic network. There is evidence for several specialist crafts at Sedgeford, as well as possible indications of imports from a considerable distance away.

Fragments of Rhenish lava-quern from northern Germany, used for producing flour, provide one example of the latter, our small assemblage of 13 sherds of vessel glass another. People in Western Europe were definitely not producing glass from raw materials at this period.

The widely accepted theory is that glass ingots were produced in the Near East on an industrial scale and shipped west. Some have been found at wreck sites of the period and production sites have been excavated in Israel. There is also evidence from the composition of glass that the Anglo-Saxons were recycling Roman material.

It is likely that people across north-western Europe were employing a mixture of imported ingots and recycled glass. This makes it very difficult to distinguish vessels worked in England from those that may have been imported from the near-Continent or Scandinavia, except occasionally on typological grounds.

Our assemblage contains material typical of the period and several fragments have strong parallels with pieces from other East Anglian sites, though there are also some unusual pieces. Most vessel forms current in the Anglo-Saxon period appear to be represented: globular beakers, claw beakers, palm/tall palm cups and possibly bowls. Either of the reticella sherds (i.e where a cross-striped pattern of coloured threads is used to create repeating diamond motifs) or the two blue sherds with opaque yellow trails could be from bowls, although globular beakers are more probable in all cases.

It is likely that the majority of the vessel glass dates to the 8th century AD, when glass consumption flourished. There are no sherds with a clear 7th century AD profile, although there are three that seem likely to be late 8th or early 9th century AD in date and are of particular interest for that reason.

On balance, it seems probable that the majority of the Sedgeford vessels were made in England from a mixture of imported ingots of glass and recycled fragments, but some may have been imported from north-western Europe as complete vessels.

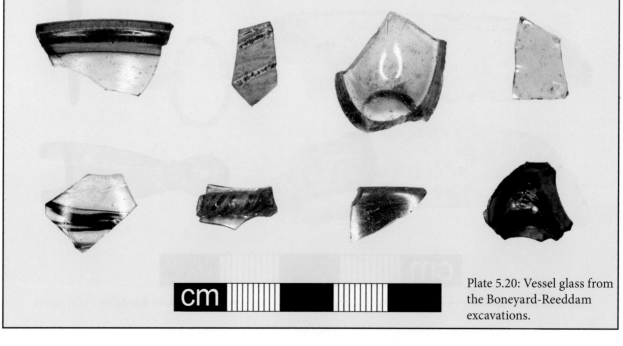

Plate 5.20: Vessel glass from the Boneyard-Reeddam excavations.

Structure H, and it is highly likely that they were not contemporary but that one replaced the other. Structure I seems to have been around 10m long and up to 5m wide, and, like its neighbour, was of post-in-trench and posthole construction.

An Anglo-Saxon thegnly residence?
Phase 7 c. AD ?900/950–?975/1025

The last phase of activity on the Boneyard-Reeddam/Lower Chalkpit site represents the third in a sequence of major transitions. The first was the appearance around AD 650/700 of a loosely ordered settlement enclosed by curvilinear boundaries associated with the earliest use of an ordered Christian-era cemetery immediately to the north. The second was the radical reorganisation of this settlement around AD 800 into a series of individual plots enclosed by rectilinear boundaries. The third, most likely in the first half of the 10th century, involved the imposition of a monumental enclosure that may have bounded the residential complex of a local lord.

On Boneyard-Reeddam, Phase 7 (Fig. 5.11) sees the replacement of the enclosure/building represented by footing trench and posthole alignment by quite substantial ditches forming a new rectilinear enclosure, again to the west of the cemetery. The fills of this enclosure ditch were dominated by Thetford-type Ware, with only residual sherds of Ipswich Ware. An arm of this enclosure which extended eastward cut through a number of burials in the south-eastern part of New Trench, strongly implying that this part of the cemetery at least had now, if not before, gone out of use.

This reorganisation may have been contemporary with the cutting of other boundary and drainage ditches further east, mainly on a north-south alignment towards the eastern limit of Boneyard Old Trench, features which also yielded a predominantly Thetford-type Ware assemblage. These ditches were re-cut many times. The final phase of ditch digging cut long swathes through the cemetery, implying that the western portion of it had now gone out of use.

North-south ditches on the same alignment and of similar form and date have also been found towards the northern limit of the Lower Chalkpit excavations. These appear to represent no less than nine successive re-impositions of the same boundary. Assuming the modern trackway dates from the Middle Anglo-Saxon period, there must have been some sort of entranceway between the Boneyard-Reeddam and Lower Chalkpit extents of the ditches.

The rectilinear plots to the south of the northern east-west boundary ditch on Lower Chalkpit seem to have remained in use on their existing alignments, but the southern east-west boundary was incorporated into the layout of a monumental D-shaped enclosure higher up the slope. The appearance of this feature is likely to have transformed the character of the settlement.

The straight side of the D extended approximately 150m east-west, following the existing alignment of the trackway and settlement. The curve of the D extended 90m up the slope, and at the highest point

Fig. 5.11: Plan of Phase 7 of the Middle Anglo-Saxon settlement on Boneyard-Reeddam/Lower Chalkpit.

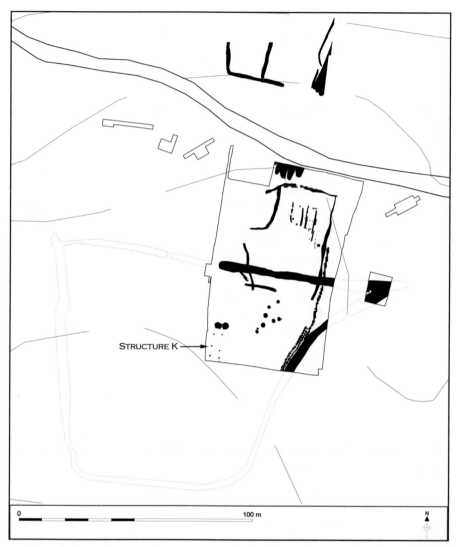

the width of the enclosure narrowed to 70m. The ditch was up to 4m wide and 2m deep (and some may have been lost to plough truncation). There is circumstantial evidence for a wide internal bank or rampart, represented by an absence of features of contemporary date immediately south of the northern ditch section. We might speculate that this would have been surmounted by a timber palisade. An entranceway was located at the western limit of excavation, and, though no obvious evidence was found, it seems reasonable to assume some sort of timber gateway.

Structure K (Fig. 5.4 and 5.12) was located inside the D-shaped enclosure towards the south-western limit of excavation. Formed of substantial but widely spaced postholes, it was aligned north-south, and was at least 12m long and about 4.5m wide. Structure K may have been associated with a steep-sided shaft measuring 2.5m across and 2m in depth. Adjacent to this was a possible working hollow and a single substantial posthole. This group of features may represent a cistern, a well, or a 'chase spring' (a hole dug to access a retreating spring), perhaps with associated lifting gear. A concentration of spinning and weaving related finds was recovered in this area, including spindle-whorls, loom-weights, pin-beaters and bone-comb fragments.

Box 5.9
Anglo-Saxon iron production and iron tools

Numerous finds of iron tools were made during the Boneyard-Reeddam excavations. Interestingly, there is strong evidence to suggest that both the production of iron and the manufacture of many of these objects took place within the settlement itself; that is, both smelting and smithing were practised by skilled local artisans.

Other excavations have shown that most Anglo-Saxon settlements would have had access to a blacksmith for the production and repair of everyday objects, but until now very few Anglo-Saxon smelting sites have been identified in England (McDonnell 1989). By contrast, known Roman-period smelting sites are relatively common. At the end of this period, however, the old centres of iron production in the Weald and the Forest of Dean seem to have been abandoned.

Most known Anglo-Saxon production centres appear to have been located away from urban settlements. Some, like Ramsbury, Flixborough, Cheddar and Lyminge, were located near ecclesiastical or high-status centres (Hamerow 2002), apparently indicating a level of control over this important commodity. The slag indicating iron production at Sedgeford may, therefore, imply a site of particular importance.

Smelting and smithing

The scale of production cannot yet be estimated, and the settlement may have been producing primarily for its own use. On the other hand, the excavations have yielded an abundance of Ipswich Ware pottery, implying a strong coastwise connection with the emporium, and a small quantity of Rhenish lava-quern and imported vessel-glass, which may also have come via Ipswich; so there is no reason to discount the possibility that Sedgeford ironwork may have made a contribution to the wider economy of the Kingdom of East Anglia in the 8th and 9th century AD.

The most likely ore source for the Sedgeford smelters was bog iron ore, which forms in river beds or marsh land, suggested by the phosphorus present in the metal (Piaskowski 1989). It is particularly useful since it is a renewable resource, refreshing itself every 15-20 years. The ore would have been placed in a furnace with charcoal and bellows used to pump air into it. The high temperatures (up to 1400° C) and reducing environment would have allowed the gangue material in the ore to react with the charcoal fuel and clay (Pleiner 2000). The process forms a waste product known as 'slag', which the excavators were able to identify on Boneyard in several different contexts (Paynter 2006).

The 'tap slag' found at Sedgeford implies that the slag furnace was tapped and the slag allowed to flow from it. During the Anglo-Saxon bloomery-smelting process, the iron was never molten. Instead, it formed as a mass of metal, known as a 'bloom', in the hottest part of the furnace near the air inlet (Pleiner 2000). Several fragments of bloom were found at Sedgeford, which is unusual, as iron was an expensive material and was rarely discarded.

Most of the slag was recovered from post-cemetery hillwash layers. The main exception was a quantity found in the fill of a ditch which cut through part of the cemetery on the lower slope of Boneyard. No firm conclusions can be drawn from this. Iron smelting may have been happening elsewhere on the site at an earlier stage and other parts of the cemetery may have continued in use beyond the cutting and infilling of this ditch.

Very little furnace lining was found with the slag, which probably means that the furnaces were not located within the area of the Boneyard-Reeddam excavation. The smelting furnaces were probably located further up the hill.

At Sedgeford two smithing-hearth bottoms have been found, both from post-cemetery hillwash

118

layers. This confirms the presence of a blacksmith in the area. Smithing is the process of turning the metal achieved from smelting into final finished objects. A smithing hearth, which need not have been a permanent structure, was used to heat the metal ready to be forged. During this process the charcoal and smithing-hearth clay would be mixed with the metal that fell off the iron and formed a smithing-hearth bottom (McDonnell 1987).

Iron bars and strips that formed the blacksmith's stock iron were also found, as were some hone stones used to sharpen iron tools. All this points to the presence of an Anglo-Saxon blacksmith in Sedgeford.

Knives

A total of 57 iron knives were found on Boneyard-Reeddam. These would have had either bone or wooden handles, and the three bone handles recovered make it clear that some of these would have been finished to a very high standard. One appears to be the terminal end of a knife handle, and has been beautifully carved into the head of a hound (see plate 5.19). Another smaller handle is made from a tube of bone and is stained with copper at one end, indicating a decorative bronze collar for what was surely an iron tool.

Most studies of iron artefacts, and particularly knives, rely heavily on typologies and classifications of shape. The cutting edge, unfortunately, is not a useful classification tool, as it can alter its shape as the knife is used or sharpened (Blakelock and McDonnell 2007). The shape of the back of the knife is therefore used instead. Here there are four basic classifications: curved-backed, angle-backed, straight-backed and incurved-backed, the shape of the knife being partly related to its function. At Sedgeford, as in Anglo-Saxon England generally, the majority of knives had a curved back.

In addition to typological classification, certain forms of scientific analysis can reveal more about the manufacturing process. Twenty-three (of which 4 were un-stratified) of the iron knives from Boneyard-Reeddam were examined by Eleanor Blakelock (2012). She used a combination of X-radiography, metallography and chemical compositional analysis to learn more about the skills of the Sedgeford blacksmiths. The results were compared with those from analysis of other Anglo-Saxon knife assemblages.

In setting out to manufacture a knife, the first step for a blacksmith was to choose an alloy from iron, phosphoric iron (iron with 0.1-2.5% phosphorus) and steel (iron with up to 1% carbon) (McDonnell 1989). Each had distinct properties. Steel was often used sparingly, presumably because it was more expensive and time-consuming to produce. Iron and phosphoric iron, while not as hard as steel, were tougher and more flexible. After the bars had been welded together, the knife was then shaped. The final process was to heat-treat the knife to increase the hardness of the steel.

The most common method of manufacturing a knife between the 7th and 10th centuries AD was to butt weld, by fire welding a small piece of hard steel to a more flexible iron or phosphoric iron back (Blakelock and McDonnell 2007). At Sedgeford this was the case with 12 of the 19 knives from stratified layers.

The majority of the knives had steel cutting-edges, and this has been the pattern observed in other Anglo-Saxon settlement assemblages. These edges were very hard, up to double the hardness of plain iron. Over half the knives had a phosphoric iron component, which indicates that a phosphorus-rich ore was most likely used, probably bog iron ore.

There were also three knives that consisted of steel sandwiched between two pieces of iron or phosphoric iron. This was a more common construction method in the 10th century AD, but was also carried out during the Middle Anglo-Saxon period. The remaining five knives were just plain iron, some of more heterogeneous composition than others.

Once shaped, the knife was then ready to be heat-treated. This quenching process, placing the object while hot in a cool liquid, increased the hardness of the steel but also made the metal brittle. To reduce the chance that the blade would shatter, the blacksmiths then tempered, that is, placed the blade back into the fire, to reduce some of the stress in the steel while retaining the hardness. In urban settlements this technique was perfected and the majority of objects were treated, but in rural settlements fewer treatments were carried out. This pattern appears to be reflected at Sedgeford, where just over 50% of the knives were treated, in contrast to more than 70% in urban settlements (Blakelock and McDonnell 2011; Blakelock 2012).

There are three possible models for the iron economy of any settlement: 1) self-sufficiency in iron production, with both smelting and smithing; 2) a complex smithy creating artefacts from imported stock iron; and 3) a basic smithy able to fashion simple artefacts and repair others, but with most ironwork imported.

At Sedgeford we have evidence for iron production in slag-tapping furnaces, implying the first model: self-sufficiency. The presence of smithing-hearth bottoms and stock iron makes it certain that there was a smithy in the settlement. This, in addition to the metallographic evidence from the knives, indicates a tradition of skilled blacksmithing within the Anglo-Saxon community at Sedgeford.

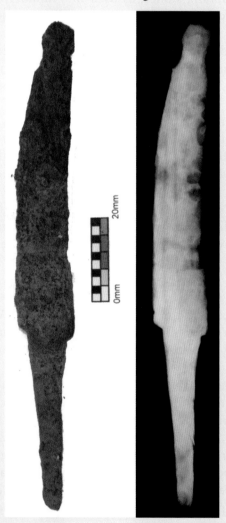

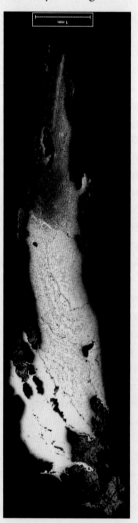

Plate 5.21: Photo and X-ray of one of the Anglo-Saxon knives from Sedgeford. The X-ray reveals otherwise invisible details indicative of how the knife was made. Note the dark horizontal lines – perhaps evidence of decoration.

Plate 5.22: The micro-structure of an iron knife from Sedgeford as revealed in section. You can clearly see the contrast between the dark red-brown steel cutting-edge and the white plain-iron back. Also note the speckled area, indicating plain iron as opposed to phosphoric iron.

Box 5.10
Anglo-Saxon whetstones and hones

A whetstone is a stone specially selected and shaped to use for sharpening metal blades. It usually consists of a bar, of rectangular, square, or more occasionally round section, with flat or angled ends, made of a fine-grained stone. It sometimes features either a suspension hole or a groove for tying a cord at one end, and occasionally a narrow channel in one face where needles and pins have been sharpened.

A hone is a smaller sharpening stone which may be of a more irregular form and possibly more often made by using whatever stone came to hand. Rubbing stones, as used in a number of craft processes, for instance in leatherworking, may also be found, and these may be difficult to separate from hones.

The presence of a small collection of whetstones, and one or two potential hones, at Sedgeford is not remarkable. They were a ubiquitous piece of equipment until recent times wherever iron blades and points were in use and needing frequent sharpening. The nature of the stones used may, however, tell us something about dating.

A number of surveys have shown that Scandinavian contact brought schist whetstones of two types into England, starting at the beginning of the 9th century AD, and that these very rapidly replaced all previous types of sharpening stone, spreading first through the Danelaw and then, by the Norman period, throughout the whole country, where they remained in use throughout the Middle Ages (Moore 1978, 61-73).

All nine of the Sedgeford whetstones/hones are sandstone and not schist. Only one is potentially a local stone; the others are imports traded from elsewhere in Britain. Not even small fragments of the imported schists have been recorded. It is therefore very likely that the stones date to the period before extensive Scandinavian contact with Norfolk – that is, they are Middle, not Late, Anglo-Saxon.

Most of the whetstones were recovered either from solidly Middle Anglo-Saxon layers or from slightly later layers which still contained large quantities of Middle Anglo-Saxon material. Another was from a Modern layer (though one that contained large quantities of Anglo-Saxon material), and the one remaining example was found on the spoil-heap. It seems relatively unproblematic to ascribe a Middle Anglo-Saxon date to the whole assemblage.

Of the individual finds, seven were made of the same material. This main group includes the best-preserved example, a complete bar-shaped whetstone with a very clear needle groove. This group is made from a fine-grained sandstone containing a lot of white mica. Suggested sources include the North Yorkshire Coast and Southern Scotland (Crosby and Mitchell 1987, 183-206). As well as the complete example, there are parts of three more bar-shaped stones in this group, a rhomboid-shaped stone (which may be the result of reworking a damaged bar-shaped one), and two flat-slab-shaped stones. The bar-shaped stones are generally considered to be for use in the hand, whereas the slab-shaped ones would have needed to be positioned on a work bench or floor and the blade or point rubbed against them.

As well as this group, there is: a single bar-shaped stone of another fine-grained, non-native sandstone which is very highly polished on all of the surviving working surfaces, but has unfortunately lost both ends; and a single round-profiled stone which is potentially a hone and may be made of a local sandstone derived from the nearby Sandringham Sands. This last may be an example of the *ad hoc* utilisation of a suitable naturally-occurring stone, rather than deliberate tool fashioning.

Box 5. 11
Anglo-Saxon textile production

Spindle-whorls

The Boneyard-Reeddam excavations yielded clear evidence for textile manufacture. Various objects associated with spinning and weaving were recovered. The spinning of yarn was attested by the presence of nine spindle-whorls made from a range of materials, three of worked bone or antler, three of stone, two of lead and one of fired clay.

The largest whorl was cut from an antler burr and is the most finely worked of the group. It has one flat face, a type which, together with whorls with two flat faces of unequal size, did not appear before the 6th century AD and emerged as the dominant type during the 7th century AD (Walton Rogers 2007, 24-25, fig. 2.18). The convex surface is decorated with two circles of engraved ring-and-dot motifs. This whorl is at the heavier end of Henry's middle range of weights for Middle and Late Anglo-Saxon England (Henry 1999, 72). These constitute around 70% of spindle-whorls of this date and would have been used to spin yarn for everyday fabrics.

The second, smaller antler whorl has two flat faces of unequal size. It fits into Henry's lighter whorls category and would have been used to spin flax fibres and high-quality wool. The third bone whorl, another middle-weight example, is a cattle femur head. Femur head whorls date from the 7th century AD onwards

Plate 5.23: Spindle-whorls from the Boneyard-Reeddam excavations.

and by the Late Anglo-Saxon period had become more common than antler whorls, probably because lighter spindle-whorls were in higher demand (Riddler and Trzaska-Nartowski forthcoming, 26-27).

Two of the three stone spindle-whorls are incomplete, but all have two flat faces of unequal size. The complete stone whorl is another middle-weight whorl for everyday yarns. It is decorated with three lightly incised lines. None of the stone whorls is obviously lathe-turned, so they probably pre-date the late 9th/ early 10th centuries AD (Henry 1999, 72).

The fired-clay spindle-whorl is also a middle-weight whorl with two flat faces of unequal size. The lead spindle-whorls are middle-weight whorls with one flat face, but they are smaller. Two of the whorls (the fired-clay example and one of the incomplete stone whorls) were found within cemetery layers but cannot be ascribed to specific graves. One of the lead whorls was found in a pit which appeared to pre-date the cemetery, and so was perhaps Late Iron Age in date. The remainder were from post-cemetery hillwash layers.

Pin-beaters

That these different qualities of yarn were then woven into garments is proven by the recovery of 15 pin-beaters from the site, a considerable number from a relatively small excavation area. Pin-beaters are smooth bone rods, usually 8-17cm in length and pointed at one or both ends, used to disentangle threads whilst weaving (Clegg-Hyer and Owen-Crocker 2011, 167).

Plate 5.24: Pin-beaters from the Boneyard-Reeddam excavations.

Six of the Boneyard-Reeddam pin-beaters are near-complete and all are double-ended (although some are incomplete they all have circular or ovate cross-sections, which single-ended pin-beaters do not). At other sites, most double-ended pin-beaters have come from contexts dating from the 7th to mid 9th century AD, although they are occasionally present up to the late 11th century, and more commonly so in rural areas (Henry 1999, 72). One of the near complete examples from Boneyard-Reeddam has one flattened end, implying that it had a special use (MacGregor 1985, 189). Another worked-bone fragment may possibly be a central section from a toothed weft-beater, a tool used with the Late Anglo-Saxon two-beam vertical loom. There is a complete comparable example from Birka in Sweden, which, like the Sedgeford fragment, is decorated with rings-and-dots (Walton Rogers 2007, 33).

Of the three pin-beaters from Jewell's 1958 excavations, two were apparently associated with burials. One fragment from the more recent excavations was within the fill of a grave, but was not recorded as being associated with the skeleton (which was, in any case, that of male aged over 45 at death, and therefore an unlikely owner). Two pin-beaters were from cemetery layers, another two were from possible Anglo-Saxon occupation layers and two were from the fills of Anglo-Saxon pits or ditches. The remainder were found in post-cemetery hillwash or ploughsoil layers. The possible toothed weft-beater fragment was from a deposit described as an occupation spread which contained Late Anglo-Saxon pottery.

Needles and loom-weights

There are also two needles made from pig fibulae which may have been used for auxiliary textile jobs, such as threading the cords that were used to fasten the edges of the cloth on a warp-weighted loom onto the uprights so as to maintain an even width (Hoffman 1964, 145-146). Such needles are common finds on Middle and Late Anglo-Saxon sites and there are similar examples from Thetford, Norwich Waterfront and York.

No loom-weights were found on the Boneyard-Reeddam site, but several have been found on Lower Chalkpit.

All this points to significant, but not abnormal, textile production at Sedgeford in the Middle Anglo-Saxon period: that is, production on the scale that one would expect on a rural site at this time, when the manufacture of cloth and clothing was a routine domestic task.

Box 5.12
Non-ferrous metalworking

During the excavations of Boneyard-Reeddam, very little evidence for non-ferrous metalworking was discovered. Two crucible fragments for melting copper alloys were found. One fragment was an Anglo-Saxon-type crucible which had been hand-made and constructed from a clay fabric with abundant quartz inclusions and some evidence for vegetable temper. It appears similar to the crucibles found at Bloodmoor Hill (Dickens *et al* 2009). Qualitative XRF analysis revealed no traces of precious metals but did reveal traces of copper. The other crucible was much larger and shallower. The centre was red but not vitrified. It had a flat base. It was presumably associated with metalworking.

No casting waste or moulds were found during the excavation. Mould fragments are rarely found as these tend to be more friable than the vitrified crucibles. It is therefore likely that some non-ferrous metalworking was taking place at Sedgeford in the Anglo-Saxon period.

Box 5.13
Anglo-Saxon writing implements

Two styli were found (see Plate 5.19) during the Boneyard-Reeddam excavations, one of copper alloy (Pestell's Class I) and one of iron (Pestell's Class II). The stylus, a pointed rod for writing, was used to scratch letters into wax writing-tablets.

Sadly, without the remarkable kind of preservation witnessed within the waterlogged areas around the Roman fort at Vindolanda, for example, we have no knowledge of the sorts of things that might have been written down in this way in Anglo-Saxon times. We can, however, hazard guesses. Information recorded on wax writing-tablets was, of course, temporary and everyday; it was not required to last for long. It seems highly likely that the development of a more complex class society – one governed by property ownership, labour obligations, tribute payment, food rents, commercial exchange and so on – created an increased need for tallies and accounts on agricultural estates.

To put this into wider context, 22 styli were found at Flixborough, three at Brandon, and they turn up occasionally on other Norfolk sites and further afield in places like York and Whitby. The dating of plain Anglo-Saxon styli is broad but where they have been found with decoration it has been Middle Anglo-Saxon in style (Evans and Loveluck 2009, 126-7). Both of the Sedgeford styli are from post-cemetery hillwash layers, but we can be certain that they were in use in the settlement during its use-life.

Finds of styli have occasionally been used to infer the site of a monastery, partly because finds have sometimes been made on sites known to have been such, but others have denied any close connection between styli and monasteries. The fact is that so few rural sites of this date have been comprehensively excavated that it is almost impossible to say what is 'normal'. Common sense suggests that the development of lordship, regardless of whether it was ecclesiastical or secular, would have necessitated record-keeping, that this need not have involved high levels of literacy, and that even if it did, monks may well have served as clerks (*sic*) on great estates. Equating styli and monasteries may be a red herring.

Box 5.14
Bones, shells and grains

The Boneyard-Reeddam excavations yielded a large assemblage of animal bone (macro-fauna) and were also extensively archaeo-environmentally sampled to recover micro-assemblages of small bones, plant remains, snail shells and other tell-tale indications of past environments, agricultural regimes and household consumption patterns.

Kris Poole has analysed almost 10,000 fragments of animal bone from stratified deposits recovered during the Lower Chalkpit evaluation in 2007. This represents by far our best 'window' so far on this class of evidence and the information it contains. There seems little doubt that analysis of the much larger assemblages from the Boneyard-Reeddam excavations would produce comparable results rather than anything radically different.

The three main domesticates – sheep/goat, cow and pig – were dominant throughout the life of the Anglo-Saxon settlement. The skeletons of sheep and goats are almost identical, so animal bones specialists are forced to lump their remains together as 'sheep/goat'. Sheep/goat was the most numerous species in each phase, but the proportion of cow and pig increased between the 8th and 10th centuries AD. In the 8th

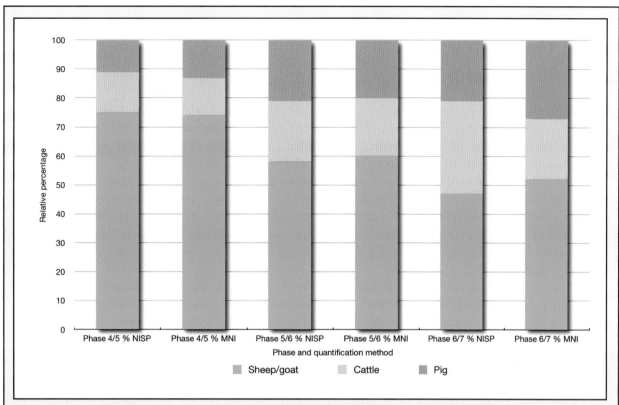

Fig. 5.12: Chart showing relative percentages of the major domesticates in successive periods represented in animal bone assemblages from the 2007 Lower Chalkpit evaluation. Three main periods are shown, and for each period data is given in two forms, the first column showing the Number of Identified Specimens (NISP), the second the Minimum Number of Individuals (MNI).

century AD the proportion of sheep/goat was 76%, in the mid to late 9th century AD 58% and in the 10th century AD 46%. Also significant was the fact that a high proportion of the sheep/goat were older animals.

The implication is that sheep (probably not goats) were being raised for wool to supply the textile production implicit in finds of spindle-whorls and pin-beaters on Boneyard-Reeddam; their meat was secondary. By contrast, a good number of the rising proportion of cattle were relatively young animals; so they were being killed for their meat (and perhaps hides), with milk production a secondary consideration.

This pattern is accompanied by a drop in the number of domestic birds in the assemblages, and an increase in wild species, such as roe deer. Mutton and chicken tend to be low status, beef, pork and venison high status. The changing composition of the animal bone assemblages may, like the rectilinear grid-planning and D-shaped enclosure on Lower Chalkpit, reflect the rise of a local elite.

Fish, on the other hand, does not seem to have featured heavily in the Anglo-Saxon diet – surprisingly, given the proximity of the sea and the active waterways and extensive wetlands in the river valley. Relatively few fish bones have been found in archaeo-environmental samples, and Lorna Corr's analysis of the stable isotope levels in the bone collagen in a sample of 45 skeletons (15 men, 15 women and 15 juveniles) indicated a predominantly terrestrial rather than a marine diet (though the shell-fish consumption implicit in the presence of numerous oysters and mussels in midden deposits would not have registered). The same analysis revealed that children under about seven years of age appear to have eaten very little meat, subsisting largely on bread (Corr 2003, 136-179). The bread, judging by the evidence of plant remains in the archaeo-environmental samples, was predominantly made from spelt wheat in the earlier phases, bread wheat in the later.

Box 5.15
Anglo-Saxon coins

Nine Anglo-Saxon coins are known to have been found in the parish of Sedgeford. Eight of these come from the main settlement and cemetery site on Boneyard-Reeddam/Lower Chalkpit, and have a date range of c. AD 700 to 985. The other is a Merovingian tremiss, an indication of Continental contact before the more obvious imports and trading activity of the 8th and 9th centuries AD.

Of the eight coins from the settlement site, five date to the 8th century AD: a Kentish Series O *sceatta* (c. AD 700-720), two East Anglian Series R *sceattas* (c. AD 730-750), a very rare denier of Pepin III, the father of Charlemagne (c. AD 755-768) and a penny of Eadwald of East Anglia (c. AD 796-798). A penny of Burgred of Mercia (c. AD 852-874) dates to the third quarter of the 9th century AD, and the final two coins bracket the 10th century AD, being a Viking-issue St Edmund memorial penny (c. AD 895-910) and a penny of Aethlered II (c. AD 975-989).

Unlike the metalwork-rich 'productive sites' of this period – sites like Bawsey that have been investigated mainly by means of metal-detector surveys of surface assemblages – Sedgeford's coin count is modest, bringing it into line with other 'non-productive sites' like Brandon in Suffolk. Though difficulties arise in comparing metal-detected sites with excavated sites, there does seem to be a distinction among Middle Anglo-Saxon sites based on relative rates of coin loss (though how one should interpret such a distinction is far from straightforward).

Another contrast is that the Sedgeford assemblage is not dominated by early *sceatta* coins, and is in fact completely devoid of early Continental *sceattas* dating between AD 680 and 750. This fits with the idea that it may have been a *de novo* foundation of the late 7th or early 8th century AD. The presence of the late East Anglian Series R sceattas perhaps hints at an economic awakening coinciding with development of the settlement during the first half of the 8th century.

Unfortunately, the assemblage is far too small to be used to reconstruct the economic fortunes of the settlement. Nevertheless, the three coin finds dating to between c. AD 755 and 874 (the penny of Eadwald of East Anglia, the penny of Burgred of Mercia and the denier of Pepin III) are of particular significance, as this is a period when the 'productive sites' are rendered almost invisible numisimatically (the exceptions being Carolingian coins from Burnham, Wormegay and Congham).

On present evidence, it is possible to suggest that, in contrast to 'productive sites', Sedgeford experienced a period of economic progression (or at least stability) during the later 8th and 9th centuries AD. The different point of origin for these three coins, and the different political situations under which they were minted (a formative Carolingian Europe, a short-lived independent East Anglia and an aggressive Mercia), provide evidence for the huge reorientations in the politico-economic landscape of Anglo-Saxon England at this time.

Plate 5.25 Naomi Payne with a London-minted coin from the time of Ethelred the Unready, found in Chalkpit.

Plate 5.26: Anglo-Saxon coins found on the Boneyard-Reeddam/Lower Chalkpit site by SHARP.

A large number of sizeable pits have also been excavated inside the D-shaped enclosure. Interpretation is uncertain, but they do not appear to have been used primarily as rubbish pits, even in their afterlife, since finds were usually sparse. The implication may be that they were dug for storage or for processing raw materials. Either way, the number and size of the pits may imply the management of surpluses on a scale not evidenced elsewhere on the site in this period or in earlier phases of occupation.

What are we to make of it? The D-shaped enclosure was contemporary with the latest phase in the life of the grid-planned settlement. The two co-existed in the 10th century AD, probably for a period of decades. Almost 700 sherds of Thetford-type Ware were recovered from the fills of the great enclosure ditches – rubbish-dumping that bears testimony to both the date of occupation and its intensity. The monumentality of the ditches is matched by the scale of some of the internal features. The implication is that the D-shaped enclosure represents control over labour and the accumulation of surpluses, either for consumption on-site or for distribution beyond. This in turn implies some form of elite control, and, perhaps, an elite presence (though an absentee lord might have been represented by a local agent).

Of what rank? Certainly that of a thegn, the Anglo-Saxon equivalent of a knight or lord of the manor. Manorialisation of the landscape seems to have been characteristic of the 10th century AD, perhaps as the great estates of the 8th century were sub-divided into smaller parcels, probably to ensure tighter control over land and labour by embattled elites dependent on flows of tribute and reserves of militia. Lower Chalkpit's D-shaped enclosure may then be the precursor to the two Medieval manors established at West Hall by the 13th century (at the latest).

A further question arises: was this great enclosure – imagine it as ditch, rampart and palisade – designed simply to dominate the landscape, to tower over the village, and to assert the rank and status of the great man within, housed amid family, dependents and estate officials? Or was it also a defence-work, perhaps raised in response to one or another of the many upsurges of conflict between Anglo-Saxon and Viking in the years after the 870s AD? Perhaps this is a false dichotomy: contemporary law codes for thegnly complexes required them to be defensible, with a gate-house to defend the entrance, a tower as a lookout and a bell within the tower to give warning to the community (Reynolds 1999, 123-135).

Whatever the case, the termination of the cemetery, village and proto-manorial complex comprising 'South Sedgeford' in the late 10th or possibly early 11th century comes as a surprise. We usually expect to find the Late Anglo-Saxon, even the Middle Anglo-Saxon settlement beneath the modern village. We regard evolution on the same site as normal and sudden relocation as exceptional.

But these were, let us remind ourselves, turbulent times, and Sedgeford occupies a marginal location, on the edge of East Anglia facing The Wash. That it might have succumbed at some point to pillage and destruction by a marauding army seems entirely possible. That there may even have been a hiatus, a period when it was an abandoned wasteland, does not seem far-fetched. In which case, when reoccupied, Sedgeford's new overlords might have found a *tabula rasa*, a blank canvas, on which to create a new settlement in a place of their choosing. Alternatively, settlement and the farming of the land may have been continuous, but new overlords, or a change in ambition and policy by existing ones, for reasons which we can only guess, may have given rise to our 'Late Anglo-Saxon shift'.

A Medieval rural landscape
Phase 8 c. AD ?975/1100+

Very few sherds of Grimston-type Ware pottery of 12th to 15th century date have been found on the Boneyard-Reeddam site. Most of the Grimston sherds were not derived from archaeological features, but from the thick layers of hill-wash which subsequently developed on the site; even then, these were vastly outnumbered by larger sherds of Middle and Late Anglo-Saxon pottery ploughed out from further up the slope.

At some point, most likely in the 11th century, another large east-west ditch was cut through the cemetery at the bottom of the slope. It seems likely that this was part of the wholesale landscape reorganisation in the river-valley associated with the construction of a causeway and dam, enabling the draining of the West Hall area to the west, the creation of the Reeddam to the east and, probably, the powering of one or more watermills. The absence of later Medieval or Early Modern pottery in association with the ditch – combined with the circumstantial evidence provided by Saxo-Norman settlement at West Hall – is suggestive of an 11th century date.

On Lower Chalkpit, at around the same time, a trackway ran alongside the partially silted up northern ditch of the D-shaped enclosure (Fig. 5.13). We know this because part of the metalled surface was found in excavation slumped into the subsiding upper fills of the ditch on its northern side. It could be dated approximately by the presence of a few sherds of Grimston-type Ware in the overlying deposit. The line of this trackway appears on the 1631 Estate Map as a field boundary or minor track running parallel to, and south of, the main trackway a short distance to the north that, as noted above, still survives today.

Interlude – A Ceramic Reconnaissance

Between 1996 and 2007, SHARP excavated a wide range of sites on both sides of the River Heacham in the central part of Sedgeford parish. The pottery recovered tells stories about both the individual sites and the parish as a whole. In the former case, ceramic insights have been embedded in the narratives of the individual sites reported elsewhere. Here, the intention is to use the ceramic assemblages as a whole to explore general developments, particularly in the Middle and Late Anglo-Saxon periods.

Key ceramic data have been summarised in the form of two tables. Table 5. 1 reports on 'South Sedgeford' – the group of sites discussed in Chapters 5

Fig. 5.13: Plan showing the Phase 8 Medieval features on the Boneyard-Reeddam/Lower Chalkpit excavations superimposed on the 1631 Estate Map. Note the minor trackway following the line of the D-shaped enclosure ditch.

and 6. Table 5.2 reports on 'North Sedgeford' – the sites discussed in Chapters 7, 8 and 9. These two sets of sites have been grouped together for the purpose of analysis because they are geographically connected and also because their respective 'ceramic signals' seem to provide a sharp and telling contrast.

A total of 16,143 sherds, together weighing 174,026 grams, have been included in the analysis, and these represent the great majority of those recovered in excavation during the first 12 years of the project. Most sherds have been assigned to one of the fabric classes in the SHARP Pottery Typology. But for the purpose of this analysis, they have been grouped by period. For each period, the pottery has been quantified by sherd count and weight.

Period Group	Sherd Count	% Share of Total Count	Sherd Weight gm	% Share of Total Weight	% Relative Ceramic Share
Iron Age	1,564	12	11,111	7	9
Roman	545	4	5,556	4	4
Middle Anglo-Saxon (Ipswich Ware)	3,514	27	60,773	38	32
Late Anglo-Saxon (Thetford-type Ware)	7,176	54	77,552	49	52
All Anglo-Saxon	10,716	81	138,533	87	84
Medieval	107	1	1,324	1	1
Post-Medieval	258	2	2,162	1	1
Total	13,190		158,478		

South Sedgeford comprises: Boneyard Old Trench, Boneyard New Trench, Reeddam, Reeddam 2 and Lower Chalkpit (up to 2007 only).

Period Group	Sherd Count	% Share of Total Count	Sherd Weight gm	% Share of Total Weight	% Relative Ceramic Share
Iron Age	271	9	1,229	8	9
Roman	96	3	617	4	4
Middle Anglo-Saxon (Ipswich Ware)	23	1	164	1	1
Late Anglo-Saxon (Thetford-type Ware)	601	20	4,700	30	26
All Anglo-Saxon	624	21	4,864	31	26
Medieval	553	19	3,988	26	22
Post-Medieval	1,409	48	4,642	30	39
Total	2,953		15,340		

North Sedgeford comprises: West Hall Paddock, Ladywell Field, Saggy Horse Field, Sedgeford Village Survey and West Hall Garden Electricity Trench.

To facilitate comparison, these quantities have then been expressed as percentages of the total. To further facilitate comparison, the percentage sherd count and weight for each period group have then been averaged. This is the meaning of 'relative ceramic share', which is designed to even out the different biases inherent in sherd counts and weights as measures of ceramic quantity (due mainly to the fact that thin-walled vessels break more easily and give higher sherd counts, while thick-walled vessels have higher weights). The last column in the tables, therefore, is the most useful for direct comparisons of relative quantities – that is, for assessing the strength of the 'ceramic signal' for each period.

The Late Iron Age and Roman periods

Approximately 9% of the pottery recovered from both North and South Sedgeford was of Iron Age date, the bulk of it probably Late Iron Age, given that the majority of sherds comprised relatively hard, well-fired, sand-tempered ceramic. The wide and even distribution of this material supports the hypothesis of a 'spurgy' *oppidum*-type zone of settlement and activity extending over a large area (as argued in Chapter 2).

The Roman period, on the other hand, is poorly represented – less than 4% of the overall assemblage. This probably indicates little more than 'background noise' – manuring spreads and the like – for this pottery-rich period. Roman sites are known elsewhere in the parish (see Chapter 3), however, so the implication may be that the settlement pattern in this period was very different from that in either the Iron Age or the Anglo-Saxon.

Dating Middle Anglo-Saxon Sedgeford

Our main preoccupation here is with events between *c*. AD 650/700 and 1100. Our main ceramic dating evidence for this period is provided by Middle Anglo-Saxon Ipswich Ware (*c*. AD 720-850) and Late Anglo-Saxon Thetford-type Ware (*c*. AD 850/925-1075/1100+). Uncertainties remain about the precise dating of these two ceramic industries.

When was Ipswich Ware first produced? The general view used to be that it was as early as *c*. AD 650. Paul Blinkhorn's view – and he is the current expert – is that it was not until *c*. AD 720 (2012). But there is then a further question: when did it first arrive at any particular site? Could it be, on the basis of Blinkhorn's start-date, as late as *c*. AD 750? We do not know: it depends on the dynamism of the distribution mechanism.

We have another problem with its end-date: the evidence from Sedgeford seems to imply some overlap between Ipswich Ware and Thetford-type Ware – that is, a short period, presumably in the mid to late 9th century, when both were arriving at the site. This conclusion was based on careful analysis of 'residuality' in a large sample of excavated assemblages.

Residuality occurs when discarded material – like broken pottery – is disturbed by later activity and re-deposited in new archaeological layers. We analysed the residuality of our pottery by assuming that it became more broken up each time it was disturbed and re-deposited – average sherd size thus became our measure of whether pottery was 'old' when it found its way into a layer or 'new'.

Comparing Ipswich Ware and Thetford-type Ware, we found that Ipswich sherds had the same average size when they constituted only 35% of the assemblage as when they constituted 100%. The implication was that the Ipswich was still 'new' even when 65% of the ceramic present in a layer was the 'later' Thetford.

This may mean that the Ipswich potters continued production for a period after the introduction of Thetford-type Ware; or that their products were stored or carefully curated for a significant period after manufacture ceased. Either way, the ceramic dating becomes blurred.

Measuring Activity

Pottery helps with dating. It may also tell us something about the function and the 'busy-ness' of a site. But there are analytical hazards to be negotiated. South

Sedgeford yielded 3,514 sherds of Ipswich Ware and 7,176 sherds of Thetford-type Ware (a ratio of 1:2.04). Is the implication that activity intensified in the Late Anglo-Saxon period? It is not. Direct comparison is insufficient. It is necessary to calibrate the ceramic signals for different periods in assessing the relative intensity of activity.

Ipswich seems to give a weaker signal than Thetford on most sites in East Anglia; there just was not as much pottery around in the earlier period. Any given level of activity, we must therefore assume, will be less 'ceramically visible' in the Middle Anglo-Saxon period than in the Late.

In 1998 Louise Barker collated the evidence from 15 published field surveys and excavations which had yielded both Ipswich and Thetford-type Wares. Some of the sites turned out to be anomalous and were subsequently excluded from the analysis, but 11 of them were accepted as representative in the sense that they appear to have been sites occupied throughout the Middle and Late Anglo-Saxon periods. Louise discovered that 12 sherds of Thetford-type Ware were being recovered for every sherd of Ipswich Ware. On the other hand, Thetford-type Ware was in use for approximately twice as long as Ipswich Ware. Taking account of this, we can estimate that one sherd of Ipswich Ware indicates a similar level of site activity as six sherds of Thetford-type Ware.

South Sedgeford's Ipswich:Thetford ratio of 1:2.04 can now be calibrated by dividing the Thetford value by six. This gives 1:0.34; that is, the Ipswich signal for South Sedgeford is three times stronger than the Thetford signal.

Two possibilities arise. Either South Sedgeford was a Middle Anglo-Saxon site which terminated fairly early in the Late Anglo-Saxon period; or it was a site whose *floruit* was in the earlier period and that what followed was a period of reduced or interrupted activity.

A Late Anglo-Saxon Shift

The calibrated Ipswich:Thetford ratio for North Sedgeford shows a strong contrast with that for South Sedgeford: at 1:4.20, it indicates a predominantly Late Anglo-Saxon site. But that is not all: the Thetford assemblage *per se* is different. In South Sedgeford, 68% of identifiable Thetford vessel forms were jars compared with 32% bowls. The corresponding figures for North Sedgeford were 54% jars and 46% bowls. Our assumption is that this difference has chronological significance: that early Thetford assemblages have two jars for every bowl, while late ones have roughly equal numbers of each. We make this assumption partly because other East Anglian archaeologists have come to the same conclusion (Andrew Rogerson, pers. comm.), and partly because an early-late distinction fits with everything else we know about the differences between South and North Sedgeford. Our small finds, our coin assemblage and our small set of radiocarbon determinations all support the broad conclusion that South Sedgeford should be dated *c.* AD 650/700 to *c.* AD 925/1075 (at the latest). There was probably the beginnings of some drift of domestic activity north across the river towards the end of this period, and possibly a period when both foci of settlement were functioning, but certainly by the 11th century North Sedgeford had become the sole settlement centre.

The main contributors to the writing of this chapter were:

Matt Hobson (principal author), Naomi Payne (principal author), Jon Cousins (principal author) and Neil Faulkner (principal author), Eleanor Blakelock, Rose Broadley, Sophie Cabot, Pamela J. Cross, Gareth Davies, Kris Poole and Martin Hatton

References

Ashby, S.P., 2007, Bone and Antler Combs, Sleaford, Finds Research Group AD 700-1700, Datasheet No. 40.

Ashby, S.P., 2011, 'An atlas of Medieval combs from northern Europe', in Internet Archaeology, No. 30.

Bates, S., 1991, 'Summary report of excavations at Sedgeford', Gressenhall, Norfolk Archaeological Unit Report, No. 35.

Blakelock, E., 2012, The Early Medieval Cutting Edge of Technology: an archaeometallurgical, technological and social study of the manufacture and use of Anglo-Saxon and Viking iron knives and their contribution to the Early Medieval iron economy, unpub. PhD thesis, University of Bradford.

Blakelock, E.S. and McDonnell, G., 2007, 'A review of the metallographic analysis of Early Medieval knives', in Historical Metallurgy, 41, 40-56.

Blakelock, E.S. and McDonnell, G., 2011, 'Early Medieval knife manufacture in Britain: a comparison between rural and urban settlements (AD 400-1000)', in J. Hošek, H. Cleere and L. Mihok (eds), *The Archaeometallurgy of Iron: recent developments in archaeological and scientific research*, Prague, Institute of Archaeology ASCR Prague, 123-136.

Blair, J., 2013, 'Grid-planning in Anglo-Saxon settlements: the short perch and the four-perch module', in Hamerow, H. (ed.) Anglo-Saxon Studies in Archaeology and History, 18, 18-61.

Blinkhorn, P., 2012, The Ipswich Ware Project: ceramics, trade and society in Middle Saxon England, Medieval Pottery Research Group Occasional Paper, No. 7.

Brugmann, B., 2004, *Glass Beads from Early Anglo-Saxon Graves: a study of the provenance and chronology of glass beads from Anglo-Saxon graves, based on visual examination*, Oxford, Oxbow.

Buckberry, J. and Cherryson, A. (eds.), 2010, *Burial in Later Anglo-Saxon England, c. 650-1100 AD*, Oxford, Oxbow.

Clegg-Hyer, M. and Owen-Crocker, G. (eds.), 2011, *The Material Culture of Daily Living in the Anglo-Saxon World*, Exeter, Exeter University Press.

Corr, L., 2003, The Evaluation of a Multi-Proxy Stable Isotope Approach to Palaeodietary Reconstruction, unpub. PhD thesis, University of Bristol.

Craig-Atkins, E., 2012, 'Chest Burial: a Middle Anglo-Saxon funerary rite from northern England', in Oxford Journal of Archaeology, 30, 317-337.

Crosby, D.D.B. and Mitchell J.G., 1987, 'A survey of British metamorphic honestones of the 9th to 15th centuries AD in the light of potassium-argon and natural remnant magnetisation studies', in Journal of Archaeological Science, 14, 183-206.

Cross, P.J., 2009, 'Horses amongst the Christians: a bio-cultural interpretation of the human-horse burial and other horse burials in the 7th-9th century cemetery at Sedgeford, Norfolk, UK', unpub. MSc dissertation, University of Bradford.

Cross, P.J., 2011, 'Horse burial in first millennium AD Britain: issues of interpretation', in European Journal of Archaeology, 14(1), 193-212.

Dickens, A., Lucy, S. and Tipper, J., 2009, The Anglo-Saxon Settlement and Cemetery at Bloodmoor Hill, Carlton Colville, Suffolk , East Anglian Archaeology 131, Cambridge, Cambridge Archaeological Unit.

Evans, D.H. and Loveluck, C. (eds.), 2009, *Life and Economy at Early Medieval Flixborough, c. AD 600-100: the artefact evidence, Volume 2, Excavations at Flixborough*, Oxford, Oxbow.

Guido, M., 1978, *The Glass Beads of the Prehistoric and Roman Periods in Britain and Ireland*, London, Society of Antiquaries of London.

Hadley, D. and Buckberry, J., 2007, 'Caring for the dead in Late Anglo-Saxon England', in F. Tinti (ed.), *Pastoral Care in Late Anglo-Saxon England*, Woodbridge, Boydell, 121-147.

Hamerow, H., 2002, *Early medieval settlements: the archaeology of rural communities in North-West Europe, 400-900*, Oxford, Oxford University Press.

Heighway, C. and Bryant, R., 1999, *The Golden Minster: the Anglo-Saxon and later Medieval Priory of St Oswald at Gloucester, York*, C.B.A. Report No. 117.

Henry, P.A., 1999, 'Development and change in Late Saxon textile production: an analysis of the evidence', in *Durham Archaeological Journal*, 14-15, 69-76.

Hinton, D.A., 1996, *The Gold, Silver and Other Non-Ferrous Alloy Objects from Hamwic, Southampton Archaeology Monographs 6*, Stroud, Alan Sutton.

Hoffmann, M., 1964, The Warp-Weighted Loom: studies in the history and technology of an ancient implement, *Studia Norvegica* No. 14, Oslo, Universitetsforlaget.

Kjølbye-Biddle, B., 1995, 'Iron bound coffins and coffin-fittings from the pre-Norman cemetery', in D. Philips and B. Heywood (eds.), *Excavations at York Minster: from Roman fortress to Norman cathedral*, Swindon, R.C.H.M.E., 489-521.

MacGregor, A., 1985, *Bone, Antler, Ivory and Horn: the technology of skeletal materials since the Roman period*, London, Croom Helm.

MacGregor, A. and Bolick, E., 1993, *Ashmolean Museum, Oxford: a summary catalogue of the Anglo-Saxon collections (non-ferrous metals)*, B.A.R. British Series No. 230, Oxford, British Archaeological Reports.

Marzinzik, S., 2003, *Early Anglo-Saxon Belt Buckles (Late Fifth to Early Eighth Centuries AD): their classification and context*, Oxford, Archaeopress.

McDonnell, G., 1987, 'The study of early iron smelting residues', in *The Crafts of the Blacksmith: essays presented to R.F. Tylecote at the 1984 symposium of the UISPP Comitâe pour la Sidâerurgie ancienne*, Belfast, UISPP Comitâe pour la Sidâerurgie ancienne, 47-52 B.G. Scott, H. Cleere and R.F. Tylecote (eds), .

McDonnell, G., 1989, 'Iron and its alloys in the fifth to eleventh centuries AD in England', in *World Archaeology*, 20, 373-382.

Moore, T.D., 1978, 'The petrography and archaeology of English honestones', in *Journal of Archaeological Science*, 5, 61-73.

Paynter, S., 2006, 'Regional variations in bloomery smelting slag of the Iron Age and Romano-British periods', in *Archaeometry*, 48, 271-292.

Piaskowski, J., 1989, 'Phosphorus in iron ore and slag and in bloomery iron', in *Archaeomaterials*, 3, 47-59.

Pleiner, R., 2000, *Iron in archaeology: the European bloomery smelters*, Praha, Archaeologický Ústav AVČR.

Reynolds, A., 1999, *Later Anglo-Saxon England: life and landscape*, Stroud, Tempus.

Reynolds, A., 2003, 'Boundaries and settlements in later sixth to eleventh-century England', in D. Griffiths, A. Reynolds and S. Semple (eds.), *Boundaries in Early Medieval Britain: Anglo-Saxon Studies in Archaeology and History*, 12, 98-136.

Reynolds, A., 2009, *Anglo-Saxon Deviant Burial Customs*, Oxford, Oxford University Press.

Riddler, I.D., 1990, 'Saxon handled combs from London', in *Transactions of the London and Middlesex Archaeological Society*, 41, 9-20.

Riddler, I.D., 2012, 'Early and Middle Saxon artefacts', in S. Wrathmell (ed.), *A History of Wharram Percy and its Neighbour Wharram: a study of settlement on the Yorkshire Wolds*, XIII, York, York University Archaeological Publications, 1515, 135-

154.

Riddler, I.D. and Trzaska-Nartowski, N.I.A., 2011, 'Working skeletal materials', in M. Clegg Hyer and G. Owen-Crocker (eds.), *The Material Culture of Daily Living in the Anglo-Saxon World*, Exeter, Exeter University Press.

Riddler, I.D. and Trzaska-Nartowski, N.I.A., forthcoming, 'Lundenwic and the Middle Saxon worked bone interlude', in *Anglo-Saxon Studies*.

Riddler, I.D., Trzaska-Nartowski, N.I.A. and Hatton, S., forthcoming, *An Early Medieval Craft: antler and bone working from Ipswich excavations, 1974-1994*, Gressenhall, East Anglian Archaeology.

Samson, R., 1999, 'The Church lends a hand', in J. Downes and T. Pollard (eds.), *The Loved Body's Corruption*, Glasgow, Cruithne Press, 120-144.

Taylor, A., 2001, *Burial Practice in Early England*, Stroud, Tempus.

Tester, A., Anderson, S., Riddler, I.D. and Carr, R., forthcoming, *Staunch Meadow, Brandon, Suffolk: a high-status Middle Saxon settlement on the Fen Edge*, Gressenhall, East Anglian Archaeology.

Thomas, G., 2003, *Late Anglo-Saxon and Viking Age Strap-Ends*, 750-1100, Part 1, Finds Research Group Datasheet No. 32.

Wade-Martins, P., 1980, *North Elmham*, East Anglian Archaeology Report, No. 9, Gressenhall, Norfolk Museums Service.

Waldron, T., 2007, *Paleoepidemiology*, Walnut Creek, California, Left Coast Press.

Walton Rogers, P., 2007, *Cloth and Clothing in Anglo-Saxon England, AD 450-700*, C.B.A. Research Report, No. 145, York, Council for British Archaeology.

6. The People of Anglo-Saxon Sedgeford

Introduction

Between 1996 and 2006, SHARP's excavations on Boneyard-Reeddam revealed the remains of 291 discrete individuals, along with a large quantity of disarticulated bone. Radiocarbon dating of some of the remains has shown that the people represented lived in the Middle Anglo-Saxon period. Their skeletal remains provide the most intimate understanding of the people themselves that archaeology can provide. They sometimes allow us, quite literally, to put human faces to the people who lived, worked and died at Sedgeford around 50 generations ago. In studying their remains we not only gain knowledge of their lives, but also make an emotive connection with fellow human-beings separated from us only by time. This chapter discusses findings and provisional conclusions drawn from the post-excavation analysis that has been completed to date.

The Sedgeford skeletons

The first study of human remains from Boneyard-Reeddam occurred in the early 20th century when the landowner, Holcombe Ingleby, sent the Royal College of Surgeons a human skeleton discovered by his gamekeeper whilst digging out a rabbit burrow (Ingleby 1922-1925, 35-36). The first major study followed excavations by Peter Jewell in 1957 and 1958 and by Don Brothwell in 1960. Skeletons from both excavations were subsequently deposited in the Duckworth Collection at Cambridge University.

There are 126 individually identified sets of bones attributed to Sedgeford in this collection (Baldry 2009). Although we believe they all came from Boneyard, we know the precise location of the original burial for only about half of the total: six came from within the area subsequently excavated by SHARP and another 54 from trenches about five metres to the east. No comprehensive report on these 126 sets of bones has yet been published.

The SHARP skeletons

Although SHARP excavated 291 sets of human remains, and earlier excavators another 126, this does not mean that 417 complete skeletons have been recovered; far from it. Human interventions (e.g. inter-cutting graves, ploughing, ditch digging) or, occasionally, natural agencies (e.g. colluvial movement, root action, burrowing by rabbits and moles) have often truncated the remains, leaving just the upper or lower half of a skeleton, or even less.

However, if the bones present in the ground are in the correct anatomical positions relative to one another – i.e. they are 'articulated' – they must have been undisturbed since burial and therefore represent the remains of one individual. Therefore, all articulated remains, however incomplete, were treated by SHARP as discrete burials. Disturbed, loose bones with no recognisable relationship to other remains, on the other hand, were classified among the 'disarticulated' remains.

Earlier excavators may have had a different policy in deciding which skeletal remains were selected for further study. By focusing on individual, discrete burials, SHARP recovered more remains without skulls that earlier excavators might have simply discounted as 'disarticulated'. Alternatively, earlier excavators may have 'privileged' skulls without post-cranial bones to a greater extent than SHARP. Evidence for this is that 42% of the individual remains in the Duckworth Collection do not have associated post-cranial bones, whereas the SHARP collection includes only 5% comprising skull only (Baldry 2009).

Methods of analysis

The skeletons excavated by SHARP, regardless of completeness, have been studied in three phases: during excavation, during post-excavation recording of the bones (presence, size, shape, features, etc.), and then during interpretation to establish what each skeleton tells us about the individual represented (e.g. age, sex, health).

A fourth phase brings together the separate results for each skeleton into a database so that demographic and other questions can be answered about the population as a whole. As our knowledge of new osteological research has developed, the SHARP recording methods have been added to or changed from time to time, even though on some occasions this has necessitated a complete review of the entire collection.

Demographics

In theory, the demographic analyses which can be performed on a living population – mortality, life expectancy, morbidity, the proportions of juveniles, of the sexes, of age groups within the population as a whole, etc. – can be performed on a skeletal population. Obtaining this demographic information is not as easy as it may seem, however. Ideally we would like to be able to establish age of death to within a five-year span, but this degree of accuracy is difficult to achieve in relation to an adult skeleton (Ubelaker 1999). Even simply determining the sex of the individual may have its challenges, particularly where the skeleton is incomplete.

Sex

Whether a skeleton is that of an adult male or female was determined on the basis of a number of observed differences between pelves and/or skulls. Using Buikstra and Ubelaker's 'Standards for Data Collection from Human Skeletal Remains' as guidance, a qualitative assessment was made for each characteristic, classing it as Male (M), Possibly/Probably Male (?M), Ambiguous (?), Possibly/Probably Female (?F), or Female (F) (Buikstra and Ubelaker 1994). Five characteristics were recorded on the pelvis and six on the skull. An overall assessment was then made by combining the individual observations. If both the skull and the pelvis were missing, or too badly damaged to permit observation of enough dimorphic features, it was not possible to sex a skeleton.

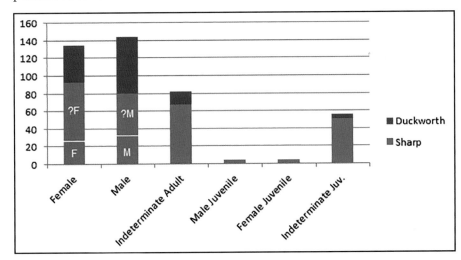

Fig. 6.1: Analysis by sex of the 417 skeletons excavated to date on Boneyard-Reeddam.

Since these differences between males and females develop only with sexual and skeletal maturity, it is not usually possible to sex sub-adults; certainly not before their late teens. It is therefore usual practice to record all juvenile skeletons as of unknown sex. However, the sex of nine of the juveniles from Sedgeford has been determined based on tooth-size (see Box 6.1).

The results of the analysis suggest that the Middle Anglo-Saxon population at Sedgeford was quite normal in its distribution between the sexes; (Fig. 6.1) neither sex is dominant, as may be found in graveyards associated with, for example, some religious or military institutions. The SHARP skeletons include slightly more females than males, those from the Duckworth Collection slightly more males. This may be the result of slightly different collection policies (see above) or it may be the result of variation across the Boneyard-Reeddam site, much of which remains unexcavated.

Age at death

Provided the relevant parts of the skeleton are present, estimation of age at death of children and adolescents is relatively simple. Dental development and fusion of the epiphyseal growth plates of bones follow well-established chronological sequences from which age can be estimated with reasonable precision (Hillson 1996, 118-147; Mays 1998, 47-49).

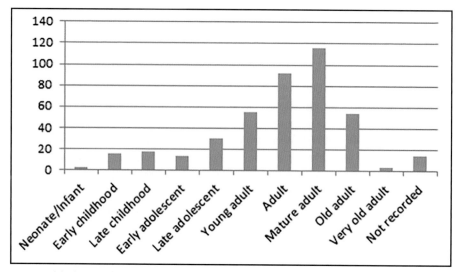

Establishing the age at death of an adult skeleton is, however, much more difficult. The methods used at Sedgeford involved comparison of the morphology of the pubic symphysis and auricular surface, and wear on the molar teeth (see Buikstra and Ubelaker 1994, 22-32; Brothwell, 1981, 72). The overall results for the whole Boneyard sample (SHARP and Duckworth) are given in Fig. 6.2 and Fig. 6.3.

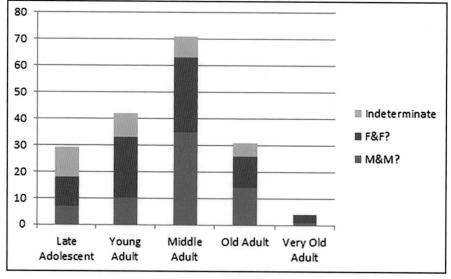

The limited accuracy of osteological ageing methods was shown by a study that compared the estimates of age at death made by skilled osteologists working on skeletons from Christ's Church, Spitalfields with their known ages recorded on coffin plates and parish records (Molleson *et al* 1993, 167-172). Yet these methods are still the only ones available.

At Sedgeford, adults have been categorised as Late Adolescent (LA), Young Adult (YA), Mature or Middle Adult (MA), Old Adult (OA) and Very Old Adult (VOA). Sometimes, because relevant bones are missing or damaged, they can be classed only as Adult (A).

These categories should be regarded as a chronological sequence. The approximate ages used as cut-off points are: <1 = Neonate/Infant; 1-5 = Early Childhood; 6-10 = Late Childhood; 11-14 = Early Adolescent; 15-24 = Late

Adolescent; 25-34 = Young Adult; 35-44 = Mature Adult; 45-54 = Old Adult; and 55+ = Very Old Adult.

Among individuals who survived into adulthood, there was a peak in female deaths in the Young Adult category, probably due to the rigours of childbirth. Of those in the Very Old Adult category, on the other hand, 75% were female.

The Spitalfields study showed that generally 'skeletons are under-aged by traditional methods' (Molleson *et al* 1993, 167). The report on the site at North Elmham, Norfolk, included a study of Anglo-Saxon ages at death recorded in historical documents (Wells and Cayton 1980, 314). This suggested that the ages for Anglo-Saxons in general were underestimated by at least a decade. Although the sample was abnormal, consisting mainly of the religious and secular elites, the average figure of 57.7 years may not have been so different from that of ordinary Anglo-Saxons. Bishops may have had long lives but kings often had violent and premature deaths. On the evidence provided by these studies, it is likely that quite a few of the Middle Anglo-Saxons in Sedgeford reached what, until very recently, would have been regarded as 'a good old age'.

Juvenile mortality

Another indication of the quality of life at Sedgeford in the Anglo-Saxon period is the relatively low child mortality. A figure of 12% (for all Boneyard-Reeddam skeletons from Neonate to Early Adolescent) would be regarded today as very significant child mortality, but it is comparable with the 19% (in a sample of 206) at contemporary North Elmham, and is substantially better than the average of 44% (in a sample of 1,195) from seven other Middle to Late Anglo-Saxon sites (Wells and Cayton 1980, 250; Buckberry 2000, 3-4). That figure, furthermore, is just for children under 12. Only two of Buckberry's seven sites have a figure below 21% and none below 16%.

The very low proportion of juvenile skeletons in the Duckworth Collection may be, like the sex ratios, the result of different collection policies or due to variation across the cemetery site. One area of the SHARP excavations was, indeed, referred to by some excavators as the 'children's cemetery' because of an apparent concentration of sub-adult skeletons. It was not, however, the only area in which juveniles were buried, nor were juveniles exclusively buried there. Our conclusion is that no specific area of the cemetery was reserved for child burials (though half or more remains unexcavated).

Diet and disease

There is more to health than diet alone, but an inadequate diet is likely to make an individual susceptible to disease. Although a good diet was potentially available to the Anglo-Saxons (Banham 2001, 190), nutritious food may not have been available all the time, or to all people equally.

The great majority of the skeletal remains from Sedgeford show good development and strong morphology, such as would be associated with a generally healthy life for those who were able to avoid the dangers of childhood mortality. Bone density is good and evidence for malnutrition-related conditions low.

Box 6.1
Boy or girl? Attributing sex to juvenile skeletons

Knowledge of how many people of each sex and age group are present is fundamental to population studies. Unfortunately, 'sex estimation of non-adult skeletons is extremely difficult, if not impossible in most circumstances' (Roberts 2009, 150). This is doubly unfortunate since 'males and females mature at different times … [Hence] … any estimated age category [for a juvenile] is necessarily wider than it would be, had the sex been known' (Scheuer and Black 2000, 15).

Within a population, however, the dimensions of the crowns of the permanent teeth, particularly the lower canines, tend to be larger in males (Cox and Mays 2000, 123-124). These teeth erupt at about 10-11 years of age and can provide a measure of juvenile sex in some instances. The method was first used at Poundbury to produce a bivariate plot of maximum bucco-lingual (BL) and mesio-distal (MD) diameters of the mandibular canines of sexed adults (see Plate 6.1) (Molleson 1993, 179).

There was reasonably clear separation between the sexes, so the sex of juveniles with permanent canines could be inferred by plotting their measured dimensions on the same graph and seeing whether they fell into the male or female range.

Although Poundbury has been described as 'exceptional' in its 'degree of sexual dimorphism in the dentition' (Mays 1998, 42), we decided to try the same method on skeletons from Boneyard-Reeddam. Based on 16 adult males and 16 adult females confidently sexed by other means, the results obtained by Eve Richardson were on a par with those from Poundbury (Fig. 6.4). When the measurements of nine juveniles with measurable permanent lower left canines were added, four fell into the male range, four into the female range and one was indeterminate.

This work has provided useful information on the Sedgeford population and a valuable test of a method that has rarely been used elsewhere since Molleson's original Poundbury study.

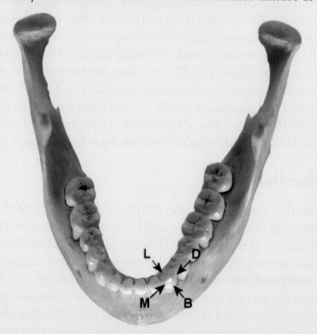

Plate 6.1: Measurement points for tooth diameters.

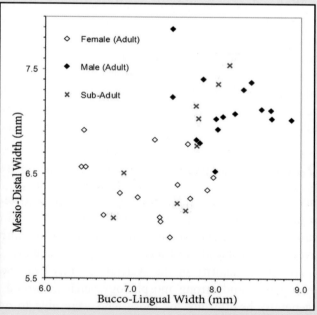

Fig. 6.4 Sexual dimorphism of Sedgeford teeth.

Stature

One broad-brush indicator of whether a population is getting the nutrition it needs is whether it is, on average, reaching its genetic potential in terms of height. Stature calculations for the Sedgeford population, using methodology first published by Trotter and Gleser, have produced average heights by sex similar to those for Anglo-Saxon populations generally and not unlike those seen in modern-day British populations (Trotter and Gleser 1952; 1958; 1977; Roberts and Cox 2003, 220)

	Mean Height Males (cm)	Mean Height Females (cm)
Sedgeford 7th-9th century	177	162
Anglo-Saxons generally	172	161
Spitalfields 18th-19th century	169	157
Britain 2002	176	162

Table 6.1: Average stature of the Sedgeford population excavated by SHARP compared with that of other populations.

Note: Figures for modern British population taken from UK Department of Health website: www.doh.gov.uk/public/summary. Figures for Spitalfields from Molleson *et al* 1993, 33. It should be noted that the modern British figure includes individuals from all ethnic backgrounds, rather than those largely of northern European ancestry, as would have been the case in Sedgeford and for the Spitalfields population.

This contradicts the popular assumption that people in the past were generally smaller than today. Whilst this was true for periods from the Late Middle Ages up until the first part of the 20th century (as shown by the example of 'the middling sort' from Spitalfields in Table 6.1), it was not true for Middle Anglo-Saxon Sedgeford.

Metabolic diseases

Although metabolic disorders have nutritional components, it is often an over simplification to attribute them solely to dietary deficiencies. Sometimes there are physiological defects that inhibit the absorption of ingested nutrients. In other instances there may be interactions with endocrine (hormonal) disturbances (Ortner 2003, 383). Nevertheless, it is worth investigating those metabolic diseases that can be detected in the skeleton to see what information may be obtained about the Sedgeford diet.

Scurvy, rickets and osteomalacia

Prolonged vitamin C deficiency causes scurvy. Vitamin D deficiency can cause rickets in children and osteomalacia in adults. All these diseases can be detected in the skeleton (Roberts and Manchester 2005, 234-240). Although 90% of the body's vitamin D requirement is produced in the skin by the action of sunlight, dietary sources such as fish-oil or animal fat may also be required in winter in Britain. Fresh fruit, a major source of vitamin C, is also less readily available in winter.

It seems, however, that any such seasonal deficiencies were insufficiently severe at Sedgeford to give rise to these particular diseases. No evidence of them has yet been observed in the Boneyard-Reeddam skeletons.

Osteoporosis

Less severe but recurring vitamin D deficiency, on the other hand, may have an accumulative effect in terms of reduced calcium levels, leading in old age to osteoporosis. This is seen in skeletons as loss of density and thinning of the bones. The fact that the few cases of osteoporosis recognised to date at Sedgeford have been associated with other mobility problems (such as Skeleton S0221, which had both a fracture of the leg and rheumatoid arthritis: see Box 6.2) may indicate that both sufficient dietary calcium and vitamin D were generally available.

Another factor, however, is that higher bone mass is seen in people who exercise regularly (Roberts and Manchester 2005, 243). Whilst the physically demanding life that these Anglo-Saxon people lived, particularly during their youth, may have had its downsides (see below), it doubtless also contributed to the strong bones generally seen in the Sedgeford population.

Cribra orbitalia and porotic hyperostosis

Two less well-known disorders that may be linked to diet are cribra orbitalia and porotic hyperostosis. Both appear as pitting in the bone, the former in the roof of the eye sockets, the latter on the outside of the skull, particularly at the sides and the front. Both are often attributed to anaemia. Although an iron-deficient diet can cause anaemia, so can excessive blood loss from injury and some chronic diseases like cancer.

A study by Chas Mifsud of all 417 skeletons excavated to date from Boneyard-Reeddam found that 38 showed signs of cribra orbitalia, giving a crude prevalence rate (CPR) of 9.1%. A meta-study of 5,334 Anglo-Saxon burials from 44 sites nationwide yielded a CPR of 7.6% (Roberts and Cox 2003, 186-187). As there is wide variability in CPRs across the 44 sites in this study, it is reasonable to interpret the prevalence at Sedgeford as 'typical'.

CPRs are often the only rate published in comparative studies. However, in cases like Sedgeford, where skeletons are often missing skulls, they underestimate the rate of cribra orbitalia since its presence can only be ascertained if an eye socket is extant. If the number of skulls present is known,

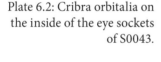
Plate 6.2: Cribra orbitalia on the inside of the eye sockets of S0043.

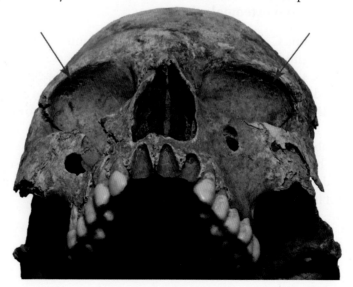

something closer to a true prevalence rate (TPR) can be determined. The true prevalences of cribra orbitalia at Sedgeford, analysed by sex and by age, are given in Tables 6.2 and 6.3.

	Male	Indeterminate	Female	Total
No. of skulls	101	40	100	241
No. with cribra	11	12	15	38
Prevalence rate	11%	30%	15%	16%

Table 6.2: Prevalence of cribra orbitalia amongst Middle Anglo-Saxons at Sedgeford by sex.

	Juvenile	Young Adult	Mature Adult	Old adult	Total
No. of skulls	25	48	102	66	241
No. with cribra	11	13	13	1	38
Prevalence rate	44%	27%	13%	2%	16%

Table 6.3: Prevalence of cribra orbitalia amongst Middle Anglo-Saxons at Sedgeford by age.

The higher prevalence of cribra orbitalia among females may be associated with menstruation, pregnancy and lactation. Even today modern women are more likely to be diagnosed with anaemia than men.

Virtually all those of indeterminate sex with cribra orbitalia were juveniles. High prevalence amongst those who die young has been recorded by other scholars (e.g. Stuart-Macadam 1985). This may indicate that the young had a diet with less iron in it than their elders (see also the discussion on stable isotopes below). Amongst those who survived longer, the bone may have remodelled, eliminating any trace of the lesions.

Plate 6.3: Porotic hyperostosis on the skull of Skeleton S1036.

Only eight Sedgeford skulls showed signs of porotic hyperostosis, about a fifth of the number with cribra orbitalia. This is the usual pattern, in 'archaeological populations in Britain the vault, i.e. the cranium, lesions are rarely seen, with cribra orbitalia being much more common' (Roberts and Manchester 2005, 230). The skulls affected at Sedgeford were those of three males, three females and two juveniles of indeterminate sex; of the adults, three were young, three mature.

Five of the skulls with porotic hyperostosis also showed signs of cribra orbitalia; the other three did not. It is therefore not clear-cut whether both are responses to the same systemic problem or whether, in some instances at least, different aetiologies, or causes, apply.

Although the idea that iron-deficiency anaemia is the common cause for both has been accepted for some time, it has recently been questioned because there is no clinical support for it in the case of cribra orbitalia (Waldron 2009).

Some have suggested that severe vitamin B12 deficiency, rather than iron deficiency, gives rise to porotic hyperostosis, either alone or in combination with cribra orbitalia. When cribra orbitalia occurs alone, as it does in 87% of cases at Sedgeford, they suggest the likely cause is multiple nutritional deficiencies, of which the most important is severe vitamin C deficiency. Both vitamin B12 and vitamin C deficiencies can, however, like iron deficiency, still have dietary origins. Also, because vitamin C is necessary for the absorption of iron, 'many people with cribra orbitalia may also have suffered from iron-deficiency anaemia' (Walker *et al* 2009, 113, 116).

Dentition: tooth wear

The condition of the teeth and dental diseases also provide information on the diet of the Sedgeford population. The most obvious feature of their teeth is the very high level of attrition. This is defined as 'the wearing away of tooth substance during mastication by rubbing of one tooth surface against another, together with the abrasive effect of any hard material present in the food' (Campbell 1939, cited in Brothwell 1981, 71).

Plate 6.4 shows a typical mouth of a Boneyard-Reeddam skeleton, with the dentine revealed by tooth wear and surrounded by a ring of enamel on each tooth. The amount of wear is much greater than would normally be found in a present-day mouth.

In broad terms, the degree of attrition correlates with how long each individual tooth has been in the mouth. Based on this principle, Brothwell published what he modestly described as 'a tentative classification of age in Neolithic to Medieval British skulls, based on molar wear' (1981, 72). The Anglo-Saxon material he used for his study was, presumably, that which he had excavated from Sedgeford. The chart he produced has been widely used in ageing British skeletons, including those in this account.

Brothwell's chart uses numerical classification but is essentially qualitative: observed wear patterns are compared with drawings of wear shown on the chart. Work by Jessica Miller in

Plate 6.4: 'Typical' tooth wear pattern in the mandible of a Sedgeford skeleton (S0021).

2007 employed a newly created quantitative method which involved the use of image-processing software to measure areas of exposed dentine and the area of original enamel on each tooth in all the SHARP excavated skulls. She found that 'at Sedgeford, though there is generally heavy attrition, it is more consistent [with the expected eruption sequence] across the dental arcade than dentitions from other sites that have been studied' (Miller, pers. comm.). She suggests that this could be a beneficial result of each Anglo-Saxon household grinding their own grain. With more control over the quality of the flour, abrasive inclusions would have been reduced. Sedgeford was compared with the site of St Nicholas Shambles in London, where anomalous dentition was found. Miller argues that this population had been eating bread made with commercially milled flour, where less care had been given to eliminating hard and abrasive inclusions.

Dentition: caries

Dental caries is the disease that we today are most likely to associate with bad diet, particularly excessive sugar consumption. In a sample of 83 skeletons excavated by SHARP, 97 of the 1,695 observable teeth had caries. This is a true prevalence rate (TPR) of 5.7% (Van Twest 2001, 93). The Sedgeford TPR is slightly greater than that of 4.2% found in a meta-study of 50 Anglo-Saxon sites with 5,035 burials and 38,911 teeth. However, the TPRs in this study ranged from 0.2% to 13.0% (Roberts and Cox 2003, 190-191), so the Sedgeford result is close to the middle of the range and might therefore be said to be 'typical'.

Stable isotopes

Information on diet can also be obtained from bone chemistry. In 2000 a study of the stable isotopes Carbon-13 (^{13}C) and Nitrogen-15 (^{15}N) in 45 Sedgeford skeletons – 15 each of males, females and juveniles – gave some insight into the amount and sources of dietary protein for the Sedgeford population (Corr

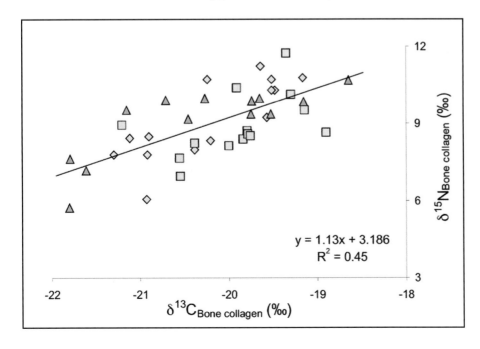

Fig. 6.5: Bone collagen (Carbon-13 and Nitrogen-15 values) for a sample of 15 males (blue diamonds), 15 females (yellow squares) and 15 juveniles (pink triangles) from the Boneyard-Reeddam skeletal assemblage.

2003). The results from analysis of bone collagen (an indicator of longer-term diet, particularly dietary protein) measured as $\delta^{13}C$ and $\delta^{15}N$ are shown in Fig. 6.5.

Values of $\delta^{13}C$ increase as the amount of marine food in a person's diet increases. The average $\delta^{13}C$ value at Sedgeford is about -20 parts per thousand (‰). This value suggests that the people of Sedgeford did not heavily exploit marine sources for dietary protein, despite their proximity to the coast.

This is consistent with the dearth of fish bones found on Boneyard-Reeddam, though not, apparently, with the abundance of oysters. However, shellfish $\delta^{13}C$ values are not as enriched as other marine species and people eating a primarily terrestrial diet who show slightly enriched $\delta^{13}C$ values, like those at Sedgeford, may have had a shellfish contribution to their diet.

Values of $\delta^{15}N$ rise with increased protein (marine or terrestrial) consumption. The average $\delta^{15}N$ value for the Sedgeford population was more than +9.1 ‰. This is close to the norm for a mainly terrestrial diet (Mays 1998, 186). However, the range of +5.7 to +11.8 ‰ is still substantial. The lowest $\delta^{15}N$ values here probably indicate diets with little or no marine/terrestrial animal protein.

Fig. 6.5 shows the most depleted $\delta^{13}C$ and $\delta^{15}N$ values as those of juveniles. Detailed examination of the data further shows that these were the youngest children, less than seven years old. This is consistent with the evidence that cereal-based foods, bread in particular, were the staple diet of young children in the Anglo-Saxon period (Hagen 1992, cited in Corr 2003, 153). It is also consistent with greater iron-deficiency in the young.

Only small differences in average $\delta^{15}N$ values were revealed between males (+9.2 ‰) and females (+8.9 ‰). This may indicate that the amount of meat consumed varied between whole families and was governed by class rather than gender. Support for this view is given by comparing the Sedgeford results with those of 76 higher status members of society from 18 different Early Anglo-Saxon sites (Mays and Bevan 2012, 868-869). In the Sedgeford sample, 16.7% had $\delta^{15}N$ levels below +8.0 ‰, whereas amongst the high-status Early Anglo-Saxons only 1.3% were this low.

Hygiene and health

Anglo-Saxon society generally was not noted for its attention to personal and community hygiene (Cameron 1993, 10). One might therefore expect levels of infection at Sedgeford to be high. Many infectious organisms, however, affect only the soft tissues and 'resolution of the infection, or death of the individual, occurs fairly rapidly and long before the infective process will have spread to the bones' (Roberts and Manchester 2005, 167). This may explain why so few examples of diseases that can undoubtedly be attributed to infection have been found in the Boneyard-Reeddam assemblage.

Osteomyelitis

Osteomyelitis is a septic infection of bone tissue leading to inflammation. It is usually contained within the marrow of the bone, and may be attributable to a number of causes, including direct bone trauma and local soft-tissue infection.

Skeleton S0044, a 20-year-old male, shows signs of systemic (whole body) infection, with the right ulna probably the primary site. This bone displays several of the discharge sinuses, or cloacae, which are the classic signs of the disease. The bone is also grossly deformed and enlarged, but there is no evidence of an injury that may have introduced the pathogen (Plate 6.5).

The right radius and right humerus also show deformation, enlargement and single cloaca, but the degree of change is much less than that on the right ulna. The extant bones of the left arm appear to be non-pathological, but allow comparison with the right side to show the extent of disease-related changes.

Other evidence for systemic infection may be seen in the skull and mandible. A swelling of the mandibular body in the region of the right second pre-molar and first and second molars appears to be pathological. It is likely that this site represents a secondary area of infection for the same disease. Bilateral lesions on the surfaces of the parietal bones indicate that there was another site of infection on the skull, probably manifesting through the scalp prior to death.

The length of time taken for such skeletal changes to occur, a minimum of two or three months, can be taken as evidence of the chronic (and no doubt agonising) character of the disease. As discussed above, it is only in chronic cases such as this that disease processes will be observable in the skeleton. Given the young age at death and the indications of systemic infection, it is almost certain that osteomyelitis was the cause of death for this young man.

Plate 6.5: Osteomyelitis of the right radius and ulna (lower arm bones) of Skeleton S0044. At the top is the proximal right radius and ulna anterior view; in the centre the proximal right radius and ulna medial view and at the bottom the proximal right radius and ulna lateral view.

Bladder stone

Bladder stones are very rarely recovered archaeologically, but Sedgeford has yielded one (Plate 6.6), the older of only two such stones so far found in Norfolk. Occurrence of bladder stones is usually linked to diet: too much grain in the case of the young and poor, and too rich a diet in the case of wealthier adults. Males are nine times as likely as females to suffer from dietary stones (Sutor *et al* 1974, 407). The chemical composition of the Sedgeford stone as shown by X-ray diffraction (XRD) analysis implied, however, that it was the result of a urinary tract infection (Beckett *et al* 2008, 407). Although infection stones are found in males and females equally, the Sedgeford stone came from the skeleton of a 13/15-year-old boy. The Sedgeford bladder stone can therefore be taken more as an indicator of poor hygiene amongst the Anglo-Saxons, and of their limited ability to treat infection, than as an indicator of poor diet.

Plate 6.6: Bladder stone from Skeleton S3010.

Work and wellbeing

Today we might link 'wellbeing' to lifestyle rather than work, though even now a person's occupation can be an important contributor to their general health. In the Anglo-Saxon era, work was the dominant activity and its physical demands were many. This could have beneficial effects: the bones of Sedgeford skeletons are dense and strong, reflecting both their genetic inheritance and the heavy physical demands placed upon them. Equally, however, the demands could be so great as to have left 'stress markers' on the bones or even injured them.

One of the most common ailments today caused by physical stress is back pain. This non-specific disorder can have many different causes and vary widely in its severity. When we look at the Sedgeford skeletons, there are various changes in the spine which may, separately or together, be manifestations of back pain and represent varying degrees of loss of flexibility.

Osteophytosis

The most commonly occurring changes are extra bony growths, called osteophytes, around the rims of the vertebrae that make up the spinal column. It can be shown that osteophytes are predominantly an age-related degenerative disease, but it has also been suggested that since they are found with greater frequency at points on the spine where stresses are greatest – where it curves backwards and forwards – stress must also be a contributory factor (Nathan 1962, 264).

A sample of 84 Sedgeford spines, made up of roughly equal numbers of each sex and a wide range of ages, was studied in detail by Lavinia Ferrante di Ruffano (2001). 92% of the individuals studied had some spinal osteophytosis, none of whom were juveniles. The study then looked further to see if the cervical, thoracic, lumbar, or sacral vertebrae were the most affected. From a total of 1,348 individual vertebrae, the prevalence of osteophytosis tended to be higher in the lower anatomical levels of the spine, i.e. among the lumbar vertebrae (Plate 6.7). The results also showed that osteophytosis increased with age, so much so that all of the sacra of the oldest age category had some osteophytes on them. Among those who survived into their middle years, the great majority of Sedgeford's Anglo-Saxon population is likely to have experienced some back problems, especially in their lower backs.

Plate 6.7: The lumbar vertebra of Skeleton S0039, lateral, superior and anterior views, showing the osteophytosis.

Osteoarthritis

Most people will be more familiar with osteoarthritis (OA) than osteophytes. This too can often be the cause of 'bad backs'. It is not confined to the back, however, and often affects any of the fully mobile synovial joints of the limbs such as the knees and elbows, the shoulders and hips and even the wrists, as well as the spine. It is a neuro-mechanical disease closely linked to overuse and 'wearing out' of the joint concerned. Primary OA is more common with increasing age; secondary OA can occur at any age in a previously damaged or mal-positioned joint (Roberts and Manchester 2005, 134). Identification of OA on the skeleton is far from straightforward. A study by Waldron and Rogers (1991) showed that even experts do not always agree as to its presence. This is borne out by work at Sedgeford.

As well as analyses of individual skeletons by many people, two studies looking at the wider population have been undertaken. The larger of the two, by Joanna Rutterford, analysed the skeletal remains of 224 adult individuals excavated by SHARP to determine the presence and distribution of osteoarthritis (Rutterford, pers. comm.). Osteoarthritis was diagnosed in a joint using the operational definition described by Waldron, based on the presence of eburnation (i.e. polish on the surface of adjoining bones caused by them rubbing together) or at least two of the following four criteria: (i) marginal osteophytes (new bone formed around the edges of the adjoining bones); (ii) new bone formation on the articular surface (i.e. a surface at the interface between the adjoining bones); (iii) alteration in the contour of the joint; or (iv) pitting on the joint surface (Waldron 2009, 34).

Table 6.4: Crude and true prevalence rates of osteoarthritis by joint site in a sample of 224 skeletons from Boneyard-Reeddam.

Site of Joint(s)	Crude Prevalence Rate %	True Prevalence Rate %
Spine	30.0	27.2
Shoulder (acromio-clavicular)	14.9	33.9
Shoulder (gleno-humeral)	10.6	14.2
Hip	8.0	10.3
Hands	6.8	12.8
Elbow	6.5	8.2
Knee	6.2	7.3
Wrist	5.9	10.6
Foot	5.9	9.4
Temporo-mandibular joint	4.3	7.4
Ankle	0.9	1.0

Table 6.5: Joints most commonly affected by osteoarthritis in a sample of 224 skeletons from Boneyard-Reeddam, analysed by sex.

Sex	Site/Joint Affected
Male	Spine, Knee, Hip, Wrist, Shoulder (acromio-clavicular) Foot
Female	Elbow, Hands, Shoulder (gleno-humeral), Temporo-mandibular joint
Equal	Ankle

A number of juveniles were also analysed but, as expected, no cases of OA were observed in this group. Of the adults, approximately 60% exhibited osteoarthritic criteria in one or more joints. The presence of OA was considered for eleven separate joints, with the proportion of the assemblage affected (the crude prevalence rate, or CPR) and the true prevalence rate (or TPR, based on how many examples of each joint were actually available for study) calculated for each (Table 6.4). In terms of crude prevalence the spine is the most common site of OA (30%). In terms of true prevalence (the proportion of cases divided by the number of joints present), the acromio-clavicular joint (i.e. a joint at the top of the shoulder between part of the shoulder blade and the collar bone) was the most commonly affected joint (40%) and the ankle the least (1%). Other joints tended to display similar levels of occurrence.

Males were most commonly affected, in contrast to the usual female predominance (Waldron 1997, 186). Furthermore, a sex-related difference was found for the relative occurrence of the disease in certain joints (Table 6.5). As in other early populations, hip OA occurred more commonly in males, while a higher proportion of females exhibited OA in the hands.

Modern clinical data show that people in particular occupations are more likely to suffer OA in some joints than others as a result of severe repeated stressing of those joints (Jurmain 1999, cited in Roberts and Manchester 2005, 143). It is not possible, however, to deduce a person's occupation from joints showing signs of OA. There are too many different activities that might produce similar stresses, and other factors than movement or trauma causing mechanical stress in the joints may result in OA. An important factor is 'genetic predisposition' to OA (Waldron 2009, 28). The same actions do not necessarily produce the same results in all people.

Notwithstanding these difficulties, we have attempted to draw some broad conclusions about the nature of work and possible division of labour at Sedgeford. A study by Ross Kendall on the Sedgeford assemblage supplemented OA data with data on enthesopathies. Entheses are the points where muscles, tendons, or ligaments insert into bones. An enthesis may become enlarged by heavy use of the muscle that inserts into it. This study showed no statistically significant differences in the rates of OA at any specific joints between males and females, perhaps implying a low level of gender role differentiation. There were, however, some possible trends, particularly in OA of the hip and lower thoracic vertebrae, and in enthesopathies of the upper arms and lower legs, which might indicate that men did more heavy lifting than women. These enthesopathies are found right the way into old age, implying that even the older members of the community were doing strenuous work. Repetitive heavy lifting has been shown to be associated with agricultural tasks in modern populations (Croft *et al* 1992, 1270), but is not peculiar to farming.

More females than males tended to show OA in the hands and temporo-mandibular joint (i.e. where the lower jaw hinges against the skull, just in front of the ears). Kendall suggested that the latter might be linked to females using their teeth as a 'tool' more often. He notes in one woman – Skeleton S0134 – a distinct groove between two teeth which he calls a 'thread biter's notch' (Kendall 2005, 91). These trends are probably indicative of women's involvement in textile production, though Kendall concluded 'that most individuals at Sedgeford participated in multiple tasks or occupations required to provide subsistence … few individuals were specialised in the specific tasks or crafts that might leave skeletal stress markers idiosyncratic to a particular occupation' (Kendall 2005, 121).

Work-related trauma

A number of cases of traumas of various types that are secondary to work or activity-related stress have also been recorded.

Spondylolysis

This condition is evident in six skeletons. It is a stress-related fracture of the lower back. Each has occurred in the fifth (lowest) lumbar vertebra and involves

154

Plate 6.8: Lumbar vertebra of Skeleton S0079 showing spondylolysis.

a fracture on the arch which attaches to the spinal muscles (Plate 6.8). This is a result of repeated bending such as can occur when digging or shovelling and then throwing the contents sideways or over the shoulder in a reversed action. The fracture does not re-join because of the repeated movement and remains a separate piece.

Osteochondritis dissecans

This is associated with young people who are active in repetitive joint actions or sudden impacts. The bone below the articular cartilage is damaged and separates, leaving an irregular round crater in the joint surface. There are three examples at Sedgeford. Two are in the knee, one a recent occurrence before death at 10 to 12 years of age and one an advanced healed example in an adult. The third is in the elbow of a young adult.

Plate 6.9: The knee joint of Skeleton S1020 showing osteochondritis dissecans.

Stress fracture of a rib

Skeleton S0083, an adult male, has a stress fracture to a first rib with secondary damage to the second (Plate 6.10). This is most likely the result of an aggressive attempt to pull on a rope or perhaps push a very resistant object. The complex arrangement of strongly developed shoulder, chest and neck muscles needed for this action, in conflict with each other, is the cause of this exceptional damage.

Plate 6.10: The right first and second ribs of Skeleton S0083 (superior view) showing an unusual stress fracture.

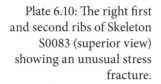

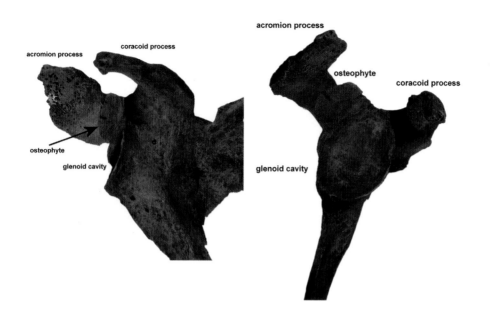

Plate 6.11: The right shoulder-blade of Skeleton S0010 showing an osteophyte caused by dislocation, bone-on-bone wear and acute arthritis.

Damage to upper arm and shoulder

A dramatic case of rotator cuff injury (i.e damage to a group of muscles and tendons that serve to provide stability to the shoulder) is seen in Skeleton S0010, a middle adult female (Plate 6.11). The supraspinatus muscle over the top of the upper arm and shoulder has been damaged.

Frequent heavy lifting compresses and weakens this muscle tendon, and this can lead to rupture in an acute incident in later years. This has resulted here in the dislocation of the humerus (upper arm bone) upwards and against the scapula (shoulder blade).

Years of continued use after this event, involving bone-on-bone wear, has resulted in severe arthritis, and the joint has remained dislocated. This is in the dominant right arm; the left shoulder shows similar but less severe signs. Other examples of this type of shoulder arthritis have been identified at Sedgeford, but no other is as extreme as that of S0010.

Os acromiale

Also related to the shoulder is os acromiale. In this the tip of the acromion of the shoulder blade (Plate 6.12) remains separate from the rest of the scapula. In some cases this may be genetic – it is found in 3-6% of modern populations (Roberts and Manchester 2005, 152) – but in others it may be induced by repetitive stress. It has been suggested that the latter might have been the case with the skeletons of the archers on board the Tudor warship *Mary Rose* (Stirland 2000, cited in Roberts and Manchester 2005, 152). The single example observed at Sedgeford could be either genetic or the result of stress.

Plate 6.12: The left shoulder-blade of Skeleton S0150 showing separation of the acromion from the rest of the bone.

Falls and fractures

Table 6.6: Cases of trauma (fractures) observed on Sedgeford skeletons excavated by SHARP.

Body Part Fractured	Skeleton/Context Number
Clavicle	S0030 [1503] [1703] [7035] [8313]
Rib	S0079 S0083 [3014]
Vertebra	[1801]
Humerus	S0061
Hand	S0177 S1016
Femur	S0221
Tibia	S0096
Fibula	S0075 [1697]
Foot	S0075[6010]
S = Skeleton (i.e. articulated individual burial) [ ] = disarticulated bone finds	

Not all the fractures suffered by the Middle Anglo-Saxon people of Sedgeford were caused by repetitively stressing their bones. Some were the result of accidental slips, falls and impacts. Others are clear evidence of interpersonal violence.

Thirty-three individual examples of bones with accidental or deliberate injuries during life have been identified (Table 6.6), with variations in healing. Old remodelled breaks and later weathering on the bones make it impossible to identify all incidents with accuracy. Those listed are the ones that show clear signs of ante- and peri-mortem damage (before and at the time of death). They include both articulated skeletons and some individual disarticulated bone finds (identified by context number).

The minor injuries seen involve successful repairs to long-passed incidents. Three are impacts causing single broken ribs, another resulted in a traumatic amputation of a middle finger leaving a stump and yet another is a fracture to a second metacarpal (hand bone).

A complicated result of a child's fall is shown in one example – Skeleton S0061 – where we see a long-standing shoulder injury resulting in a slipped epiphysis (growth plate) on the right upper arm bone. This injury fractured through the epiphysis and damaged the blood supply to the upper end of the bone. Avascular necrosis (bone death by lack of blood supply) then went on to stop growth at that point, and a new misshapen joint with limited function has been formed. By comparing the length with the fully-grown adult side, an age of approximately 12 to 15 years can be proposed for the incident.

Fractures of the clavicle (collar bone) are most commonly the result of falls directly onto the shoulder. Five examples are present, with degrees of healing from a few months to several years. All have some displacement but are soundly and successfully healed, making it impossible to ascertain at what age they occurred.

Falls from a height are represented by two injuries. The first is a wedge-shaped compressed fracture on a low thoracic vertebra resulting in a marked kyphosis (abrupt forward curvature) of the spine. This old injury has healed and consolidated.

In comparison, Skeleton S0096 displays a healed fracture of the lateral tibial plateau (lower part of knee joint). This injury can occur as the result of jumping or falling from a height and landing on the feet, where the impact causes the femoral condyle at the knee to punch a hole into the tibia and fracture it vertically. Although the fracture has healed soundly, the depressed knee-joint surface has caused general osteoarthritis arising from walking on the imperfectly shaped and misaligned joint.

Ankle and foot injuries can happen in many ways, but fractures are commonly caused by slips and sudden twists. There are two examples of fractures of the fibula (outside lower leg), but not all the bones of the ankle joint are present, so it is difficult to assess them fully. Both are very soundly healed without serious displacement. They are situated above the ankle joint line, suggesting rotational forces.

A close parallel to the ankle injuries is an avulsion fracture on the base of a fifth metatarsal (outer side of the foot). This is caused by the tendon inserted here pulling off a piece of the bone when the foot is twisted in a fall.

The most severe and disabling injury noted is a long oblique fracture to the right femur (upper leg bone) of Skeleton S0221. Although misshapen by the tension of large leg muscles acting on the grossly unstable bone, there is good evidence of healing. This man's new bone callus is thick and advanced enough to provide some stability to the leg (Plate 6.15).

Further analysis of the skeleton reveals very disabled hands, arms and feet from rheumatoid arthritis (see Box 6.2). This kind of fracture is often a consequence of already weakened bones being impacted by falls on the part of older people unsteady on their legs. As this injury results in large amounts of blood loss, incapacity and pain, this man would have needed constant nursing care for many weeks.

The displaced position of the mend is the result of passive bed-rest; it is not compatible with walking or normal weight-bearing at the time of death. This is likely to have followed a few months after the probable fall. He most likely finally succumbed to general ill-health from his previous physical condition, exacerbated by weakness due to his long period of enforced bed-rest.

Box 6.2
Rheumatoid arthritis

Skeleton S0221 is a very rare archaeological example of rheumatoid arthritis (Mckinnon *et al* 2013). It is probably currently unique for the Anglo-Saxon period. The remains of S0221 consisted only of the upper legs, arms and some parts of the hands and feet, because of disturbance by later graves and ditches. On closer study, there was evidence that this was a male, aged at least 55 years old, and approximately 179cm tall.

He showed evidence of a number of arthritic conditions, according to the accepted operational definitions as described by Tony Waldron (2009). The bones indicate significant rheumatoid arthritis in the wrists, hands and feet, with symmetrical marginal erosions, eburnation (polishing of the bone surface), osteophytosis (bony spurs) and ankylosis (bone fusion) all observed. Osteoporosis is also evident around the affected joints, and there is a partially healed fracture of the right femur.

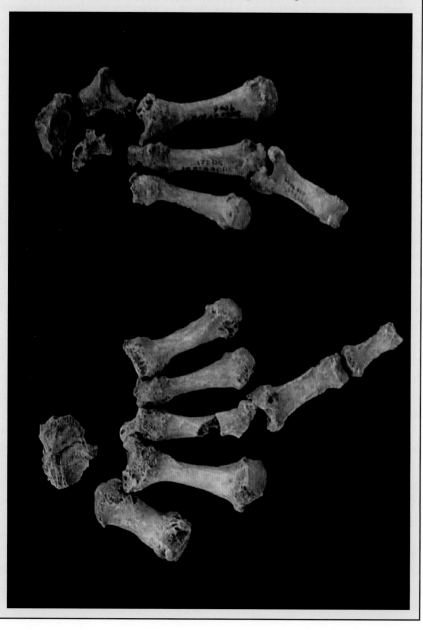

The co-existence of osteoporosis was perhaps related to the reduced mobility caused by his arthritis, though there is some evidence from patients with rheumatoid arthritis today that there is a direct link between the two diseases: peri-articular osteoporosis (bone thinning around the joint) on radiograph is expected clinically. The current prevalence of concurrent osteoporosis in patients with rheumatoid arthritis is 50%, and it is a significant cause of morbidity today (Hafez *et al* 2011, 87), so there is no reason to believe that this was not also true in the past.

S0221 suffered from rheumatoid arthritis and osteoarthritis for some time,

Plate 6.13: Rheumatoid arthritis in the hands of Skeleton S0221.

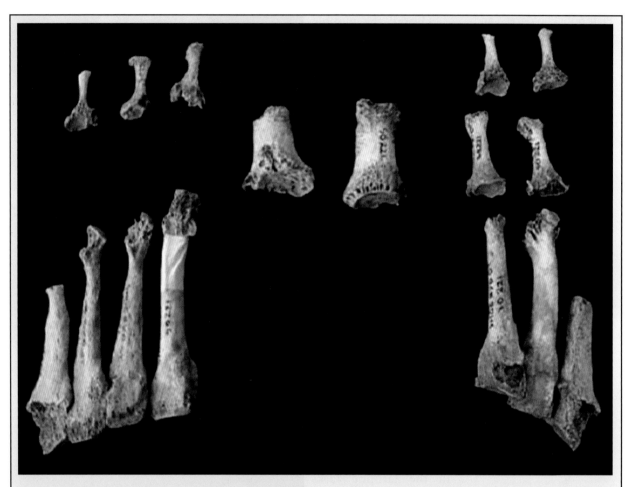

Plate 6.14: Rheumatoid arthritis in the feet of Skeleton S0221.

and the degree of change, particularly at the wrist, suggests that he would have been in significant pain and had restricted movement. He may have used a crutch to help with mobility, perhaps due to the arthritic changes to his feet, since his right humerus (upper arm bone) is more developed than his left.

Although rheumatoid arthritis nowadays has a prevalence of 0.5-1% (Ortner 2003, 561), it is poorly represented in the archaeological record compared to osteoarthritis, with the few possible examples debatable (Roberts and Manchester 2005, 156). Some people, indeed, believe that the disease did not even exist before the 17th century (Short 1974, 204). If rheumatoid arthritis did not exist in Europe until quite recently, this may be important epidemiologically, suggesting an environmental change acting as a trigger.

It is possible that the small number of cases recognised in the archaeological records represents not a disease that has only existed recently, but the difficulties in diagnosis and differentiation between the various erosive joint disorders. Or alternatively, the way rheumatoid arthritis manifests in the bones may have influenced identification, particularly if earlier ages at death precluded the disease from progressing enough to leave visible changes. It is also possible that the relevant bones are too often those lost to archaeology, namely the hand and foot bones, making convincing diagnosis impossible.

This example is therefore important in establishing an earlier date for the appearance of rheumatoid arthritis in Britain, as well as the rest of the world. Understanding the disease history could help to develop new treatments for this potentially debilitating condition.

Plate 6.15: Photograph and radiograph of the posterior side of the right upper leg bone of Skeleton S0221, showing the healing bone callus from a severe and disabling fracture.

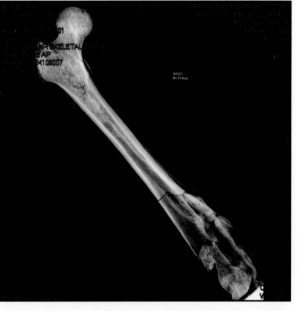

Overall the number of each type of accidental fracture is small, as is normally the case at Anglo-Saxon sites (Roberts and Cox 2003, 203-208). They are the sorts of injuries that could result from stumbling over rough ploughed ground or being kicked or butted by farm animals. Even today the most frequent of these fractures – broken collar-bones – are often the result of falls from horses.

Of the nine articulated skeletons that sustained fractures listed in Table 6.6, six were male and three female. This may indicate some gender differentiation in the farming tasks undertaken, but the numbers are too small to be conclusive.

What is clear from the fact that these people survived fractures is that they were members of a society with at least some knowledge of how to cope with such injuries, and with the capacity and compassion to perform the necessary healing work. This is especially evident in the case of Skeleton S0221.

Cuts and conflict

This indication of the care given to the injured in the Sedgeford community contrasts with the level of violence apparent in some of the cranial trauma cases (Table 6.7). In a study of 134 skeletons excavated by SHARP, 12 were identified as having suffered cranial trauma (Stillwell 2002, 1). Of these, five were described as 'ante-mortem blunt force trauma'.

Such blows to the head could be the result either of accidents, such as falls, or of violent force. It is difficult to be certain of the cause of blunt trauma to the head when it is not immediately lethal (as in these cases), because the healing process changes the contours of the wound over time. Distortion and crushing in the ground after burial can also mimic these processes.

In seven other cases, however, there can be no doubt: we are dealing with individuals who were killed violently. There are six who can have their deaths directly attributed to violently inflicted traumas from the sharp edge of a blade, presumably the result of interpersonal conflicts of unknown magnitude – a one-on-one scuffle, a group fight, or an all-out battle.

	S0067	S0086	S1016	S1018	S1033	S0023	S1049
Cranium	●	●	●	●	●	●	●
Ulna	●	●	●●	●			
Radius	●	●●					
Scapula				●			
Fibula				●			
Ribs		●					
Mandible	●					●	
Cervical Vertebra						●●	

Table 6.7: Sedgeford skeletons with cranial traumas from sharp-edged weapons and associated post-cranial traumas.

Five were tall, strong males aged around 30 to 40 years. Although three were buried close together and can be tentatively linked, there is not the evidence to establish how many incidents are represented and when they took place. The sixth example – Skeleton S0023 – is younger, aged 18 to 25 years and of indeterminate sex. The injuries on this person do not follow the same pattern as the others. The seventh – Skeleton S1049 – did not die immediately. A single long sharp cut to the centre of his cranium shows healing had been progressing for several weeks prior to death (Plate 6.16).

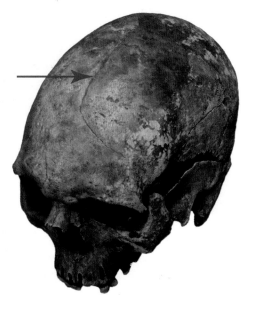

Plate 6.16: Healed sharp-edged blade injury to the top of the skull of Skeleton S1049.

Plate 6.17: Fractures in both the left and right ulnae (lower arm bones) of Skeleton S1016, implying attempts to parry blows.

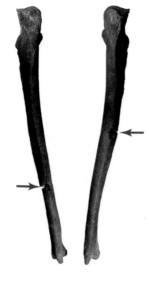

Although the five older men died of sharp weapon injuries to their heads, they also display several injuries to their limbs. These are examples of warding blows, attempts to protect themselves from attack, or injuries sustained in attempting to attack their opponent. Unhealed fractures can be seen that confirm the injuries happened peri-mortem (around the time of death). Sharp cutting wounds and associated fractures had been directed at the wrists of two men. These suggest an attempt to disarm them (Plates 6.17 and 6.18).

Plate 6.18: Injuries to the left wrist of Skeleton S0067, implying an attempt to disarm him during combat.

The extensive skull and rib fractures represent heavy unconscious falls as well as direct blows. Of the three who suffered the most severe and grotesque head injuries, two have received singular fractures to the mid forearm that suggests an attempt at unarmed defence against a weapon attack to their heads prior to death.

One individual, Skeleton S1018, has a combination of cranial, lower leg and shoulder injuries consistent with a fighting stance, where both combatants are face-to-face and at least one may have held a shield.

Plate 6.19: Injuries to Skeleton S1018. At the top left is the cranium with a sharp weapon injury, top right is a fracture of the left fibula (a lower leg bone), bottom left are two views of the left ulna (a lower arm bone) and at the bottom right is the injury to the right shoulder as viewed from above.

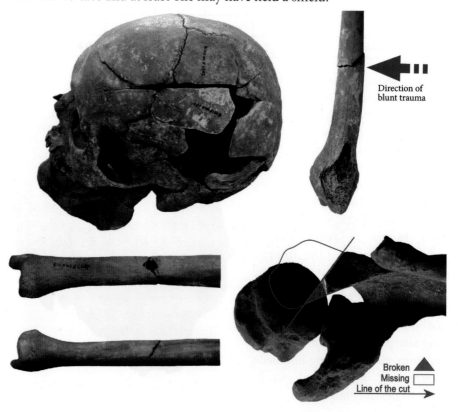

The youngest victim was either a tall woman or slim man. Analysis is inconclusive, but sex could be relevant to the interpretation of the violence indicated. Four fine cuts were directed at the face with what appears to have been a large knife, possibly a seax – the quintessential Anglo-Saxon weapon. Among the wounds is a fracture of the lower jaw. No other fractures are apparent, but the conclusion to the attack seems to have been a direct and precise lethal cut to the throat deep enough to damage two neck bones (Plate 6.20).

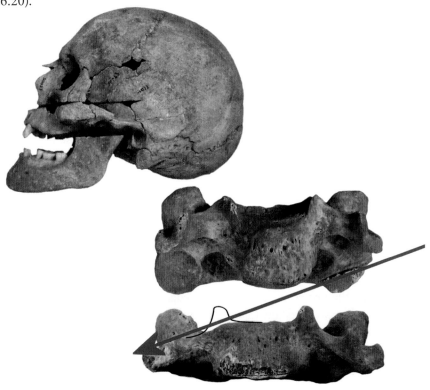

Plate 6.20: Injuries to Skeleton S0023. Above is the skull with horizontal cuts across the face and below is the cut which damaged the third and fourth cervical vertebrae. The red arrow indicates the direction of the knife blade.

The extreme violence experienced by all of these people suggests serious conflict rather than petty disputes. The Middle Anglo-Saxon period was characterised by attempts to create unified kingdoms and by wars between these kingdoms. This was followed after AD 865 by a series of Viking incursions and the conquest of East Anglia by what the *Anglo-Saxon Chronicle* calls 'the great raiding army'; intensive conflict between Viking and Anglo-Saxon then dominated the succeeding half century.

These conflicts were associated with a process of state formation based on kingship, the Church, great estates and the *fyrd*, a militia into which any free man might be conscripted for active service. The men of Sedgeford almost certainly saw occasional service as part of the *fyrd* of the Kingdom of East Anglia, and perhaps, as political authority changed, under other auspices.

The trauma could represent several incidents over a number of decades, or perhaps just one or two episodes in quick succession. Our dating methods are insufficiently precise to enable us to decide. There is little evidence to imply veteran soldiers. The bones display no old healed injuries. And the likelihood must be that they died in a local conflict – the difficulty of transporting the dead, and concerns about decomposition, make it almost certain that these men were killed close to their village.

Conclusions

The good preservation conditions at the Boneyard-Reeddam site have provided an opportunity for an in-depth study of a cemetery population spanning an approximate 200-year period between *c.* AD 650/725 and 850/875 (at the latest). Although the cemetery has not been completely excavated, the proportion sampled is sufficiently large to enable some general conclusions to be drawn about the daily lives of the people who lived at Sedgeford during the Middle Anglo-Saxon period.

The evidence from the hundreds of discrete burials and large amounts of disarticulated bone has revealed that the population were a hardworking, robust community who exploited a varied terrestrial and marine diet. On the other hand, they were not without health issues – an effect of their physically demanding lifestyle and lack of medical treatment for conditions such as infection.

The people buried represent all ages and both sexes. Young children are under-represented, as is commonly found in cemetery sites, but there are examples of people living far into old age. There is some evidence of gender differentiation. Both men and women exhibited stress markers on their bones but the sites of osteoarthritis could show that women were involved in different activities requiring more use of hands and jaws. The most obvious role difference was during conflict, where violent injuries are seen on the skeletons of males. The small numbers involved imply that violence was not a common occurrence, and there seem to have been no professional soldiers among the population. On the whole, the skeletal population at Sedgeford shows less evidence for bony disease and trauma than might be expected for the time.

In summary, the people of Anglo-Saxon Sedgeford lived in an environment which included disease, hardship, injury and sudden death. At all levels of society they were hard-working and life could be difficult, but they had the benefit of abundant nutritious food and, when unable to care for themselves, the support of their community.

The authors of this chapter were:

Ray Baldry, Sophie Beckett, Martin Hatton, Lorraine Horsley, Katie Mckinnon and Melanie Van Twest. In addition to the cited sources they also drew upon unpublished research by all previous human remains supervisors and many volunteers.

References

Baldry, R., 2009, 'Sedgeford skeletons held at the Leverhulme Centre for Human Evolutionary Anatomy, Cambridge - A quantity and quality survey on behalf of SHARP', unpub. SHARP report.

Banham, D., 2001, 'Food and drink' in M. Lapidge, J. Blair, S. Keynes and D. Scragg (eds.), *The Blackwell Encyclopaedia of Anglo-Saxon England*, Oxford, Blackwell, 190-191.

Beckett, S., Hatton, M. and Rogers, K., 2008, 'The discovery and analysis of a urinary calculus from an Anglo-Saxon burial in Sedgeford, Norfolk', in *Norfolk Archaeology, XLV (III)*, 397-409.

Brothwell, D., 1981, *Digging up Bones*, 3rd edition, Ithaca, New York, Cornell University Press.

Buckberry, J., 2000, 'Missing, presumed buried? Bone diagenesis and the under-

representation of Anglo-Saxon children', Research Articles @ www.ads.ahds.ac.uk/
catalogue/adsdata/assemblage/html/5/buckberr, accessed on 15/08/2012.

Buikstra, J. and Ubelaker, D., 1994, *Standards for Data Collection from Human
Skeletal Remains, Arkansas*, Arkansas Archaeological Survey Research Series, No. 44.

Cameron, M., 1993, *Anglo-Saxon Medicine*, Cambridge, Cambridge University Press.

Campbell, T., 1939, 'Food, food values and food habits of the Australian Aborigines
in relation to their dental conditions', in *Australian Journal of Dentistry*,
Melbourne, 43, 1,45,73,141,177.

Corr, L., 2003, 'The Evaluation of a Multi-Proxy Stable Isotope Approach to
Palaeodietary Reconstruction', unpub. PhD thesis, University of Bristol.

Cox, M. and Mays, S., *2000, Human Osteology in Archaeology and Forensic Science*,
London, Greenwich Medical Media.

Croft, C., Coggen, D., Cruddas, M. and Cooper, C., 1992, 'Osteoarthritis of the hip:
an occupational disease in farmers', in *British Medical Journal*, 304, 1269-1272.

Ferrante di Ruffano, L., 2001, 'A comparative analysis of spinal pathology', unpub. BSc
dissertation, University College London.

Hafez, E.A., Mansour, H.E., Hamza, S.H., Moftah, S.G., Younes, T.B., Ismail, M.A.,
2011, 'Bone mineral density changes in patients with recent-onset rheumatoid
arthritis', in *Clinical Medicine Insights: arthritis and musculoskeletal disorders*, 4,
87-94.

Hagen, A., 1992, *A Handbook of Anglo-Saxon Food: processing and consumption,
Norfolk*, Anglo-Saxon Books.

Hillson, S., 1996, *Dental Anthropology*, Cambridge, Cambridge University Press.
www.doh.gov.uk/public/summary

Ingleby, H., 1922-1925, *The Charm of a Village, an account of Sedgeford with its
history and its carnivals*, London, Clement Ingleby.

Jurmain, R., 1999, S*tories from the Skeleton: behavioural reconstruction in human
osteology*, Amsterdam, Gordon and Breach Publishers.

Kendall, R., 2005, 'Inferring activity from skeletal modification in a Middle Anglo-
Saxon population', unpub. MA dissertation, Western Washington University.

Mays, S., 1998, *The Archaeology of Human Bones*, London, Routledge.

Mays, S. and Bevan, N., 2012, 'An investigation of diet in early Anglo-Saxon England
using carbon and nitrogen stable isotope analysis of human bone collagen', in
Journal of Archaeological Science, 39, 867-874.

Mckinnon, K., Van Twest, M. and Hatton, M., 2013, 'A probable case of rheumatoid
arthritis from the Middle Anglo-Saxon period', in *International Journal of
Palaeopathology,* 3(2), 122-127.

Molleson, T., 1993, 'The human remains', in D. Farwell and T. Molleson, Excavations
at Poundbury, 1966-80, Volume II, The Cemeteries, Dorchester, *Dorset Natural
History and Archaeology Society Monograph Series, No. 11*, 142-214.

Molleson, T. and Cox, M., with Waldron, A. and Whittaker, D., 1993, *The Spitalfields
Project, Volume 2, The Anthropology: the middling sort*, York, Council for British
Archaeology Research Report, No. 86.

Nathan, A., 1962, 'Osteophytes of the vertebral column', in *Journal of Bone and Joint
Surgery,* 44A(2), 243-268.

Ortner, D., 2003, *Identification of Pathological Condition in Human Skeletal Remains*,
San Diego, California, Academic Press.

Roberts, C., 2009, *Human Remains in Archaeology: a handbook*, York, Council for
British Archaeology, C.B.A. Practical Handbook, No. 19.

Roberts, C. and Cox, M., 2003, *Health and Disease in Britain from Prehistory to the
Present Day*, Stroud, Sutton Publishing.

Roberts, C. and Manchester, K., 2005, *The Archaeology of Disease*, 3rd edition,
Stroud, Sutton Publishing.

Scheuer, L. and Black, S., 2000, *Developmental Juvenile Osteology*, London, Academic Press.

166

Short, C., 1974, 'The antiquity of rheumatoid arthritis', in *Arthritis and Rheumatism*, 17(3), 193-205.

Stillwell, B., 2002, 'An investigation into cranial trauma from the Anglo-Saxon cemetery at Sedgeford, Norfolk', unpub. BSc dissertation, Bournemouth University.

Stirland, A., 2000, *Raising the Dead: the skeleton crew of Henry VIII's great ship, the Mary Rose*, Chichester, John Wiley.

Stuart-Macadam, P., 1985, 'Porotic hyperostosis: representative of a childhood condition', in *American Journal of Physical Anthropology*, 66, 391-398.

Sutor, D. J., Wooley, S. E. and Illingworth, J. J., 1974, 'A geographical and historical survey of the composition of urinary Stones', in *British Journal of Urology*, 46, 393-407.

Swanton, M., 2000, *The Anglo-Saxon Chronicles*, London, Phoenix Press.

Trotter, M. and Gleser, G., 1952, 'Estimation of stature from long bones of American whites and negroes', in *American Journal of Physical Anthropology*, 10, 463-514.

Trotter, M. and Gleser, G., 1958, 'A re-evaluation of estimation based on measurements of stature taken during life and of long bones after death', in *American Journal of Physical Anthropology*, 16, 79-123.

Trotter, M. and Gleser, G., 1977, 'Corrigenda to "estimation of stature from long bones of American whites and negroes"', in *American Journal of Physical Anthropology*, 47, 355-356.

Ubelaker, D., 1999, *Human Skeletal Remains: excavation, analysis, interpretation*, Aldine Manuals on Archeology, 3rd edition, Washington DC, Taraxacum.

Van Twest, M., 2001, 'Restoring Identity: A study of the population of Anglo-Saxon Sedgeford, Norfolk, through the analysis of human skeletal remains', unpub. MA dissertation, University of Melbourne.

Waldron, T., 1997, 'OA of the hip in past populations', in *International Journal of Osteoarchaeology*, 7, 186-189.

Waldron, T., 2009, *Palaeopathology*, Cambridge, Cambridge University Press.

Waldron, T. and Rogers, J., 1991, 'Inter-observer variation in coding osteoarthritis in human skeletal remains', in *International Journal of Osteoarchaeology*, 1, 49-46.

Walker, P., Bathurst,R., Richman,R., Gjerdrum,T. and Andrusko,V., 2009, 'The causes of porotic hyperostosis and cribra orbitalia: a reappraisal of the iron-deficiency-anemia hypothesis', in *American Journal of Physical Anthropology*, 139, 109-125.

Wells, C. and Cayton, H., 1980, 'The human bones', in P. Wade-Martins, *Excavations in North Elmham Park, 1967-1972*, East Anglian Archaeology Report, No. 9, Gressenhall, Norfolk Museums Service.

7. A Medieval Parish Church: St Mary the Virgin, Sedgeford

Introduction

Standing some 500m to the west of Boneyard-Reeddam, the church of St Mary the Virgin and its churchyard occupy the north-western corner of a square block of land which also encompasses West Hall House and West Hall Farm (Plates 7.1 and 7.2). The oldest surviving building in Sedgeford, the church sits low down on the side of the valley and is not widely visible from the surrounding landscape. It has been the focus of the social and spiritual

Plate 7.1: Sedgeford church from the north-west.

lives of Sedgeford's residents for a millennium, and the relative rises and falls in the parish's fortunes are clearly reflected in the fabric of the building.

The church was a primary research focus during SHARP's first five years. In that time a number of different strands of investigation were pursued, with varying degrees of success. The floor-plan and exterior of the building have been recorded at a scale of 1:50, and the interior studied in great detail, using a combination of measured sketches, scale drawings, photographs and written descriptions to record its features. This work has culminated in a detailed understanding of the structural history of the building, the results of which are summarised here.

As well as being a focus of research, the church has also played a very important role in SHARP's own history. It was the venue for the public meeting at which the idea of the project was first discussed in 1995, and since 1996 it has played host to weekly lectures held during the summer excavation seasons. Between 1996 and 2000 the church kitchen functioned as a storeroom and welcome shelter for the teams working on the West Hall Paddock excavations.

The church has also been used by SHARP as the base for several school visits and taught courses, including field history (1998), church archaeology (1999, 2000 and 2001) and geophysical survey (2001). Several of these courses were accredited by the University of East Anglia and resulted in SHARP winning the Graham Webster Laurels for its outstanding contribution to education in archaeology at the 2002 British Archaeological Awards.

Research at the Church

The fabric of the church has been thoroughly recorded, in words and pictures, both inside and out. During SHARP's first season in 1996 a detailed floor-plan of the entire building was surveyed at a scale of 1:50 using a survey grid which surrounded the outside of the building and extended through the north and south doors to allow the interior to be surveyed as well (Fig. 7.1). More details

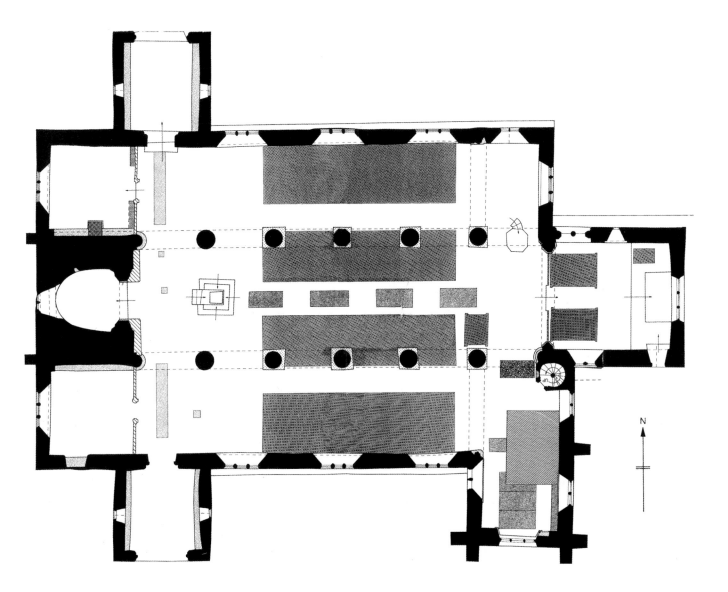

Fig. 7.1: The floor-plan of the church at 1:200.

were added to this plan in subsequent years when we realised that patterns in the flagstone floor of the church preserved the outline of ghost walls from earlier phases of the building.

Work was also begun recording the exterior elevations of the church in 1996, and after a couple of false starts the exterior record was completed in 1999. The work commenced with an attempt at a photo-mosaic survey of the west wall using a large-format plate camera, but the resulting images were not sufficiently detailed (Plate 7.3). Likewise, initial attempts to produce a stone-by-stone record of the building's flint-rubble exterior were also rapidly abandoned when we realised that the work would take over 30 seasons to complete!

Instead of focussing on detailed recording, a series of exterior elevations were drawn at a scale 1:50 by Dominic Andrews during the 1998 and 1999

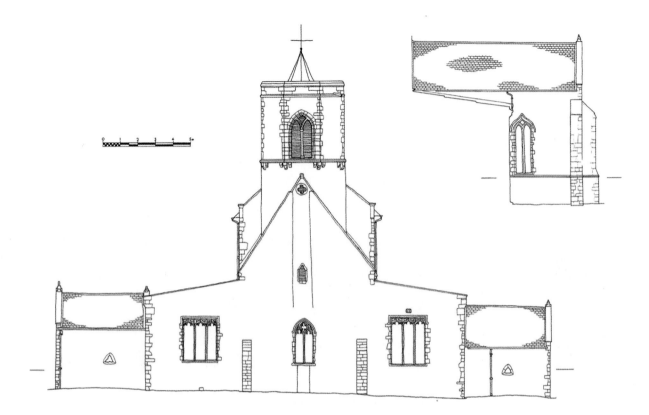

Fig. 7.2: The west-facing elevation of the church at 1:200.

summer seasons, and these were subsequently used to record the various phases evident in the building's fabric (Figures 7.2, 7.3, 7.4 and 7.5).

Accurate surveying of these elevations was achieved by establishing a datum line around the entire church from which vertical measurements could be taken. Wherever possible, accurate measurements were taken from the ground or from ladders. Triangulation was used to calculate unreachable points. To reach the higher levels of the building, members of the project team climbed onto the roofs of the aisles and several measurements were taken from the roof and windows of the tower. The elevation drawings were complemented by a photographic survey which recorded all of the exterior walls, window and door openings, and other architectural details of note.

Once complete, the elevations and floor-plan were used to record the various building phases evident in the masonry fabric. In this fashion over 450 individual building elements were identified and interrelated using a Harris Matrix to create a detailed picture of the building's structural history (Hoggett 2000).

Whereas it was relatively easy to create a detailed and extensive survey of the exterior of the building, we encountered greater difficulty recording the interior. The entirety of the interior of the building is plastered, obscuring many of the structural details, and we therefore decided that a series of measured sketches accompanied by written descriptions would have to provide a sufficiently detailed record.

The interior of the building was recorded during the 1998 season on a cell-by-cell basis, with recorders working in a clockwise direction around the building. In addition to providing a visual and verbal record of the building's interior, this detailed internal examination would enable some light to be shed

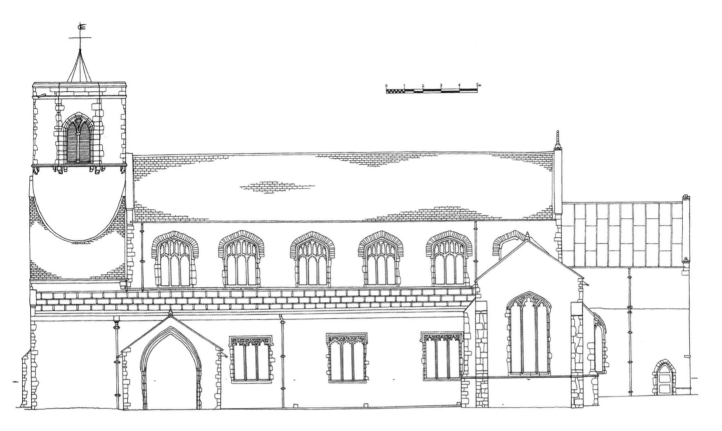

Fig. 7.3: The south-facing elevation of the church at 1:200.

upon the wider developmental sequence of the building, complementing that which could be derived from the exterior fabric.

In addition to our studies of the building, the churchyard has also been the focus of a great deal of activity. SHARP's first season saw a comprehensive written and photographic record made of the surviving gravestones, complementing records which had been made by the local branch of the Women's Institute in the 1970s. Many of the gravestones recorded in 1996 have since been moved or have weathered away, meaning that SHARP's archive now provides the only record of them.

It has long been recognised that substantial architectural remains lie buried in the churchyard, and SHARP conducted geophysical resistance surveys on two occasions. Small areas of the north transept were surveyed in 1998 by the late Peter Carnell, and an extensive survey of the eastern half of the graveyard was carried out by students on a taught course in 2001. The latter produced a detailed plan of the missing north transept and the shortened chancel (Fig. 7.6). The same students also produced an accompanying earthwork plot of the graveyard, along with a survey of the surviving trees, both of which help to put the building into its immediate landscape context.

The existing historical documentation regarding the church held by the Norfolk Record Office has been thoroughly researched and found to contain many details of two 19th-century restorations, and a few earlier references, although documentary history is generally lacking with regard to earlier periods of the building's history. A brief study of the bequests made to the church in the wills of 16th- and 17th-century villagers has shed some light upon its history during that period (Fogarty 2001). Ultimately, however, it is

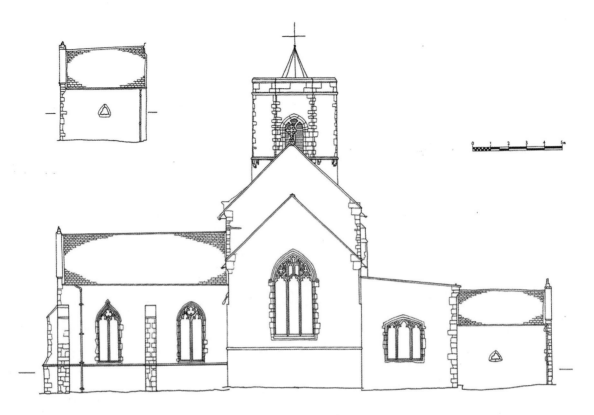

Fig. 7.4: The east-facing elevation of the church at 1:200.

the architectural stratigraphy of the building itself which has been used to piece together its structural history.

The development of the building

Detailed architectural and archaeological analysis of the structure of the building has given rise to a multi-phase interpretation of the church's development. It should be stressed that much of this sequence is a relative chronology, in true archaeological fashion, although there are parts of the sequence which are able to be dated with recourse to architectural styling and/or corroborative historic documents.

We are not the only people to have studied Sedgeford church. In particular, St Mary's was the subject of an interpretative article by Stephen Hart published in the June 2001 issue of *The Round Tower*, the newsletter of the Round Tower Churches Society (Hart 2001). More recently, the church has also been the subject of a Conservation-Based Research and Analysis report written by Stephen Heywood (2010). The architectural schemes put forward in both reports broadly comply with that identified during the fieldwork described here, albeit with slight differences of opinion about the exact chronology.

Phase 0: the earliest church
c.1000–1250

The Middle to Late Anglo-Saxon Christian cemetery excavated on the Boneyard-Reeddam site appears to have fallen out of use by the mid-10th

century at the latest, perhaps some time before a new settlement focus was established in the West Hall area. This period of upheaval perhaps coincided with the reconquest of the eastern Danelaw by the emergent English, and may also be connected with the Sedgeford estate coming into royal hands, as it certainly had by the time of the Norman Conquest. We know that Sedgeford was granted to the Bishop of Elmham after the Conquest, and that by 1086 it was in the hands of the Bishop of Thetford, the episcopal see having been transferred there in 1070 (Brown 1984, 10:20).

It would be very surprising for either a Late Anglo-Saxon royal estate or an Early Norman episcopal estate not to feature a church and attendant churchyard, and we should not be misled by the fact that the Domesday account of Sedgeford does not make any mention of one. Although an unusually high number of churches are recorded in Norfolk's Domesday entries, and they were evidently common features in the Late Anglo-Saxon landscape, the way in which they were recorded was very inconsistent and the absence of a mention cannot be taken to indicate that none existed (Hoggett 2007, 126-132). Indeed, it is worth noting that the only church recorded in the entire Smethdon (Smithdon) Hundred in which Sedgeford lies, was that at Hunstanton, suggesting that the local Domesday recorders were not interested in distinguishing churches from the rest of the manorial holdings (Brown 1984, 49:02).

Greater substance is offered by the documentary records of Norwich Cathedral Priory, which record that Bishop Turbe of Norwich (1146/7-1174) gave the Manor of Sedgeford to Norwich Cathedral Priory during his episcopate (Virgoe 1996, 342-3). It would seem that the bishopric retained the rights to the church at this point, for our first definite documentary reference

Fig. 7.5: The north-facing elevation of the Church at 1:200.

Fig. 7.6: Results of the 2001 geophysical resistance survey of the churchyard at 1:200, showing the traces of the shortened chancel and the ruined north transept. The resistance is given in Ohms, red being the higher resistance and green the lowest.

Plate 7.3: The unsuccessful 1997 photo-mosaic of the western wall.

Plate 7.4: The tower encased by the later westward extension of the nave and aisles. Note how only a small strip of the tower remains visible and the 'Anglo-Saxon' window at first-floor level.

to a church in Sedgeford dates from 1205, when Bishop de Gray granted the Priory's cellarer the income from Sedgeford church (Virgoe 1996, 349).

We must assume that a church – though not necessarily the church – was well established in the village by this date. None of the surviving fabric of the extant building appears to date from before the 13th century. If this is the case, the church referred to in these early medieval documents may be the mortar-floored structure identified in the West Hall Paddock excavations immediately to the south of the current churchyard wall (see Chapter 8 below).

The former presence of at least three burials in the interior of the structure (one of which produced a calibrated radiocarbon date of 1010-1180 at 95% probability) is a testament to the building's ecclesiastical purpose, and there is a strong likelihood that any associated cemetery extended to the north, into the area currently occupied by the present churchyard.

The fact that this building may have had a timber superstructure, perhaps with beams laid on flint rubble foundations, is entirely in keeping with what we know of ecclesiastical architecture in the region during this time, and the building's careful dismantling and the exhumation of at least one of its burials, presumably for reburial in a later church, would all suggest that the building was superseded rather than its being allowed to fall out of use (Hoggett 2007, 153-162).

Such a sequence would also explain why the present church stands to the north of the West Hall Paddock site. Presumably the then existing church could have continued in use while the new one was built. The massive programme of rebuilding represented was surely a direct result of the Cathedral Priory investing in the infrastructure of their most profitable manor.

Phase 1: the first masonry building
c.1250-1300

It is clear from the fabric of the building that the earliest surviving masonry element of the church is the round tower, which is constructed from flint-rubble laid in mortar. It is difficult to see much of the lower portion of the tower, as the later addition of the vestry and kitchen at the western ends of the north and south aisles respectively has encased its base. At the very western extent of the circular tower, a thin vertical strip of original masonry has been left visible between the two westward extensions (Plate 7.4).

There has been much discussion about the possible foundation date of the tower, with various commentators opting for Late Anglo-Saxon, Saxo-Norman, Norman/Early Medieval and High Medieval construction dates (Goode 1982, 1994; Heywood 1988; Hart 2003). The circular shape of the tower cannot be taken in and of itself to indicate Late Anglo-Saxon origin. There are few who would now consider this to be the case, and some, indeed, would go so far as to suggest that most if not all round towers are of post-Conquest foundation (Heywood 1988; Hart 2003, 166-171).

Similarly, the presence of a west-facing triangular-headed window in the first floor of the tower, and another looking south into the void between the tower and the wall of the kitchen, cannot be taken to indicate Late Anglo-Saxon origin (Taylor and Taylor 1965, 720; Hart 2001, 78). Such window forms remained common into the medieval period, and the fact that the examples here are faced with dressed stone would further suggest that they are of post-Conquest origin.

Both Hart and Heywood are of the opinion that the round tower and the 13th-century octagonal belfry which sits atop it are of a single coherent build, and that the entire tower is therefore a late 13th-century structure (Hart 2001, 76-78; Heywood 2010, 2-3). There are certainly no signs of any earlier belfry stage lower down the tower, as might be expected if the octagonal belfry were a later addition, and the style of stonework is consistent throughout the height of the tower and into the belfry itself.

Further evidence that the tower is late 13th century is provided by its shape and the way in which it is joined to the west wall of the nave. There are traces of a blocked doorway from the tower into the nave at first-floor level, which must have given access to the roof-space of the original nave (Plate 7.5). The later encasing of the base of the tower renders it impossible to see the junction between the tower and the nave – so often used to discern the relative relationship between the two structural elements – but the 1996 floor-plan of the building clearly indicates that the tower actually has a horseshoe-shaped footprint on the ground, only becoming truly circular by the time it reaches first-floor level.

Plate 7.5: The view looking west along the interior of the nave.

The implication here is that the tower cannot have been a free-standing, circular structure to which a later church was added; rather, it was originally constructed along with the nave wall as a coherent build. The amount of re-engineering required to reshape a free-standing round tower into this horseshoe shape would have made the whole enterprise prohibitively expensive, if not physically impossible.

If we accept that tower, belfry and west wall of the nave are contemporary structures, then by implication the whole of the nave and its surviving arcades must also belong to the same late 13th-century build. The north and south arcades are of identical construction, with the exception of the central pillar of the north arcade, which is octagonal rather than circular, indicating that the arcades are contemporary with each other (Plate 7.5).

The arches of the arcades fit perfectly within the length of the nave, suggesting that they too are an intrinsic part of the same phase of building and are not later insertions, and there are no traces of earlier walls through

which the arcades might have been cut. Indeed, an indication that the arcading was specifically tailored to the space is given by the western halves of the westernmost columns where they abut the western wall of the nave. Here the later addition of the kitchen and vestry has exposed the western halves of these capitals and revealed that they have been deliberately finished to fit the space (Plates 7.6 and 7.7).

Daniel Secker has recently re-examined the fabric of the church and he too sees no evidence of pre-Norman work. It seems curious that, given the propensity of Herbert de Losinga, the Bishop of Norwich, for new ecclesiastical building projects, that we can detect no evidence for new work at Sedgeford. It is just possible that a structure might have been built on the site of the present church, all traces of which have been removed or concealed by the present St Mary the Virgin. However, this speculation would be dependent upon the date of the West Hall

chapel, and its dismantling, lying earlier, rather than later, in the date range of 1010-1180 we have for the skeleton in the chapel (see Chapter 8 below).

Secker also believes he has detected some evidence to suggest an early 13th-century date for the arcades, perhaps associated with earlier, narrower and now vanished aisles, a date coinciding with the transfer of ownership from the Bishops of Norwich to the Cathedral Priory, thus providing a suitable context for such a programme of building, though making a 'missing church' less likely. This would have the effect of 'stretching' the chronology of the building sequence backwards, whereas Richard Hoggett, SHARP's leading church archaeologist, favours a 'tight' sequence beginning in the late 13th-century.

Whether part of the original design or later insertions, the arcades indicate the presence of aisles at an early date, though we cannot be sure of their width as later alterations have removed all trace of them. It is extremely likely that they were narrower than the present aisles and that the steeply pitched thatched roof of the nave would have spanned the nave and aisles together. Taking the lean-to roofs which enclose the sides of the tower as an indication of the original pitch and height of the nave's thatched roof, it is possible to project the roofline along the building and infer that the aisles themselves were perhaps half as wide as they are today.

It seems that an incarnation of the present chancel belongs to an early phase of building, judging by the presence of a surviving lancet window in its north wall (Plate 7.10) and traces of the internal splay of a blocked lancet window visible in its internal southern wall. These windows would suggest that the present width of the chancel reflects its original dimensions, and in turn one can infer that the width of the chancel arch is likewise consistent with the original design.

It is also possible to discern something of the height and pitch of the original chancel roof from the three dressed stones which are to be found built into the east wall of the south transept at the point at which it joins the south wall of the chancel. These three stones are all that remains of a drip course which must have protected the join between the chancel and the nave when the transepts were added, and it is presumed that this reflects the original line of the roof.

Plate 7.8: A thin line of flagstones at the eastern end of the north aisle preserves the line of a former wall. There is a marked change of floor level on either side of this line.

Phase 2: the transepts
c.1300–1350

It appears that the first phase of the masonry church we see today was constructed without transepts, but it is clear from the structure that these were soon added, sometime during the early 14th century. The south transept still stands, albeit in an altered state, but the north transept was later demolished and now survives only as sub-surface remains.

Both transepts left the aisles at right angles at the level of the final column of the arcades, where additional arches may have been constructed spanning the aisles in order to accommodate the new transepts. The architectural and geophysical evidence clearly indicates that the two transepts were not of the same dimensions, giving the church a slightly lopsided cruciform plan. What is less clear is exactly how the roofs of the transepts, chancel and nave would have come together, and one possible suggestion, in part supported by the structural evidence surrounding the transepts, is that their earliest incarnations had flat roofs which sloped outwards from the thatched roof of the nave.

One can be relatively certain that the dimensions of the surviving south transept reflect its original extent, although there is clear evidence that the roof was subsequently raised. A piscina is built into the south-eastern corner of the transept, indicating its use as a side chapel, and it now houses the organ and the rood-stair turret.

The builders of the south transept clearly struggled to make it as large as possible without impacting on the existing architectural scheme of the chancel. The east wall of the transept abuts the south wall of the chancel so close to the chancel's westernmost window that the stonework actually

Plate 7.9: The junction of the south transept and the chancel showing the drip course of the earlier chancel roof. Note how the transept wall butts onto the frame of the chancel window.

overlies the dressed stone of the window jamb (Plate 7.9)

Although the north transept no longer survives, there is sufficient architectural and archaeological evidence for us to be able to reconstruct its dimensions and say something about its construction. The western wall of the north transept left the aisles at a right angle on the line of the final arcade. Geophysical surveys of the churchyard indicate that the north transept was broadly the same length, along its north-south axis, as the south transept. Interestingly, something of the line of the western wall of the north transept is preserved in the floor of the north aisle, where there is a distinctive step downwards as one moves from the aisle proper into what remains of the north transept (Plate 7.8).

In 2011 new drains were laid out around the outside of the church, necessitating a circuit of trenches which were subject to an archaeological watching-brief. At the time of writing, a report on this is still awaited, but it was observed on a site visit during the works that the ruinous foundations of the north transept survive beneath the surface.

It appears from the geophysical survey and the traces of masonry protruding from the ground to the north of the chancel that the north transept extended further to the east than its opposing number. This would go some way to explaining the presence of a most unusual window, which is to be found tucked into the join of the north aisle and the north wall of the chancel. This window is ornately carved from a very soft stone and was clearly never intended to be an external window, since the central pillar or tracery is decorated on all sides and sits at the centre of the frame rather than being flush with the exterior face of wall. Although it is now glazed, this window was presumably an internal, unglazed opening which allowed a view from the chapel in the north transept through into the chancel (Plate 7.10).

Plate 7.10: The earthworks of the north transept and the curious former internal window in the north wall of the chancel. Note the original 13th-century lancet window to the east and the build line from the shortening of the chancel c.1770.

Phase 3: the widened aisles c.1350 – 1400

In the late 14th century the original narrow aisles were widened to their current width and both aisles were extended westwards with the addition of the cells now used as the kitchen and vestry. It was at this point that the base of the tower was enclosed and the first incarnation of the sloping roofs which flank the tower were constructed, presumably continuing the height and pitch of the thatched roof of the nave.

When both of the aisles were widened, they encroached upon the western walls of the two existing transepts. All traces of the relationship between the north transept and the north aisle wall have subsequently been removed, but the surviving junction of the south wall of the south aisle and the west wall of the south transept indicates that the aisles were widened as far as they could be, so that the wall abutted the window jamb of the south transept (Plate 7.11).

Internally, the widening of the aisles called for the reconstruction of the arches which span the aisles and form the western walls of the transepts. With narrower aisles, these arches would have been of conventional gothic proportions, mirroring those of the arcades themselves. With the widening, they had to be extended laterally, but without the roof-space to allow them to be extended upwards to maintain their proportions, such that the resultant arches are flatter and more elongated than they should be and look decidedly badly built.

Plate 7.11: The wall of the widened south aisle butting against the west wall of the south transept. Note how the aisle wall almost encroaches onto the frame of the transept window.

It seems likely that the two porches were also added at this time, and the door within the south porch may well have been reused and reset from the earlier aisle wall. It should be noted that the current windows in the north and south aisles are later insertions.

Phase 4: the demolition of the north transept
c.1400-1500

One of the floating elements in the church's chronology is the date at which the north transept was demolished and the eastern end of the north aisle reinstated in its place. The areas of blocking, complete with reset windows, can easily be picked out in the walls of the north aisle (Plate 7.12)

Documentary references indicate that the transept was ruinous by the late 18th century at the very latest, and had probably been so for some time at this point (Parkin 1809, 389). Hart places the demolition in the mid 15th-century, before the construction of the clerestory, based on the observation that the blocking of the aisle had occurred before the walls of the aisles were raised to accommodate the lower roof pitch needed to facilitate the insertion of the clerestory (Hart 2001, 80-1).

Close observation of the fabric of the east wall of the north aisle reveals

182

Plate 7.12: The eastern end of the northern wall of the north aisle, showing the blocking and reset window which filled the gap left by the removal of the north transept. Note the build-line visible above the blocking which is indicative of the lowering of the pitch of the aisle roof.

that a tantalising fragment of gravestone has been reset into the wall, but unfortunately detailed examination has failed to reveal any details or markings on this fragment which might have given a *terminus post quem* (earliest date) for the wall. For the time being, at least, the exact demolition date of the transept remains a mystery.

Phase 5: the clerestory
c.1450–1500

The clerestory, which was added to the church in the later 15th century, is the most lavish and skilfully executed element of the building. Its creation would have transformed the experience of the church.

The roof of the nave was removed, the nave walls raised and faced with neatly-laid dressed flint flushwork, and a row of six large windows inserted on each side of the church. Standing in the church, it is still possible to appreciate something of the feeling of space and light which the clerestory introduced in a church which must previously have seemed much more claustrophobic and poorly lit.

It was at this point in the church's history that the roof of the nave first overlapped with the eastern face of the belfry, as it still does today. At the same time, the pitch of the aisle roofs must have been lowered to accommodate the new windows, with the outside edges of the aisle walls being raised accordingly. The build-lines from this work are clearly visible.

As a result of the higher nave roof, the chancel arch was also able to be heightened, with the roof of the chancel being lifted in turn to accommodate it. This new arch would have allowed for the construction of a new rood screen and rood loft at a greater height than had previously been the case.

The church now achieved its greatest scale, with both aisles at their widest, both transepts intact, a chancel twice as long as that which survives now, and a newly installed clerestory with substantive windows and lavish dressed flint. It must have been a sight to behold.

Unfortunately, from this point onwards, the church began a period of gradual decline which has continued in one form or another to the present-day, despite the best efforts of the Victorians.

Phase 6: the raising of the south transept
c.1450 – 1550

There is clear evidence that the walls and roof of the south transept were raised at some point after the insertion of the clerestory, presumably during the late 15th or early 16th century, as there is a clear build-line in the fabric and the new roofline of the transept blocks the easternmost window of the southern half of the clerestory (Plate 7.13).

There has been much discussion about why this would have been done, and the negative impact which it had on the aesthetics of the church. One possibility is that more space was needed to accommodate the construction of the rood stair within the south transept, as is suggested by the fact that the top of the

rood stair is level with the height of the raised transept walls. Another possible explanation might be the replacement of a previously flat transept roof with a pitched roof, perhaps to aid with weatherproofing and drainage.

Plate 7.13: The raised roof of the south transept blocking the easternmost window of the clerestory.

Phase 7: the truncated chancel
1770

It is clear from an examination of the eastern end of the chancel as it currently stands that a substantial programme of rebuilding has taken place, with the priest's door unusually close to the eastern end of the chancel and the east wall itself effectively having been replaced along with the eastern ends of the north and south walls of the chancel.

This episode in the Church's structural history is one of very few for which there is an explanatory historical document. The Norfolk Record Office contains a faculty dated 9 March 1770 (NRO PD 601/28/1) which retrospectively summarises the nature of the work and identifies Edmund Rolfe as the party responsible:

> *The chancel did contain in length 47 foot and in width 24 foot and height to the wall-plate 21 foot – that the said chancel, being very old and decayed in the walls, roof and lead could not be repaired according to such dimensions without great expense, that you have contracted the said chancel and made the same only 20 foot in length, 24 foot in width and 18 foot in height under the wall-plate, and have built a strong gable at the east end there of 4 bricks thick to the water table, 3 bricks thick to the height of the plates or level walls, and 1 brick and a half with a gable part, with a proper window, and have repaired the side walls and topped the same with bricks under the plates 2 foot deep, and have put on a new roof of fir with oak plates thereon, the principals whereof are 10 foot by 7, and have covered such roof with lead that the old lead being so thin by length of time as to be rendered unfit for use.*
>
> *You did therefore take down the old lead and sell the same and*

purchased the said new lead that the expense of repairing the said chancel and covering the same with lead as above, exclusive of the old lead, amounted to £60 and upwards, that the said chancel is now large enough for every purpose and is in a decent, proper and substantial condition and likely so to continue for many years.

Plate 7.14: Looking north along the drainage trench excavated across the buried chancel in 2011. Note the foundations of the south and north walls of the chancel in the trench.

In 1991 a drainage pipe was laid across the ground beyond the eastern end of the chancel, cutting into the archaeological and architectural deposits which lay sealed beneath. The east-facing section of this trench was drawn and it shows the north and south walls of the old chancel surviving beneath the ground, flanking a red-tiled floor with a flat limestone tombstone set into it (NHER 1615). Subsequent excavation did not reveal a burial beneath this stone.

Further evidence of the surviving extent of the remains of the chancel was revealed by the geophysical survey undertaken by SHARP in 2001, which seemed to indicate that the complete footprint of the chancel described in the faculty survived beneath the ground. Confirmation of this survival came during the 2011 drainage excavations, which exposed the foundations of the north and south walls of the chancel, as well as cutting a cross-section though the chancel floor (Plate 7.14).

Phase 8: Victorian restorations
1842 and 1882

The church was struck by lightning in July 1819, causing some damage to the tower and resulting in the death of a young girl who had been attending evening school in the vestry at the time (as reported in *The Times* on 21 July 1819). By the mid-19th century the church was in a sorry state.

There is a considerable number of documents in the Norfolk Record Office which describe the condition of the building and the two Victorian restoration efforts, the first in 1842, the second in 1882 (NRO PD 601/35). Although not the main subject of the work conducted by SHARP, summaries of these restorations are included here for the sake of completeness.

A particularly vivid account of the state of the church before the 1842 restoration was written by Charles Fawcett Neville Rolfe, who described the situation thus:

In no part could you sit without drops of rain which fall now on your head, now on your book. A foul and damp smell rose from the green broken floor. Many vaults had fallen in, tilting their memory stones on one side. The earth was within six inches of the windows. The walls [were] covered with centuries of whitewash wherever not preoccupied with green mould. The seats, built as each man listed, were an array of nonconformity. The pulpit door [was] so narrow that the Rector of Ringstead, after vainly attempting to enter it, either straightways or crabfashion was obliged to elevate himself by its doorposts and pass his legs through the aperture which would not admit his body.

The screen bore marks of mending, many steps worse than total neglect; every vestige of nail has disappeared, and the Communion table, surmounted by a three-light wooden window, was any rate suitable, if not to the comfort of our own houses, at least to the desolation of the rest of the building. The only chancel furniture was some desks and forms, whereof old the alumni of the village had been taught to read and write.

The God's-acre around, sown with the harvest of the resurrection, was unwalled and in every way profaned. The tower, lightening stricken, threatened the roofs, and these, in turn, the seats and aisles.

The Dean of Norwich, being Bishop and Patron, managed the whole concern, appointing me his commissary, but as he seldom listened to my complaints and as we differed in our notion of church architecture, many things were done and many left undone without any fault of mine. The repairs cost about £1,700.

As stated by Rolfe, the 1842 restoration cost £1,700 and saw general repairs, re-roofing, the installation of new seating and the insertion of a new screen, although the details of the work are difficult to reconstruct.

Rolfe's reservations about the quality of the earlier restoration work proved to be well founded, and a second programme of restoration was undertaken in 1882 under the direction of architects Frederick Preedy and Ewan Christian. This programme was much more wide-ranging and included the re-leading of the aisle and chancel roofs, the almost total replacement of the timber roof of the nave, the rebuilding of the north porch, the re-facing of the east end of the chancel, and the replacement of the east window. Having been replaced in 1842, the interior seating was again replaced, and this time set on a well ventilated wooden platform to prevent it rotting in the damp. The total cost of the works was in excess of £2,200.

Conclusions

The church of St Mary the Virgin has stood at the centre of village life in Sedgeford for the best part of a thousand years and in that time has borne witness to great changes in the fortunes of the parish. These have been reflected in the fabric of the church itself, which grew considerably throughout the medieval period while Sedgeford enjoyed strong links with Norwich Cathedral Priory.

The dissolution of the Priory in the mid-16th century sounded the death-knell of this age of prosperity, and Sedgeford church entered a period of decline from which it has never truly emerged. Having grown too big to be easily maintained by a parish of Sedgeford's size, parts of the building were allowed to fall into disrepair and were eventually demolished, reducing the size of the church in an attempt to fix the problem.

So dire had the situation become by the middle decades of the 19th century that two programmes of restoration were required to bring the church back from the brink. We owe those Victorian residents of Sedgeford a great debt, for without their efforts there is no doubt that the Sedgeford church we know today would be largely ruinous.

The main contributors to the writing of this chapter were:

Richard Hoggett (principal author) with additional research by Dominic Andrews, Pauline Fogarty and Daniel Secker.

References

Brown, P., 1984, *Domesday Book: Norfolk*, 2 vols., Chichester, Phillimore.

Fogarty, P., 2001, 'Sedgeford: parish and manor', unpub. MA dissertation, Royal Holloway, University of London.

Goode, W., 1982, *East Anglian Round Towers and Their Churches*, Lowestoft, Friends of the Round Tower Churches Society.

Goode, W., 1994, *Round Tower Churches of South East England*, Burnham Market, Round Tower Churches Society.

Hart, S., 2001, 'Sedgeford, St Mary the Virgin', in *The Round Tower*, XXVIII, No. 4, 76-82.

Hart, S., 2003, *The Round Towers of England*, Ipswich, Lucas Books.

Heywood, S., 1988, 'The round towers of East Anglia', in J. Blair (ed.), *Minsters and Parish Churches*, Oxford, Oxford University Committee for Archaeology, 169-177.

Heywood, S., 2010, 'The Church of St Mary, Sedgeford: conservation-based research and analysis report', unpub. Norfolk County Council Historic Environment Service report.

Hoggett, R., 2000, 'Principles and practice: the application of the Harris Matrix to standing building recording', unpub. BA dissertation, University of Bristol.

Hoggett, R., 2001, 'The origin and early development of Sedgeford, Norfolk', unpub. MA dissertation, University of Bristol.

Hoggett, R., 2007, 'Changing Beliefs: the archaeology of the East Anglian conversion', unpub. PhD thesis, University of East Anglia.

Parkin, C., 1809, *An Essay towards a Topographical History of the County of Norfolk*, Volume 10, London.

Taylor, H. and Taylor, J., 1965, *Anglo-Saxon Architecture*, 2 vols., Cambridge, Cambridge University Press.

Virgoe, R., 1996, 'The estates of Norwich Cathedral Priory, 1101-1538', in I. Atherton, E. Fernie, C. Harper-Bill and H. Smith (eds.), *Norwich Cathedral: church, city and diocese, 1096–1996*, London, Hambledon Press, 339-359.

8. Power and Piety in Medieval Sedgeford

In the summer season of 1996 the opportunity arose, thanks to the kind permission of Andrew and Katharine Ramsey, owners of West Hall, to undertake preliminary exploration of Sedgeford's Medieval centre. What began as a season-long investigation comprising four small evaluation trenches evolved into five years' work in two small area excavations in West Hall Paddock, with an additional evaluation trench in the adjacent Ladywell Field in 1998.

West Hall Paddock lies immediately south of Sedgeford's Early Medieval parish church, and work here was intended to provide information about what was thought to be the secular centre of the village during the Medieval period. A major aim was to learn more about the date and purpose of the 'Late Anglo-Saxon shift' from south to north of the river.

We were later able to expand the investigation with two small area

Fig. 8.1: Location of the 1996 evaluation trenches and 1997-2000 area excavations in West Hall Paddock.

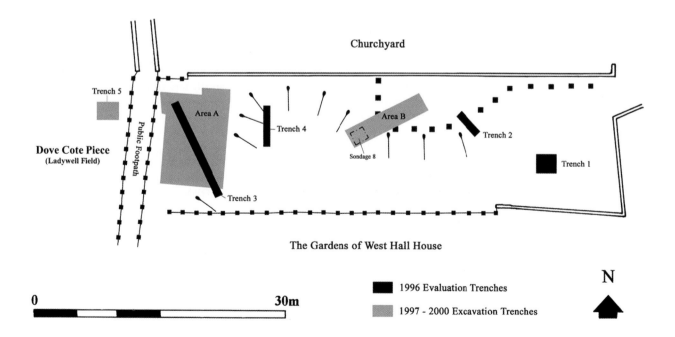

188

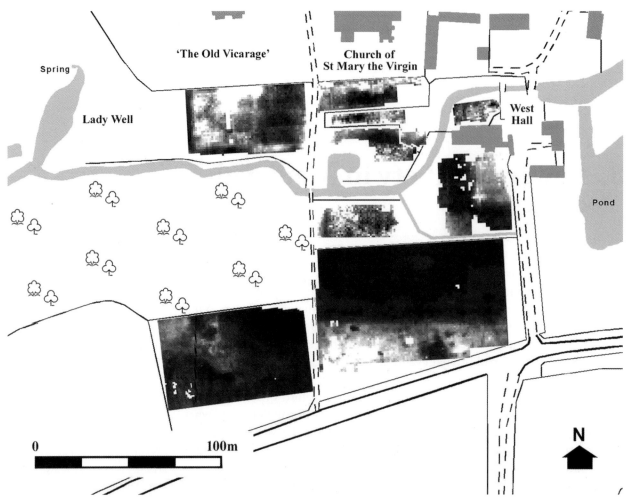

Fig. 8.2: The results of electrical resistivity surveys undertaken in and around the West Hall study area between 1996 and 2003.

excavations in Ladywell Field, which lies immediately west of West Hall Paddock, in 2002 (with the kind permission of Janet Hammond and Tim Snelling). This was further supplemented by two evaluation trenches, in 2003, in what is technically 'the eastern portion of West Hall Long Meadow', but which came to be known as 'Saggy Horse Field' (in honour of a former aged occupant!). This lies south of West Hall house and south of the river, and the purpose here was to give us a clearer idea about the immediate relationship between the zones south and north of the river, and about activity and change in the valley bottom, both human and topographical.

During the period 1996 to 2003 much of the area was subjected to electrical resistivity survey. The overall results can be seen in Fig. 8.2. The most revealing thing at this scale is the dampness of the ground, especially in the extensive areas to the south of the present course of the river.

Environment and settlement shift

Trenches 2 and 5 showed evidence of early waterlogging, but the primary evidence for this appeared in Area A (see Fig. 8.1). Here we had drainage ditches augmented with rocks, and an extensive layer of wet, black, organic-rich mud between 0.07 and 0.24m thick, thinning out to the north and west of the trench.

This deposit appears to have been widespread, since identical material was observed 30m to the east in the 1996 Evaluation Trench 2, 15m to the east in Area B, Sondage 8, and 8m to the west in the 1998 Evaluation Trench 5. In addition, the deposit was similar in composition to the fills of a ditch and two gullies within Area A.

All the indications therefore point to a large area of waterlogging. The leaching of some deposits also indicates fluctuations in the water-table as they were forming. None of the lower deposits in either the evaluation trenches or the area excavations were fully excavated due to time pressures. Further excavation would, in any case, have been difficult due to present-day waterlogging at depths of more than a metre.

Datable material, primarily pottery, in the layers immediately above the black waterlogging deposits is of Late Anglo-Saxon or Early Medieval (or 'Saxo-Norman') date. Thus it appears that the area around the Paddock was unusable for a sustained period before Late Anglo-Saxon times. The recovery of an assemblage of sizeable Roman potsherds from the lowest levels in Area A implies that this phase of waterlogging may have begun at the end of the Roman period.

In the Saxo-Norman period, episodes of waste dumping are clearly visible in both the test pits at the eastern end of the Paddock. Oyster shell, flint, animal bone and other domestic waste are widely present in the dumps. The layers containing such material are, however, somewhat thicker in Trench 2, suggesting that it is closer to the main focus of dumping. Given the increased building activity a few metres to the west of this area, the dumping may have been undertaken to bring the area up to the level of the buildings' sand hard-standing.

Layers sealing the dumped material can be securely dated to the 13th to 16th centuries, when activity in the area was much increased, and apparently continuous. The silty-sandy soil, containing some domestic debris, suggests backyard cultivation, possibly a vegetable garden. After this, land use changed, probably to pasture.

The apparent hiatus between the Late Roman and Late Anglo-Saxon periods is also seen across the river in Saggy Horse Field. Here the resistivity survey clearly distinguished between the lowest area of the field, equating with the flood-plain of the river, and the slightly higher ground of the field's southern third. A similar difference between the very lowest levels, nearest the river, and the slightly higher ground, where burials took place, has also been noted with respect to the Boneyard-Reeddam cemetery site (see Chapter 5). In neither West Hall Paddock nor Saggy Horse Field was there any substantial evidence for activity in either the Early or Middle Anglo-Saxon period.

The two small evaluation trenches opened in Saggy Horse Field in 2003 were designed to test the geophysical survey results. Trench 1, measuring 7m x 5m metres, was in the south-west of the field on the higher ground, whilst Trench 2, measuring 1.6m x 20m, was sited further north on the river's flood-plain (see Fig. 8.1).

Trench 1 revealed some Late-Anglo Saxon activity, including some shallow gullies running downslope from south to north towards the river, interpreted as drainage ditches, similar in form to those found on the main Boneyard-Reeddam site to the east. Evidence of Iron Age activity was also found in the trench, including a possible boundary ditch, which had been re-cut.

Trench 2 was focused on what proved to be a large ditch of Medieval date, perhaps with its origins in the Late Anglo-Saxon period, and certainly associated with Medieval water-management schemes in the valley. Apart from the ditch, there was only minimal evidence of Late Anglo-Saxon activity.

Iron Age material was much more abundant, and there was evidence of prolonged activity. Yet here, south of the river, it would appear that the area was abandoned by the Roman period, with some activity resuming only in the Late Anglo-Saxon period.

The implication, then, is extensive areas of riverine marsh and wetland in the vicinity of West Hall during the first millennium AD. The shift in settlement focus from south to north of the river appears as a definite break rather than a gradual change. Whatever the reasons for this, we can speculate that prior to it this low-lying area had been rendered unmanageable by the collapse of water-management systems.

The worsening climate in the Late Roman period and the rise in sea-level that reached its climax in the Middle Anglo-Saxon period (see Chapter 1) will have had an effect on the river systems of west Norfolk and may have been the underlying cause of the wetter conditions represented in the excavations.

Whether the subsequent Late Anglo-Saxon shift was driven by environmental factors or by political agency – or perhaps some combination of the two, with drier conditions making it possible for new landowners to effect the change – remains uncertain. What is clear is that a chalk outcrop above the valley flood-plain may well have been a major attraction, and that the construction of the causeway on which the final north-south extent of the road from Snettisham now enters Sedgeford village, probably in the Late Anglo-Saxon period, may have been designed in part to drain land and canalise water immediately to its west, creating a new settlement zone.

Late Anglo-Saxon society was quite capable of major feats of land re-engineering, and at the time of Domesday Book the estate was held by Gyrth, King Harold's brother. If this land-holding pattern reflects ownership in the earlier part of the Late Anglo-Saxon period, then one can assume a powerful magnate with the wealth to effect major changes in the landscape. Relevant to this is the fact that four watermills were recorded on the estate in Sedgeford at the time of Domesday, one of which at least must be associated with the ponding that would inevitably have followed the creation of the causeway.

Whatever the details, there can be no doubt that by the Saxo-Norman period, the main religious and secular centres of Sedgeford were firmly established to the north of the river.

Box 8.1
Black mud

Plate 8.1: The waterlogged black deposit towards the base of the excavated sequence of deposits in Trench 1, West Hall Paddock.

The extensive layer of black, silty-sandy, organic-rich mud representing the Early and Middle Anglo-Saxon inundation in the West Hall area contained a wide range of material including: occasional chalk, flint and oyster shell; a moderate assemblage of animal bone; a fragment of tile; three fragments of well-dressed stone; seven fragments of Romano-British pottery; and three intrusive (that is, originally from a higher level) fragments of Anglo-Saxon Thetford-type Ware.

Archaeo-environmental sampling revealed that it also contained significant floral and faunal fossils including: beetle remains, small mammal bones, amphibian bones, and caddis larval cases (indicative of flowing water); Elderberry seeds; a range of common wild species such as Vervain, Henbane, Musk Thistle, Stinging Nettle, Hemp Nettle and Wild Radish; a range of wetland and aquatic plants such as Sedge, Water Crowfoot, Wild Celery and Lesser Spearwort; and some charred cereal grains of Oat, Barley and Wheat.

West Hall Paddock and Ladywell Field were clearly subjected to prolonged periods of flooding. The black mud was the result of this flooding, and the presence of caddis larval cases and watercress seeds shows that the land contained areas of flowing water. On the other hand, the presence of common weed macrofossils implies that areas near Area A, probably to the north where the land slopes naturally upwards, may still have been relatively dry. Overall, though, the area was transformed in this period from a zone of damp grassland into one of boggy marginal land unable to support settlement, cultivation or grazing..

An expression of piety

Trench 3 was opened in West Hall Paddock near its western boundary, but at an angle to it, to test the geophysical survey results. Although at its greatest depth it was taken down to 0.75m, the most significant discovery was the presence of a randomly coursed chalk wall, some 0.46m wide, which ran diagonally through part of the trench.

This became the focus of a small area excavation (Area A), measuring 7.5m by 12m, which was opened in 1997, and worked on during our summer seasons until 2000. Unlike the eastern half of West Hall Paddock, which had been used for tipping and waste disposal, the land uncovered in Area A had been raised and levelled using iron-rich sand and some deposits of soil. This levelling may well have taken place in the Late Anglo-Saxon period, and certainly occurred at some point in the Saxo-Norman period, at the time the settlement focus was shifting from south to north of the river.

The mammoth task of backfilling and levelling the land would have taken time, resources and command of labour. The use of an iron-rich sand which bonds to form a hard, concreted surface indicates an important building. Indeed, this iron-rich sand is still used in the local construction and landscaping industry to create a hard-standing on which to build (Janet Hammond and Tim Snelling, pers. comm.).

Table 8.1: Table giving dimensions of known Late Anglo-Saxon churches.

Excavated Buildings		
Site	Length	Width
Raunds Furnells	5.5m	4.4m
Cheddar, Somerset	*c.* 7.0m	*c.* 5.0m
Wharram Percy	*c.* 8.5m	*c.* 6.0m
Rivenhall, Essex	*c.* 9.0m	*c.* 4.5m
Norwich Castle	*c.* 10.0m	*c.* 5.0m
Thetford, Norfolk	*c.* 11.2m	*c.* 5.0m
Flixborough, Lincs	*c.* 14.0m	*c.* 7.0m
Barton-on-Humber	*c.* 18.0m	*c.* 7.0m

Extant Buildings			
Site	Length	Width	Height (if known)
Escomb, County Durham	7.0m	5.56m	
Bradford-on-Avon	7.5m	4.05m	7.5m

The nearest possible source for this sand is a seam of carstone roughly a kilometre from the site, where a possible small quarry has been identified. Otherwise the nearest source of carstone is near Snettisham, nearly three kilometres away (Janet Hammond, pers. comm.). Only a wealthy and influential member of the community could have organised the quarrying, transportation and spreading of material that seems to be implied.

The hard-standing obviously supported a structure, but the limits of

Plate 8.2: Work in progress on the Area A excavation in West Hall Paddock between 1997 and 2000.

excavation, heavy truncation of features and later activity meant that its form could not be determined. The main evidence for a structure was a mortar and flint layer placed directly on the hard-standing, thus most likely a floor. No evidence of earth-fast walls or of any wall foundations was seen, but a spread of medium- to large-sized flint was recorded within surrounding layers, appearing to radiate out from the mortar and flint floor.

The flint spread may represent the disturbed remains of walls or, alternatively, the building could have been of non-earth-fast sleeper beam construction, which would have left little or no archaeological signature. A potential parallel can be seen at Flixborough, where the whole of Building 1A had a gravel foundation, believed to have carried a structure based on wooden sills and supported by postholes (Loveluck and Atkinson 2007, 47).

As only a small portion of the eastern side of the building was uncovered, we cannot exclude the possibility of earth-fast postholes at the corners of the structure, or indeed in the remainder of the building as a whole. Indeed, two postholes were recorded within the structure, though their function was not understood.

We can, however, be more certain of the religious nature of the building. Our excavation revealed two grave cuts dug through the mortar and flint

Fig. 8.3: Reconstruction of West Hall Chapel as a simple, single-cell structure.

floor, with a third just visible, but lying mostly beyond the limits of excavation. Having a west-east orientation, the three grave cuts were arranged regularly along, and at right angles to, the structure's eastern edge. Interior burials such as these must indicate a religious or funerary function for the building, particularly as their alignment strongly suggests that the people interred here were Christian.

A skeleton recovered from one of the graves (see Box 8.2) produced a radiocarbon age of between 1010 and 1180 (cal. 95% probability). The church/chapel can thus be given an 11th or 12th century date – a date which would place its construction towards the end of the burst of 10th/11th century church-building prompted by the emergence of a thegnly class (Gem 1988). During this period local lords were beginning to establish small churches at their manorial centres; indeed, possession of a chapel became one of the conditions for acquiring thegnly status. In part this was simply a matter of providing a permanent local religious focus – as opposed to remaining dependent on a distant minster church and its peripatetic canons. But churches were also status symbols and sources of income for the emerging class of manorial lords.

In Sedgeford's case, the emergence of an Anglo-Scandinavian elite under the authority of the Danelaw in the late 9th century AD may have been responsible for the settlement changes imprinted on the archaeological record, including both the foundation of the manorial centres at West Hall and the establishment of a chapel or church. Alternatively, the Anglo-Saxon Reconquest of the early 10th century AD might provide a context, or even the Danish Conquest of the early 11th. In any of these cases, we may have unrecorded changes of ownership and an incoming elite keen to make its mark on the landscape; and our dating is not tight enough to say which of these occasions is the most likely.

Although the Area A excavations did not determine the full size of the structure, revealing only its eastern edge, it may have been around 7.5m by 5m. A test-pit dug to the west of Area A in Ladywell Field (Trench 5) revealed no structural evidence in this direction, thus limiting the church/chapel's length to less than 8m (a size paralleled by some other known Late Anglo-Saxon ecclesiastical structures).

We can also estimate the width of the building. The three graves were regularly spaced, being 0.8m and 0.9m apart, whilst the width of the cuts themselves varied between 0.64m and 0.83m, giving a total width of around 4.5 to 5 metres. This is a standard width in known Late Anglo-Saxon churches. Besides, any further unobserved burials associated with the building would have given it a square shape, a very unusual form for the period. Thus we can be reasonably confident that the chapel contained just the three graves.

The plan and superstructure of the building remain unknown. The comparative examples range from the single-celled, rubble-built structure excavated at Raunds Furnells, through the two-celled timber building at Rivenhall, to the three-celled 'turriform' masonry church of St Peter at Barton-on-Humber (Boddington 1996; Platt 1994; Waldron 2007). The size of the West Hall church/chapel would, though, indicate a simpler form. The fact that our structure contained burials would not preclude a small, simple building (our reconstruction shows it as a single cell structure, Fig. 8.3). Although intramural burial was usually the province of the higher secular and ecclesiastical aristocracy in the Late Anglo-Saxon period, the recent excavation of smaller early churches has shown that lesser nobles were also being interred inside them (Gilchrist 2009).

A good example of this can be found at Flixborough, where three adults and an infant were buried along the inside edges of Building 1A – unusually, two adults and an infant in the western cell and a single adult in the eastern cell. Only two external burials were found associated with this building, so it has been interpreted as a mortuary chapel for a single family (Loveluck and Atkinson 2007, 51). We may have at Sedgeford a similar two-celled structure, with the chancel containing the remains of the elite local family and founders.

Only two of the possible three grave-cuts were excavated at West Hall Paddock: the third lay mostly beyond the excavation area. The first grave contained the remains of a female aged between 30 and 35 years, whose skeleton was extremely deformed (see Box 8.2). In general 'disadvantaged individuals' gravitated towards larger towns and cities to try to support themselves by begging. Norwich has yielded clusters of burials of deformed people, for instance at St Michael-at-Thorn and at St Margaret's Church (Waldron 2007). Moreover, skeletons showing evidence of physical disability sometimes appear to have been treated with less respect than those of able-bodied members of the population (Hadley and Buckberry 2007; Boddington 1996, 69).

Why, then, was this particular disabled woman – dubbed 'Red Rose' by the excavators – living in Sedgeford, and why was she buried in what we must assume was an estate church or chapel? One possibility is that she was living a religious life, though there is no archaeological or documentary evidence to support this. Her careful Christian burial within the church shows that she was greatly respected and was certainly not treated any differently because of her deformities. On the contrary, the burial of this woman within the manorial church/chapel, especially at a time when intramural burial was rare, may well imply that she belonged to the class of thegns (Anglo-Saxon knights), who likely formed the village elite at this time.

The second grave contained no articulated skeletal remains, but rather an assemblage of 23 fragmentary and complete disarticulated human bones, recovered from the grave fill. This collection has been shown to contain the remains of at least two individuals, an older adult and a juvenile, and is also likely to include the disarticulated human remains of other individuals from surrounding contexts. The dark, almost black colour of some of the adult bones is comparable with that of the bones of Red Rose, so it can be inferred that they come from similar depositional environments. Thus, these darker bones likely originate from the second grave and probably represent all that remains of the interment. It thus appears that the original occupant of the grave was deliberately removed long enough after burial for the body to have decomposed. The redundancy of the West Hall church/chapel is probably the reason this individual was removed from its grave.

Although information is sparse for the Anglo-Saxon period, documentary evidence for the Medieval period shows that re-interment was not uncommon for individuals of high status, for both religious and political reasons (Daniell 1997). Bartlett cites several incidences of re-interment of highly respected individuals from graveyard to church, to a more prestigious part of the church,

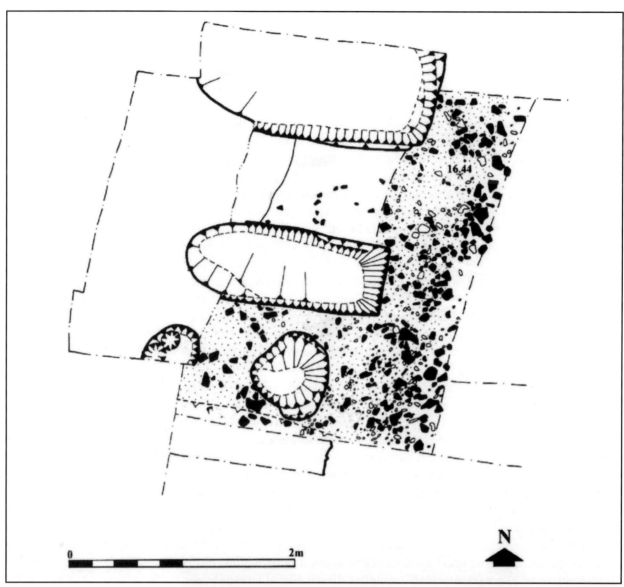

Fig. 8.4 Plan showing grave cuts and post pits in the Chapel.

Plate: 8.3 Red Rose grave cut fully excavated and the large interior post pit.

or even due to the rebuilding of a church, as with Archbishop Lanfranc for example (Bartlett 2000).

This, of course, raises the question: 'Why was the deformed woman (Red Rose) not also removed at the same time?' One possibility is that she was not of such elevated status. Perhaps she was the mother, sister, or daughter of a thegn; perhaps she was the founder of the church/chapel.

The building itself looks to have been deliberately removed. There is no evidence of a naturally collapsed structure, no deposits suggesting rotted wood beams, posts, or thatch. Flint that possibly came from the structure appears to have been spread around the former building, and the larger of the two postholes recorded inside the structure appears to have had its post completely removed. This removal may account for the comparatively large size of the hole for an internal post – this having been enlarged as the post was wrenched free – and the amount of mortar in the fill – evidence, perhaps, of contemporary demolition work. All of the evidence, such as we have it, points to a systematic dismantling of the building and its contents.

The abandonment of the church/chapel probably resulted from the need for a larger and more impressive church that could serve the needs of a wider and perhaps growing community. Platt maintains that such upgrading and rebuilding of churches was not uncommon by the late 10th century, and Gem recognises a 'Great Rebuilding' of churches in the second half of the 11th century (Platt 1994; Gem 1988). Platt also highlights the fact that rebuilding often occurred after a change in ownership from a secular to an ecclesiastical body.

Prior to the Conquest, Gyrth Godwinson, Earl of East Anglia and brother to King Harold, held the manorial lands of Sedgeford. (We do not know, however, for how long he, or one of his men, managed the estate before the Conquest. Was there a previous ecclesiastical owner?). At the Conquest, Earl Gyrth's lands fell to the Bishop of Elmham, Æthelmær (Ælmer), and remained in the hands of his successors (later the Bishops of Thetford, following the transfer of the episcopal seat) until Herbert de Losinga, the first Bishop of Norwich, gained the land and its church in the late 11th or early 12th century.

Whether Losinga was responsible for the building of a significantly improved parish church in Sedgeford is impossible to say. Richard Hoggett's analysis of the standing fabric clearly implies a much later date for the impressive church of St. Mary the Virgin we see today (see Chapter 7 above). However, Losinga was certainly responsible for a spate of church building during his episcopate. What is more certain is that he is unlikely to have been responsible for the removal of the body from the chapel. The Anglo-Saxon aristocracy was comprehensively dispossessed after the Conquest, and the common people of England came to think of themselves as living under 'the Norman yoke'. Norman appropriation of the landscape must have militated strongly against any honouring of former Anglo-Saxon lords.

This adds weight to the possibility of a 'missing' church post-dating the original church/chapel where Red Rose was laid to rest, but pre-dating the present stone-built structure. In general, when churches were rebuilt in the Saxo-Norman period, the original site was reused. At Sedgeford, however, the estate church/chapel was probably replaced by a building sited almost 40m to the north-east. Such a site, higher up the valley side, on a chalk outcrop,

Box 8.2
'Red Rose'

During the 1999 season a most unexpected find was made in West Hall Paddock, south of the Church. Three grave-cuts were located under a western boundary path of Medieval date within a layer of hard-standing that appears to have once supported the floor of a small structure. Remarkably, one grave was completely preserved, and the occupant was identified as a young to middle-aged woman.

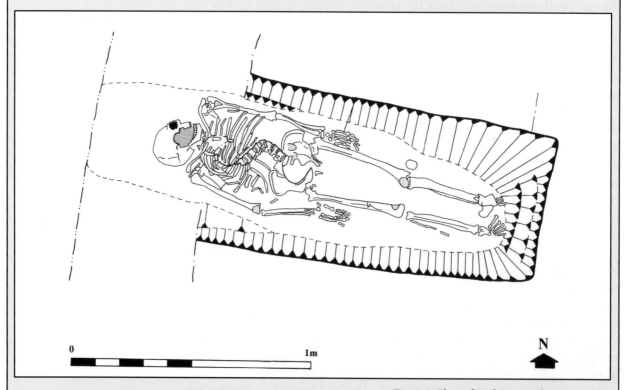

0   1m   N

Fig. 8.5: Plan of Red Rose in her grave cut.

She was almost immediately dubbed 'Red Rose': 'red' because of the iron-staining that had leached into her bones from the surrounding soil, and 'Rose' for a prominent member of the family that was known to have had a Medieval manor house close by. Radiocarbon dating indicates that her death probably occurred in the 11th century AD.

Although the skeleton appeared to be complete, aside from some crushing damage to the right side of the face, the bone was seen to be very friable. For that reason a large amount of recording was undertaken at the graveside, in case information was lost during and after the excavation of the skeleton.

The most remarkable feature of the skeleton was immediately apparent: the woman had suffered a significant physical deformity, namely gross curvature of the spine – scoliosis. The plan and photo from the excavation show it clearly: the marked curvature of the thoracic spine to the right, and the compensatory curve of the lumbar spine to the left. The placement of the ribs also shows that the right lung would have been compressed and possibly non-functional; the left lung, however, would probably have been enlarged to compensate, and the heart would have been relatively unaffected.

Post-excavation study of the skeleton indicates that the spinal curvature was likely not a congenital defect, but may have developed as a response to another problem that was. The right hip appears to have been malformed, with a tilted pelvis – again evident in the plans and photos. Measurement of the bones of the left and right leg show the latter to have been significantly less robust, suggesting bone underdevelopment as a result of disuse. In addition the tarsal (ankle) bones of the right foot seem to have been fused in an abnormal arrangement, which may have been a clubfoot (talipes equinovarus).

Research into the causes of scoliosis suggests that Red Rose's spinal deformity is actually a secondary development from her congenital hip and leg malformation, and that in all likelihood her spine was normal at birth. She may, in fact, have been born with a congenitally dislocated right hip, a common enough finding in modern infants, such that all babies in developed countries are routinely screened to allow immediate corrective management.

Plate 8.4: Red Rose fully revealed by excavation.

During her infancy there would have been no barriers to her normal development. However, once she began to crawl, and later to walk, the unstable right hip joint would have discouraged her from placing much weight on it, resulting in less robust bone development. Even today, untreated hip dislocation will result in deformation of the hip joint with stiffness, and usually shortening, of the affected leg.

The most likely explanation for Red Rose's scoliosis, therefore, is that it began to form after she started walking. Her uneven leg length would have tilted her pelvis and placed her upper body at an angle, but as the natural instinct is to keep the head and eyes horizontal, she would have unconsciously twisted her upper spine in order to straighten her shoulders. The resulting imbalance of muscles would have begun to pull her spine out of its vertical alignment: as the muscles and ligaments became stronger on one side, the effect would have accelerated, until it stabilised in adolescence as her skeleton matured.

The implications for Red Rose's quality of life are, of course, significant. The scoliosis is evidence that she was mobile, but with her shortened right leg she likely walked with a pronounced limp and may have used a crutch. Presumably she would not have been able to perform any physically demanding occupation. She should, however, have had equal capability in any sedentary occupation with able-bodied people, and in a Medieval community, for a woman in particular, these would have been many.

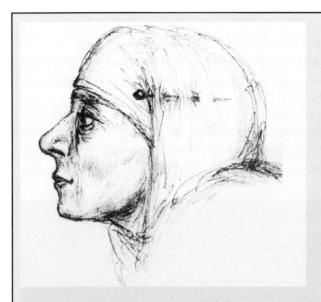 

Fig. 8.6: Reconstruction of Red Rose

The abnormalities in her lung size and capacity may have made her prone to respiratory diseases. The condition of her bones – aside from responses to congenital problems and the effect of taphonomic conditions – is quite good, and there is no sign of malnutrition, so it must be assumed that Red Rose was either able to care for herself, or had someone to provide adequate care for her, from earliest childhood. The implication is that there were no barriers to her acceptance into the Medieval village community despite her physical disabilities, and she was therefore able to live relatively normally until her death, probably aged between 30 and 35 years.

During the 2000 excavation season, a simple ceremony was held to reinter the remains of Skeleton S5001, and a red rose bush was planted over the site. The opportunity to study the individual we knew as 'Red Rose' gave us a valuable insight into the health and life of a woman with a disability in Medieval Sedgeford.

Plate 8.5: Detail of Red Rose's skull and curved spine

would have been more suited to a larger structure, whether of timber or stone, and may have allowed easier access for the wider community. In contrast, the church/chapel in West Hall Paddock lay on low-lying, previously marshy and largely reclaimed land – not ideal for building a large structure or for symbolising wealth and status. Presumably, then, the slight movement of the religious focus of the settlement was down to the ambition to build a larger church and the practical matter of finding a more stable site.

Eventually, by the 13th century, ownership of the manorial lands of Sedgeford passed from the Bishop to Norwich Cathedral Priory, and Sedgeford became one of the Priory's main assets during the High Medieval period. This would provide a context for the wholesale church rebuilding that may be represented by the whole of the standing fabric we can now see.

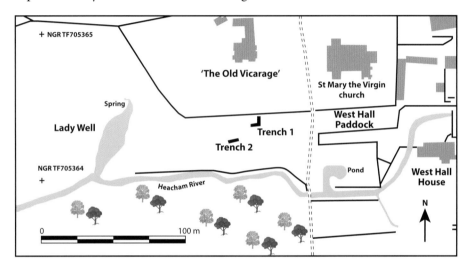

Fig. 8.7: Location of 2002 excavation trenches in Ladywell Field.

Manors and moats

After the dismantling of the church/chapel in West Hall Paddock, activity resumed in the 12th or 13th century, and most intensively at the western end of the site. Here a new boundary wall of chalk was erected, running from the edge of the churchyard (at least) southwards towards the river. Peter Carnell's 1997 geophysical survey, moreover, appears to map the remains of this wall continuing from West Hall Paddock all the way to the river. Thetford-type Ware and six fragments of unglazed Grimston-type Ware, recovered from within the fabric of the wall, provide the dating evidence for its construction.

By the Norman period some historical documentation is available for Sedgeford, and we can track the changing ownership of ecclesiastical and manorial lands in the parish. This allows us to speculate about the historical context for activity represented in the archaeological record.

Since the Conquest, let us recall, the major landowners were, successively, the Bishops of Elmham, Thetford and Norwich. These lands consisted of one major manor, an outlier at Fring, and several other unidentified outliers.

From 1066 William Bellofago (Beaufeu) owned a further, minor manor in Sedgeford, and it is thought that both manors were amalgamated at around 1086, after William became the Bishop of Thetford and consequently gained control of all of Sedgeford's manorial lands. By the 1100s these amalgamated manors were held by Herbert de Losinga, along with the manor of Gnatingdon (in the eastern part of Sedgeford parish and later known as East Hall); the latter he gave to Norwich Cathedral Priory (Hammond 1984).

By the mid 12th century Bishop William Turbe held the amalgamated manor, and some time before 1166 had divided off two small manors from the main manorial lands, whilst leasing the main manor to Norwich Cathedral Priory (Janet Hammond, pers. comm.). Both of the new small manors were of

Fig. 8.8: Plan of the walls in Trench 1 presumed to belong to the de Sechefords' manorial complex in Ladywell Field, as revealed by excavation in 2002.

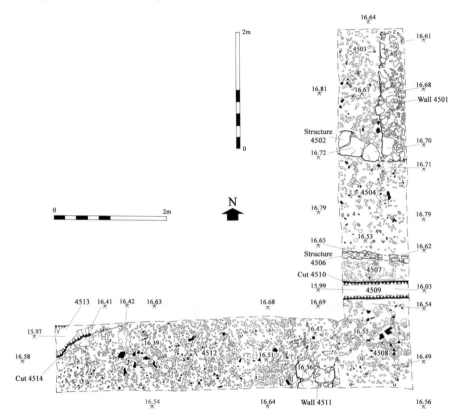

a half-knight's fee. One became known as Sedgeford's Manor, held by William de Secheford, and the other as Bradestone's Manor, which later became Caston's Manor (Janet Hammond, pers. comm.).

Finally, on 2 June 1205, John de Gray, the fifth Bishop of Norwich, granted the Church of St Mary the Virgin and the full rights to the manorial lands of Sedgeford to Norwich Cathedral Priory. The lands were to continue in Church hands until the 19th century.

The boundary wall seen in the excavations may, then, have been built to formalise the division of land when Sedgeford's Manor was created. Several historic maps and documents label the land immediately to the west of the Paddock as 'Sedgefords', and it is likely that the land was part of the manor awarded by Bishop Turbe to the de Secheford family in the mid-12th century.

An entry in a 'field book' for Sedgeford dated 1546 implies that the de Sechefords built a house and associated buildings on the land, and this is supported by the results of a landscape and geophysical survey of Ladywell Field, and by evaluation excavations undertaken on the site in 2002 (NRO LEST/IB 83).

Alternatively, the creation of the boundary may reflect either the

Fig. 8.9: Plan of the Medieval boundary wall and metalled track revealed in Area A, West Hall Paddock, 1997-2000.

Fig. 8.10: Results of the electrical resistivity survey of Ladywell Field undertaken by Peter Snelling in 2002.

consolidation and reorganisation of the manorial lands under the administration of Norwich Cathedral Priory, or a slightly later decision to invest in the improvement and development of the manor. Although no remains of the Priory's manor buildings have been found, the 13th century saw similar improvements being made by the Priory in its associated church of St Mary the Virgin (see Chapter 7).

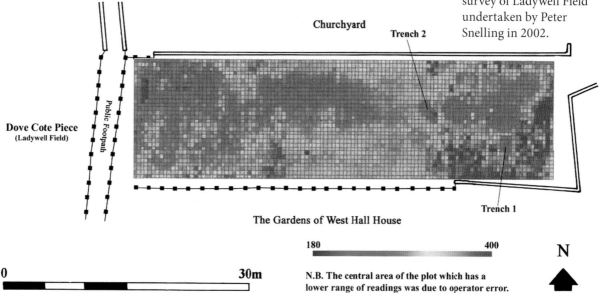
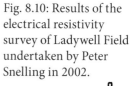

Plate 8.6: An excavated
wall of the de Sechefords'
manor in the Ladywell Field
excavations.

Plate 8.7: 'Church Lane' –
this track, running down
one side of a boundary wall
and connecting a footbridge
over the River Heacham
with St Mary the Virgin
Church, is referenced in
a 16th century field book,
and also appears on a 17th
century estate map.

Bailiffs' accounts survive for the period 1255 to 1352 and a reference in the 1255 account roll notes the '... constructing 15 perches of stone walling towards the church ... coping the wall' (quoted in Carnell 1998). Coping may indicate prestige display, but it is likely to have had a practical function, particularly if porous material like chalk was used, as was the case here. Indeed, several accounts from 13th century Sedgeford refer to the coping of walls with ridge-tiles or coping-stones (NRO DCN 60/33/3).

Contemporary with the wall, a metalled pathway was laid down following the line of the wall from the river to the Church. This pathway provided a route from the southern side of the river to the Church, over a crossing point which is still spanned by a small wooden footbridge today. In fact, the 1546 field book refers to this path as 'Church Lane', a name also used for the continuation of the path south of the river on the 1631 Le Strange estate map (NRO LEST/OC 1)

As the wall and pathway appear contemporary, it is likely that the Priory created the pathway to enable worshippers living on the south side of the river and in the nearby hamlet of Eaton to get to church. The boundary, established with this wall, appears to remain intact until the 17th century. In various guises it appears as wall and path, then wall and ditch, then fence and path and finally as a path with a new wall.

That second phase, however, when a large and deep ditch was dug in line with, and to the west of, the chalk wall, involved the destruction of the pathway. The ditch respects the line of the wall and provides an embellishment to this existing boundary, flanking the wall for its entire length until it empties into the river. Yaxley's work on the documents of the Priory Manor has shown that

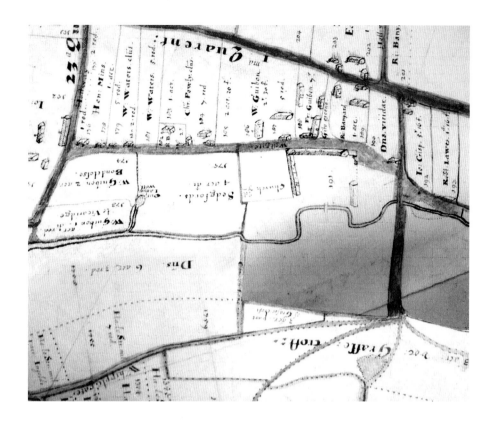

Plate 8.8: West Hall in 1631. Extract from the 1631 Le Strange Estate Map showing the core of the village – a composite of two adjoining portions. The map is here oriented to the north.

Plate 8.9: West Hall in 1736. Extracts from Church Commissioners Map (taken from the 1736 Le Strange Sedgeford Map Book) – a composite of two maps detailing adjoining land north and south of the river. The map is here oriented to the north..

206

Plate 8.10: West Hall in 1797. Extract from a 1926 copy, traced by T. H. Gordon Wright, Surveyor, Norwich, of the 1797 Inclosure Map of Sedgeford.

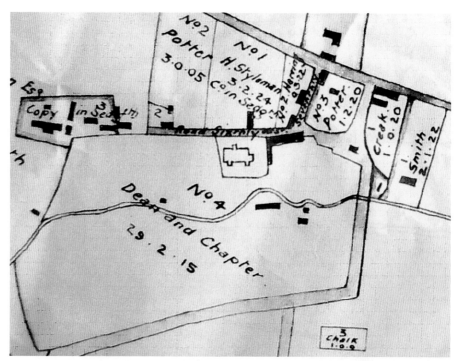

it was moated into two courts, an east and west court. There was '... a thatched wall inside the moat...', and we can safely assume that our wall and ditch was part of this moated complex (Yaxley 1988).

The accepted site of the manor's buildings is to the immediate south-east of the Paddock where West Hall house now stands, a building dated to the later 16th or early 17th century (Fogarty 2001). Although no archaeological evidence of the Medieval manorial buildings has been found, the bailiffs' accounts paint a typical picture of the range of buildings that would have formed the Medieval manor complex.

The earlier Ordnance Survey sheets show the western arm of this east court

Plate 8.11: West Hall in 1840. Extract from the 1840 Tithe Map.

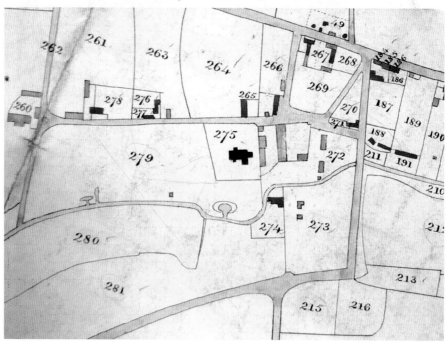

continuing southwards beyond the main course of the river and turning east to form the southern arm of the moat. Today this portion of the moat only survives as a damp and silted ditch and is indicated on the current Ordnance Survey map simply as a drain.

Geophysical survey results of the area to the east of this 'drain' clearly show this southern arm of the moat continuing to the east and spanned by a causeway giving access to the enclosure. The eastern arm of the moat, however, is no longer visible, and extensive garden landscaping in recent years is likely to have removed any trace of Medieval features.

The west court is sited slightly further north than the east court containing the manor house, though the river flowing south at this point forms the shared arm of the two courts. The river then turns westwards to form the southern arm of the west court, before bending sharply to the north just beyond the modern footbridge, at the point where the boundary wall recorded in the Paddock would have terminated on reaching the river. The ditch dug to the west of the wall would also have joined the river here to form the western arm of the moat surrounding the west court. It is unlikely that the west court had a northern arm as the land rises steeply upwards to St Mary's Church, and its churchyard bounds the northern side of the second court.

During the era of the moated manor at Sedgeford, and throughout the rest of the Medieval period, the remainder of the study area appears to be devoid of significant activity. Both Area B and the 1996 evaluation test-pits revealed only occupation layers containing general domestic waste, probably manuring spreads, and no other features. The implication is that the west court of the manor complex was primarily used to supply the immediate needs of the manor house, such as for fruit and vegetables.

Yaxley's study of the bailiffs' accounts tells us that one of the courts produced a whole range of fruits and vegetables, and he notes that an ash-grove was sited in one of the courts, and that there was also a 'herbage' (1988, 21-22). The manor house and some of its associated outbuildings must have stood in the east court, where West Hall now sits, contra Yaxley's view.

A double-moated manor house is not rare – Madingley in Cambridgeshire, Hales in South Norfolk and Chanons Hall at Tibenham in Norfolk, all have double moats. But the story of Sedgeford's moats grows, and becomes more complicated.

The Lady Well

Resistivity surveys in Ladywell Field revealed an area of high resistance that we interpreted as a building platform, whilst to the west of this platform a long linear area of low resistance ran down towards the river (Fig. 8.10). This appeared to be a wide ditch or moat flanking the building platform, indicating the possibility of another moated manor complex.

If this was such, then the river would have formed another southern arm of moating. The river flows westward in a straight line from the Priory Manor until adjacent to its junction with this north-south ditch or moat identified in the geophysical survey. Here there is a kink, or double right-angled bend, before it resumes its straight course westwards, until it is joined by the waters of the Lady Well itself, which forms the western arm of the further moated court.

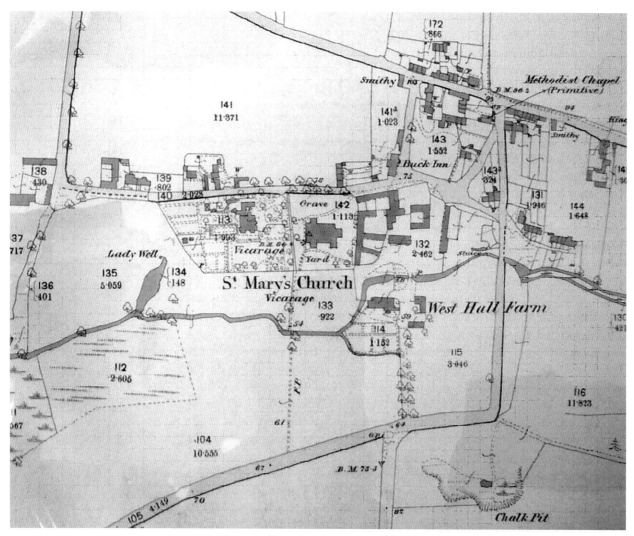

Plate 8.12: West Hall in 1886. Extract from the 1886 25-inch FirstEdition Ordnance Survey Map.

At the south-western corner of the area surveyed the course of the river curves into the Lady Well, which extends northwards, cutting deeply into the chalk outcrop of the valley side.

Originally the Lady Well was probably a small natural spring-channel, ideal for enlarging into a wide, north-south aligned moat fed by several plentiful springs.

The name of the feature implies ancient religious significance. The dedication of the adjacent Medieval Church – to St Mary the Virgin – reinforces this. The current form of the Lady Well, however – a wide, deep, linear cut into the chalk bedrock of the valley side – is undoubtedly a deliberate, man-made feature. It has been further modified since by cleaning over the years; the current owners have themselves dredged it (Janet Hammond and Tim Snelling, pers. comm.).

The eastern arm of the easterly court is likely to have been shared with the Priory Manor, and both this and the central arm would have terminated where the chalk outcrop rises up to form the valley side, in a similar fashion to the Lady Well channel.

Ladywell Field, then, has revealed a double, open-sided, E-shaped, moated site. The builders used the chosen location of the moated complex to their great

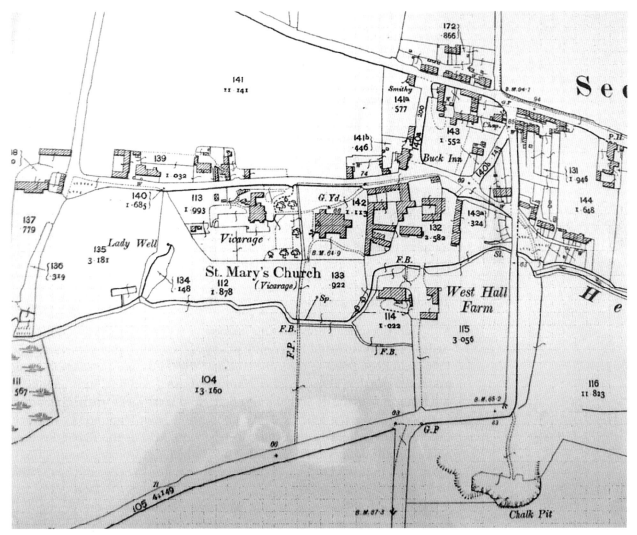

Plate 8.13: West Hall in 1905. Extract from the 1905 25-inch Second Edition Ordnance Survey Map.

advantage. They modified and incorporated the river for the long axis and dug two north-south arms (the third being part of the Priory Manor complex), cutting into the chalk outcrop of the valley side, leaving the northern side of the complex unenclosed, but utilising the steep valley side as a natural boundary.

The numerous springs were also used to their best advantage, as Lady Well was incorporated into the moat system and the other north-south arms were almost certainly fed by their own springs. Moreover, the low-lying site was an advantage, because at between 15m and 16m above Ordnance Datum (OD: sea-level) the builders could rely on groundwater to help fill the moat.

Indeed, most moated sites in Norfolk were built on the poorly draining clay lands towards the centre and south, while few moats were built in drier, well-draining areas like north-west Norfolk. Consequently, landowners wishing to construct a moated site here needed to take advantage of groundwater, and all of the known sites within a 10km radius of the study area are sited below 25m above OD between the coastal flats and the chalk scarp of West Norfolk. Shernborne Hall, for example, lies directly south of Sedgeford at about 25m above OD, while the three separate moated sites in Dersingham lie between 6m and 15m above OD.

The open-sided character of the Ladywell Field complex is quite rare but not unknown. Many moated sites only survive as a two- or three-sided earthwork, but some were originally constructed in this way. Attlebridge Hall in Norfolk (NHER 7751) was identified in 1978 as the site of a possible three-sided moat, whilst it has been shown that Gamlingay in Cambridgeshire was originally dug with only three sides. Taylor maintains that such sites may have been designed like this to save money or may simply have been left unfinished (Taylor 1978, 8). In the case of Sedgeford, however, the character of the moats was almost certainly determined by the siting.

It is thus possible that we are looking at a unique quadruple-moated site, but it is much more likely that we have adjacent double-moated manors, likely sharing one moated arm as the boundary between the two complexes. It certainly seems more plausible that the western pair of moats forms a separate complex reflecting the separation of the half-knight's fee manor awarded by Bishop Turbe to the de Secheford family.

The de Secheford manor

Although documentation for this manor is sparse, the site is labelled as 'Sedgefordyard' on a mid 16th century copy of the 1490 Rental Survey, and the 1546 Field Book refers to the same land as 'Sedgefords one messuage in times past built' (Yaxley 1998, 21; Janet Hammond, pers. comm.). Such references can relate only to the de Secheford/de Sedgeford family who are first recorded in the village during 1107/1108. We know from Janet Hammond's research into the Proceedings in the Court of Chancery held at the Public Records Office that the de Sedgeford family had accumulated reasonable landholdings, including a mill, dovecotes, outbuildings and a house in Sedgeford by the mid 15th century (pers. comm).

Both the trenches dug on the platform examined by the geophysical survey as noted above revealed evidence of structures (Fig. 8.7). Although the trenches were too small to permit the reconstruction of building plans, there was sufficient quantity and quality of evidence to support the contention that this was indeed the site of a manor complex, and therefore the likely home manor of the de Secheford family.

Dating of the Medieval deposits was necessarily broad as few diagnostic pieces of pottery were recovered to give more specific dates within the general 12th to 15th century period attributed to Grimston-type Ware. Nonetheless, evidence for at least four Medieval stone-built structures was uncovered, along with a curbed surface and other associated deposits.

Trench 1 in Ladywell Field yielded a sequence of three phases of building, the earliest of which was an east-west aligned chalk wall preserved to at least four courses high (Fig. 8.8). This wall remains undated but appears to have been early, since it is overlain by quite a depth of accumulated waste, above which was a layer of cockle and mussel shell with a pottery date of 13th to 14th century. A second, north-south chalk wall had been constructed immediately on top of this. These chalk walls are spatially and temporally unrelated, and because only a small section of each wall was uncovered, no other structural relationships could be established.

The final structural phase of Medieval activity unearthed in Trench 1 is more easily interpreted. It consists of an 11th to 14th century chalk surface with a curb along its northern edge, running parallel to, and contemporary with, the south-eastern corner of a building constructed of chalk. The southern return of the chalk building was assembled with large flat chalk slabs and was faced only on its south side. It looks, therefore, like a threshold into the south-east corner of a building, which opens out southwards onto a curbed chalk yard.

Only one wall was revealed in Trench 2 (Plate 8.6), but its history and scale seem more remarkable than any of those found in Trench 1. Again primarily constructed of chalk, the wall was preserved to between five and eight courses, and a foundation cut for its construction was identified. An extra, faced, structure of chalk had been built against and keyed into its eastern face. Butting this was a naturally accumulated deposit and a dump of domestic debris and heat-affected daub. The domestic debris included unabraded fragments of 13th to 16th century decorated glazed Grimston-type Ware. The western face of the wall was butted by undated, naturally accumulated deposits.

The presence of a foundation cut and the size of the wall indicate a substantial structure. The addition of chalk facing to the east would have widened and strengthened the wall, increasing its load-bearing capacity. The wall may have been part of a large building that developed over time, possibly with the addition of an upper storey. Certainly this wall differs in form and construction from the other walls discovered on site, which are slimmer, built directly onto the ground surface, and are best interpreted as boundaries. The limits of excavation precluded, however, the revelation of any floors or living surfaces suggestive of internal space east of the wall.

Chalk is the most common building material in the walls recorded at both Ladywell Field and West Hall Paddock. Chalk can be seen used in conjunction with flint, carstone and brick in the construction of buildings throughout north-west Norfolk. Yet the soft, soluble nature of chalk, even in the case of the harder variety known as 'clunch', makes it inferior to other harder-wearing materials. Certainly there are none of the expensively imported limestones found in the adjacent church, and little use of the flint or carstone found more locally.

All this suggests that, despite the scale of the Ladywell Field moated courts, the buildings inside were erected with a tight hand on the purse-strings. Indeed, the superstructure may well have been timber-framed. This would certainly fit with the status and resources of a lesser landowning family such as the de Sechefords.

The Priory Manor

No evidence has been found for any of the neighbouring Priory manor buildings. Probably none ever will be: if anything survives, it is likely to lie beneath the present West Hall. But it is quite possible that it, too, was constructed in a similar form to the de Sechefords'. A religious organisation may well have spent more on its church than its manor, particularly if it was occupied by a local steward and only visited by a Priory cleric occasionally. Dyer tells us that the custom of feeding harvest workers *ad mensam* (at the lord's table) may explain why estates maintained manor houses rarely visited by their owners (Dyer 2000, 86-87). No need to expend large sums on what was primarily a producer estate, however valuable.

Why and when the Priory decided to moat its manor at Sedgeford is unclear. No precise dating evidence was found during excavations in the Paddock, nor is there a record of the initial digging of the moat in the bailiffs' accounts for the Priory Manor, which date to between 1255 and 1352. There are, however, several references in the accounts to the cleaning of moats and ditches, whilst the 1299/1300 accounts describe the moat of the east court as being 20ft wide (Yaxley 1988, 21; Janet Hammond, pers. comm).

A moat may even have been dug by 1265 to 1266, when 8d was paid 'for cleaning out the ditches' (NRO DCN 60/33/3). If this earlier date was proven to refer to the moat ditches, it would put the moating of the Priory Manor back to the turbulent reign of Henry III (1207-1272). The only one of the four moated courts that is fully enclosed is the one that now surrounds West Hall House. It may be that this predates any of the others, with the second Priory moat perhaps predating those of the de Sechefords.

The moats may, therefore, have had a defensive function to begin with, given the violent nature of the period. Certainly, during the Barons' Revolt of 1264-1267, Roger Bigod, the Earl of Norfolk, was a principal supporter of the rebels under Simon de Montfort, whereas the Bishop of Norfolk, Simon de Walton, remained a staunch royalist (Maddicott 1995, 186-7). This would surely have made Sedgeford a target for de Montfort's supporters.

On the other hand, this was the era of the moated manor house, and certainly the impression of wealth and power such complexes exude would have played its part in decisions made to construct them. And once the Priory had moated its manor, it is quite likely that the de Secheford's would have felt obliged to follow suit to maintain status. Moats also served an economic function as breeding grounds for fish; trout can still occasionally be seen in the much reduced waters of the River Heacham at Sedgeford.

There was probably close co-operation between the two manors. Certainly this would have been necessary if they in fact shared the central moated arm. A close working relationship does in fact appear to be the case. During the 13th century members of the de Secheford family exchanged several pieces of land with the Priory, whilst Albin de Stanford, a member of the de Secheford family, signed charters across the county as a steward of the Priory (Griffiths 1985). Moating the manors would also have benefitted both owners by helping to drain the low-lying lands on which their respective manors stood.

Parts of the moated system, at least the western arm of the western Priory court, eventually went out of use. This arm was filled in with the demolished remains of the chalk wall found in the Paddock – though no precise dating evidence for this event was found during excavation. A fence, probably of wattle, replaced this boundary.

Why the moated system, with its interior curtain wall, became redundant is uncertain, but it shows that the need for such an impressive and defensive boundary had passed. From the mid 14th to 15th centuries, few new moated sites were constructed and those already in use were being modified by the needs of the moment (Yaxley 1988, 21-22). Certainly by this period the political situation was more stable and the need for defence gone. There is also evidence that the Priory estate was declining, its Sedgeford landholding having fallen from its pre-Black Death 400 acres to barely half that by 1424 (Dyer 2000, 82). On the other hand, the character of elite status display was changing in this period. It now depended less on mimicking the style of the local warrior-knight and more on following courtly fashion in clothes, furniture, wall-hangings and haute cuisine.

Inevitably, the fence also fell into disrepair and was either left to rot or was snapped off at ground-level. Even so, at some point during this period of neglect the pathway to the church was reinstated. It ran along the line of the earlier timber fence and was laid over the top of its remains. Four phases of this well-used pathway were observed, showing that aspects of the manorial complex were certainly being maintained. It might well have been the case that the boundary, in whatever form, was reinstated on the western side of the path beyond the limits of excavation.

A single estate

The archaeological record implies a restoration in the fortunes for the Priory Manor by the 15th century. A chalk wall, similar to the first, was built along the western edge of the path, enclosing the path within the manor grounds. The northern part of the wall was constructed upon a hard-standing of demolition debris. The debris included mortar, painted wall plaster, medieval roof tile, roofing lead and a piece of twisted Grimston-type jug handle that can be securely dated to the 15th century or later.

A boundary can be seen on the 1631 Le Strange Estate Map, and this may indicate that the wall was still upstanding at this time and ran from the river to the churchyard. The erection of the new boundary wall and the evidence for the demolition and/or alterations to a prominent high-status building elsewhere on the estate seems to indicate a resurgence of activity and therefore perhaps an improvement in fortunes.

Conversely, dating evidence and the stratigraphic sequence recorded during the evaluation of Ladywell Field shows that the de Secheford manor had gone out of use by the 15th or 16th century. This is consistent with the general decline and abandonment of most moated sites in Britain, but in this case there may have been particular causes (Janet Hammond, pers. comm.). By the late 1420s the Priory Manor was let to an unknown tenant (Pauline Fogarty, pers. comm.), and in 1491 the lease came into the hands of the Le Strange family. By the late 15th century the de Secheford family had sold their interests in Sedgeford to the Duke of Suffolk, who in turn leased the land to the Le Stranges (Hammond 2002). Both sets of land were thus at last reunited under one tenant, so that only one manorial centre was now required. The size and status of the former Priory manor would have made it the obvious choice for this centre, and this seems to be reflected in the archaeological record.

At some point after the early 17th century, the boundary between the two pieces of land again fell into disrepair, eventually disappearing until reinstated during the late 20th century as a fence along its present line.

The four side-by-side moated courts divided between two owners remain remarkable, however, not only for being, as yet, unparalleled, but also as one of only nine moated sites in Norfolk ever to have been sampled by excavation.

The main contributors to the writing of this chapter were:

Andrea Beckham (née Cox), Keith Robinson (principal authors) and Melanie Van Twest

References

Bartlett, R., 2000, *England under the Norman and Angevin Kings, 1075-1225*, New Oxford History of England, Oxford, Clarendon.

Boddington, A., 1996, *Raunds Furnells: the Anglo-Saxon Church and Churchyard*, English Heritage Archaeological Report, No. 7, London, English Heritage.

Carnell, P., 1998, 'Sedgeford: a non-invasive search for a lost manor', *The Annual*, No. 7, Norfolk Archaeological and Historical Research Group.

Daniell, C., 1997, *Death and Burial in Medieval England*, New York, Routledge.

Dark, K. and Dark, P., 1997, *The Landscape of Roman Britain*, Stroud, Sutton Publishing.

Dyer, C., 2000, *Everyday Life in Medieval England*, London, Hambledon.

Fogarty, P., 2001, 'Sedgeford: parish and manor', unpub. MA dissertation, Royal Holloway, University of London.

Sedgeford, Norfolk: An Assessment. September 2000, unpub. report.

Gem, R., 1988, 'The English parish church in the eleventh and early twelfth centuries: a great rebuilding', in Blair, J. (ed.), *Minsters and Parish Churches: the local Church in transition, 950-1200*, Oxford, Oxford University Committee for Archaeology, 21-30.

Gilchrist, R., 2009, 'Landscapes of the Middle Ages: churches, castles and monasteries', in J. Hunter and I. Ralston, I. (eds.), *The Archaeology of Britain: an introduction from the Upper Palaeolithic to the Industrial Revolution*, 2nd edition, London, Routledge.

Griffiths, G.R., 1985, 'Three Norfolk Estates: a study of their development and economic performance', unpub. MPhil thesis, University of Nottingham.

Hadley, D. and Buckberry, J., 2007, 'Caring for the dead in Late Anglo-Saxon England', in F. Tinti (ed.), *Pastoral Care in Late Anglo-Saxon England*, Woodbridge, Boydell, 121-147.

Hammond, J. 1984, 'Gnatingdon, DMV or Mislaid Manor', *N.A.H.R.G. News*, 37, Norfolk, Norfolk Archaeological and Historical Research Group.

Hammond, J. 2002, 'Where are they now? The de Secheford family 1108-1460 and the lands of their half Knight's Fee 1108-2002', in *Smithdon Hundred Local History Forum Miscellany*, Volume 2, Sedgeford.

Loveluck, C. and Atkinson, D., 2007, *Excavations at Flixborough, Volume 1, The Early Medieval Settlement Remains from Flixborough, Lincolnshire: the occupation sequence, c.AD 600 to 1000*. Oxford, Oxbow Books

Maddicott, J.R.,1995, *Simon De Montfort*, 2nd edition, Cambridge, Cambridge University Press.

NRO DCN 60/33/3 ? Sedgeford. William de Kirkby 1. 1272-3 no. 5233

NRO LEST/IB 83 – 1546 Le Strange Manor of Sedgeford Field Book.

NRO LEST/OC 1 – 1631 Le Strange Estate Map

Platt, C., 1994, *Medieval England: a social history and archaeology from the Conquest to 1600 AD*, 3rd edition, London, Routledge.

Taylor, C.C., 1978, 'Moated sites: their definition, form and classification', in F.A. Aberg (ed.), *Medieval Moated Sites*, C.B.A. Research Report, No. 17, York, Council for British Archaeology.

Waldron, T., 2007, *St Peter's, Barton-upon-Humber, Lincolnshire: a parish church and its community. Volume 2, The human remains*, Oxford, Oxbow Books.

Yaxley, D., 1988, *The Prior's Manor Houses: inventories of eleven of the manor-houses of the Prior of Norwich made in the year 1352 AD*, Dereham, Larks Press.

9. The Spread of the Medieval Village

In two summer seasons of excavation in 2003 and 2004, the Sedgeford Village Survey (SVS) excavated 49 test-pits in gardens and open areas around the village of Sedgeford. The principal aim was to date the development, expansion and eventual merging of what were originally separate settlements to form the modern-day village of Sedgeford. This was done by collecting datable pottery and other artefacts from a random spread of sites.

As noted previously, Sedgeford parish is a river valley, with the Heacham River bisecting it from east to west and a number of natural springs feeding into the river along its course. The underlying geology is principally chalk, greensand and sandstone. The village lies on the north bank of the river, on the

Plate 9.1 Sedgeford from the air, looking west, April 2013.

Fig. 9.1: Map showing the location of the Sedgeford Village Survey test-pits between 2002 and 2004.

south-facing valley slope. In contrast, the Boneyard-Reeddam Middle Anglo-Saxon settlement and cemetery are on the southern bank, on the north-facing slope. The shift from south to north in the Late Anglo-Saxon period is one of the changes the SHARP Team is attempting to understand.

Having emerged out of the amalgamation of pre-existing components, the village of Sedgeford nowadays forms an irregular sideways 'Y' shape, following the contours of the river valley. It is roughly a mile from east to west, and around a quarter of a mile from north to south.

The background to the SVS excavations is provided by local maps dating from 1631 to the present. The modern village is shown to have been formed around five principal centres: the West Hall area near the Church; Cole Green around the war memorial; Eastgate along the Docking Road; Littleport further towards Docking; and the area around Sedgeford Hall, south-east along the Fring Road. Two other outlying settlements are now largely deserted: East Hall (the former Gnatingdon) beyond Littleport to the north-east; and Eaton, about a mile west of the centre of the modern village.

Map evidence from the 20th century shows that it is only in the last 25 years or so that extensive construction work in and around Sedgeford has largely completed the amalgamation of the three central components, West Hall, Cole Green and Eastgate, into a single entity. Sedgeford Hall and Littleport remain semi-detached.

Survey methods

While a great deal of work has been done on failed or deserted settlements such as Wharram Percy, the study of successful settlements like Sedgeford is at a relatively undeveloped stage. Archaeological interventions in extant villages and towns are difficult for the obvious reason that accessible open space is restricted. In this respect, the Sedgeford Village Survey is following a trail blazed by projects at Shapwick in Somerset (1988-2000), at Whittlewood

Plates 9.2-9.4: Community archaeology in action. SHARP archaeologists work with the local community digging test-pits in people's gardens to recover the history of the village.

in Buckinghamshire/Northamptonshire (2000-2005) and even by Channel Four's *Big Dig* in 2003 (Aston 1998; Dyer 2001; Faulkner 2005).

Each of these projects involved garden, backyard and open-space test-pitting in living settlements. At Shapwick, however, the 22 test-pits dug in the existing village were intended only to establish an approximate age for the village as a whole, not to chart its developmental history. At Whittlewood, on the other hand, the test-pitting extended over 12 parishes, included farmland and woodland as well as villages, and was designed with landscape characterisation rather than settlement chronology in mind (Moshenska 2005, 160-161).

The Sedgeford Village Survey was different again, being a concentrated effort to test-pit a village with a view to plotting the settlement's evolution over time. The sample was created by sending a questionnaire to every household and, amongst other things, seeking permission to excavate a test-pit on the property. Roughly 40% of villagers returned completed questionnaires, many with agreement to a test-pit. Around 10% of village properties were subsequently dug, and the overall coverage, while somewhat uneven, was extensive enough to allow provisional conclusions.

The SVS excavations were carried out by a team of two supervisors, Gabe Moshenska and Zannah Baldry, working with between two and seven volunteers at any one time. The test-pits were all one-metre square or equivalent. These were usually dug in spits of 10cm with spades and mattocks. All soil from the test-pits was sieved to recover as large a sample of artefacts as possible. Turf was stacked and spoil piled on sheeting so that gardens could be made good at the end of each excavation.

Recording was done by context, although in almost every case this took the form of topsoil/subsoil/natural. Each test-pit was measured in to fixed points in each garden, and the location was then transferred to digital maps for archiving and for recording at the NHER (Norfolk Historic Environment Record). Most of the finds were bulk-finds, often in enormous quantities. The most significant of these, and the ones on which this report is based, were the datable potsherds.

The mapping of the potsherds onto phase maps of the village is the principal result of the SVS excavations. The phases are determined by diagnostic pottery types rather than recognised historical periods, so there is some divergence between period name and date range. The results have then been plotted by period on a series of village maps.

Fig. 9.2: Iron Age, *c*. 700 BC-AD 60.

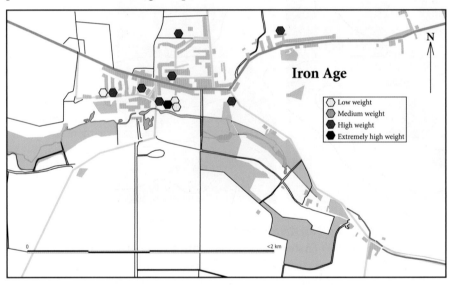

The SVS assemblage for the 43 out of 49 test-pits that yielded pottery totalled 11,288gm. This breaks down as follows: 120gm Iron Age; 80gm Roman; 17gm Early Anglo-Saxon; 19gm Middle Anglo-Saxon; 573gm Late Anglo-Saxon; 808gm Early/High Medieval; 467gm High Medieval; 3,553gm Early Modern; and 5,651gm Late Modern.

Before reviewing the results, we must enter some caveats. The keyhole nature of test-pit surveys means that the sample is tiny and its representativeness can be questioned. The pottery itself can be ambivalent in meaning. Does a given quantity of small abraded sherds represent a village-centre backyard or an open-field manuring spread? Does a collection of large, fresh-looking sherds imply rubbish dumped in a backyard or rubbish dumped beyond the edge of a settlement? We must allow that our SVS pottery distributions offer only an uncertain glimpse into the history of Medieval Sedgeford.

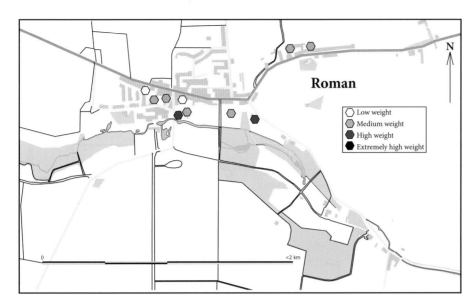

Fig. 9.3: Roman,
c. AD 60-400.

A potted history of Sedgeford

There is a wide but sparse scatter of Iron Age find-spots along the north side of the river, with a cluster of richer spots where SVS interventions come closest to the bank (Fig. 9.2). This corresponds with both our general knowledge of the Iron Age preoccupation with water and watery locations, and with our particular knowledge of the intensity of Iron Age activity on the south side of the river in the central part of Sedgeford.

The Roman distribution closely parallels the Iron Age one: the cluster close to the river remains, as does the generally wide but sparse scatter elsewhere (Fig. 9.3).

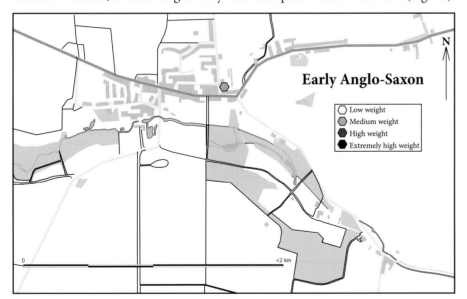

Fig. 9.4: Early Anglo-Saxon,
c. AD 400/450-650/700.

With only a single sherd, it is impossible to say anything definitive about the Early Anglo-Saxon period (Fig. 9.4). However, the sherd in question comprised a large, fresh fragment of cremation urn, adding a little weight to antiquarian reports of Early Anglo-Saxon cemeteries in Sedgeford, the precise locations of which still elude us. The absence of domestic pottery may be inconclusive; pottery use in this period was modest in scale, and buried settlement sites are sometimes archaeologically invisible in routine surveys.

The extreme scarcity of diagnostically Middle Anglo-Saxon Ipswich Ware in the SVS assemblages is remarkable given its abundance on the Boneyard-Reeddam site south of the river (Fig. 9.5). Find-spots are few and no test-pit produced more than one or two sherds. These can easily be written off as 'background noise'.

Fig. 9.5: Middle Anglo-Saxon, *c.* AD 650/700-850/875.

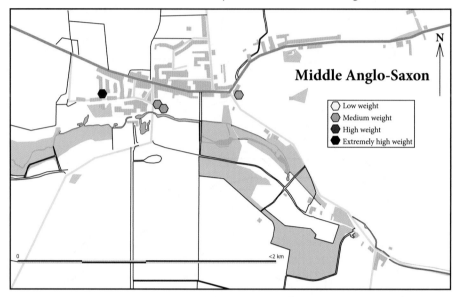

A small but significant assemblage of diagnostically Late Anglo-Saxon Thetford-type Ware almost certainly represents the first phase in the development of the modern village of Sedgeford – 'North Sedgeford' as opposed to Middle Anglo-Saxon 'South Sedgeford' (Fig. 9.6)

Fig. 9.6: Late Anglo-Saxon, *c.* AD 850/875-1100.

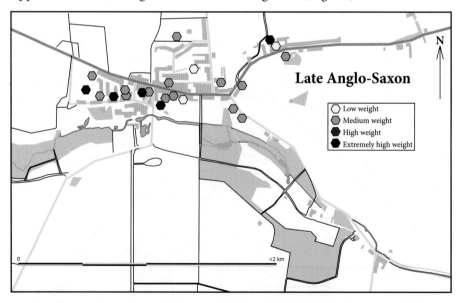

The focus of the scatter is around West Hall and the church – which we understand to be the historic core of the village. The other, sparser, scatters can be interpreted in a number of ways; some sherds may simply be misidentified unglazed Grimston-type Ware of later Medieval date; those that are indeed Late Anglo-Saxon may represent manuring spreads.

The focus on West Hall fits with the findings of other work by SHARP, especially the West Hall Paddock excavations, and further sharpens the contrast between Ipswich-Ware-rich 'South Sedgeford' and Ipswich-Ware-poor 'North Sedgeford'.

In marked contrast to the Thetford-type Ware distribution, that for unglazed Grimston-type Ware extends beyond West Hall and the church to Cole Green and along the Docking and Fring Roads. This fairly even spread into many areas of the modern village implies that the 12th century was a period of exceptional expansion.

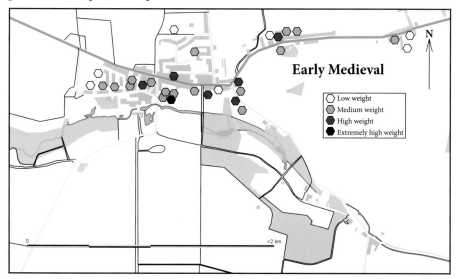

Fig. 9.7: Early Medieval, *c.* AD 1100-1250.

The only caveat here is that our key ceramic dating evidence depends upon a rather slippery distinction. Glazed Grimston-type Ware can be broadly dated to *c.* AD 1250-1500 (though it sometimes occurs earlier). But many vessels were glazed only in part, and glaze sometimes wears away in heavily disturbed deposits; we cannot be certain, therefore, that a small, abraded unglazed Grimston-type sherd does not in fact date from the 14th or 15th century. Our Early Medieval date for the rapid expansion of Sedgeford is, therefore, somewhat tentative.

Nor should 'expansion' be equated with prosperity. The area under

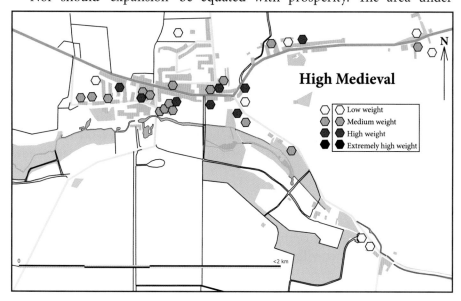

Fig. 9.8: High Medieval, *c.* AD 1250-1500.

residential occupation may have increased, and the implication of that is likely to be population growth. But we know that there was growing pressure on food supplies in the High Medieval period, culminating in a series of severe shortages that are believed to have contributed to the virulence of the Black Death in the mid 14th century as it impacted upon a weakened population. Medieval Sedgeford may have been growing in size, but not necessarily in general well-being.

There is strong continuity between the unglazed and glazed Grimston-type Ware distributions, with the foci at West Hall, Cole Green and Eastgate continuing, along with the smaller ceramic 'signal' at Littleport. The only new focus is a small signal further down the Fring Road at Sedgeford Hall.

The Early Modern period is marked by the appearance of stonewares and earthenwares in the pottery assemblages. Once again the distribution matches closely the morphology of the modern village, though the settled areas at Littleport and Sedgeford Hall are now much more clearly defined, and the south-east area of Cole Green, on the road to Sedgeford Hall, seems to have declined somewhat.

A multi-focal Medieval and Modern village

West Hall

Parts of West Hall, especially its eastern extent, seem to have been active in the Iron Age and Roman periods, when there may have been a river-crossing here. If so, there was perhaps a hiatus afterwards, and a resumption of activity of some sort in the Middle Anglo-Saxon period, since three of the four SVS find-spots for Ipswich Ware were at West Hall. Even so, there are no good grounds for assuming actual settlement at this time.

In the Late Anglo-Saxon period, West Hall became a major centre of occupation, with a number of significant find-spots of Thetford-type Ware clustered in a fairly small area. In addition, SVS finds at West Hall included a worked antler awl of Anglo-Saxon or Viking date, and a posthole 17cm across and 30cm deep cut into the chalk bedrock.

In the period immediately following (*c.* AD 1100-1250), West Hall remained a major focus, but with growing activity in the northern extent of the area, and other areas of activity developing further afield. Occupation has continued unbroken to the present-day, with a sizeable housing development in the last 20 years.

The role of St Mary the Virgin church has, of course, been highly significant in maintaining West Hall's importance, but this has not prevented a marked shift in the village's centre of gravity over time, with the church's location now somewhat peripheral.

Cole Green

Cole Green, the effective centre of the modern village and the site of the war memorial and former village shop, produced only a weak ceramic signal for the Iron Age and Roman periods. It was, however, the site of the only unequivocally Early Anglo-Saxon find in the village: a large, fresh, unabraded sherd of cremation urn, decorated with stamps and grooves.

Very little is known about Early Anglo-Saxon activity in the village, though some complete urns were found in the south of the parish in the early 20th century (see Chapter 4). This discovery is therefore of potential significance.

The single Ipswich Ware find-spot at Cole Green, on the other hand, probably represents nothing more than a manuring spread. Thetford-type Ware is more prevalent and widely dispersed, but again it is not present in sufficient quantity as to suggest occupation.

In the post-Conquest period, on the other hand, Cole Green blossomed, with strong ceramic signals in several test-pits across a relatively small area. It is perhaps no coincidence that this coincides with a slight decrease in the intensity of the signal at West Hall. Perhaps a movement away from this area contributed to the emergence of Cole Green?

This elevated level of activity is also apparent on the south-eastern edge of Cole Green, a short distance along the Fring Road. In the later Medieval period the whole area maintained a high level of activity. But in the Early Modern period occupation along the Fring Road seems to have vanished; today it is a small pasture. Aside from this, the level of activity at Cole Green seems to have changed little since *c.* AD 1100.

Eastgate

There were few Iron Age or Roman finds along the part of the Docking Road that makes up Eastgate, an area which in the last ten years has expanded, becoming an extension of Cole Green as construction has filled in the gaps between houses. Modest Late Anglo-Saxon finds probably imply manuring, but then the ceramic signal is strong from *c.* AD 1100. The significance of the area continued into the later Medieval and Early Modern periods, and on into the present.

Littleport

The Littleport area further along the Docking Road from Eastgate registers fairly late in the story, with no pottery earlier than *c.* AD 1100. Activity remained at a low ebb throughout the Medieval period, spread across a relatively small area. Only in the Early Modern period does a stronger signal register – in an area which historical documents record as active during the English Revolution of the mid 17th century.

Sedgeford Hall

The pattern of activity in the Fring Road area closely mirrors that at Littleport. A weak signal registers in the post-Conquest period, growing stronger later in the Medieval period, but only in the Early Modern period does there appear to have been relatively intensive activity, continuing to some degree into the present.

One of the earlier structures in this area, 'Smithy Cottage', raises the possibility of a local smithy – significant because none other has been found in the village.

Together with the Littleport results, these findings suggest a shift eastwards away from the previous centres at West Hall and Cole Green in the Early Modern period.

Overview

We can define the village of Sedgeford as a 'polyfocal agglomeration' – that is, it contains more than one centre and represents the amalgamation of once-separate small settlements.

We can identify four 'bursts' of village development: the establishment of West Hall in the 11th century; the spread to Cole Green and Eastgate in the 12th and 13th; the further spread to Littleport and Sedgeford Hall in the 16th and 17th centuries; and finally the rolling waves of housing development since 1945, especially in the last 25 years or so.

Another way of viewing matters might be to regard West Hall as the primary centre, Cole Green and Eastgate as secondary settlements, and Littleport and Sedgeford Hall as tertiary ones.

Account must also be taken of the two distant outliers, Eaton and East Hall/Gnatingdon, both failed and now deserted settlements. Their rise and fall must somehow be integrated into the history of human settlement in the parish of Sedgeford.

We have a narrative framework. The task ahead is to make better sense of why the village of Sedgeford developed in the way that it did, when it did.

The main contributors to the writing of this chapter were:

Gabriel Moshenska (principal author), Zannah Salter (née Baldry) (principal author) and Neil Faulkner

References

Aston, M., 1998, 'General Introduction', in M. Aston, T. A. Hall and C. M. Gerrard (eds.), *The Shapwick Project: an archaeological, historical and topographical study*, 8th Report, University of Bristol Department of Continuing Education, 7-8.

Dyer, C., 2001, 'The Whittlewood Proejct', in *Society for Medieval Landscape Studies Newsletter*, Spring/Summer 2001, 7-8.

Faulkner, N., 2005, 'Roman Big Dig or National Archaeology Week: which do you prefer?', in *Current Archaeology*, 196, 177-178.

Moshenska, G., 2005, 'The Sedgeford Village Survey: digging for local history in the back garden', in *The Local Historian*, 35 (3), 159-167.

Conclusion

The parish of Sedgeford represents a small slice of fairly typical English landscape. The combination of winding, marshy river valley, rolling chalk downland and rural village of a few hundred or so must be replicated in a thousand places across the south-eastern part of the British Isles.

Partly because it seemed so 'normal', we chose it almost two decades ago as a place in which to explore changing settlement and land-use over what some historians like to call *la longue durée* ('the long age'). The value of its presumed normality was that it ought to be representative of a wider whole.

Normal does not mean dull. Typical does not mean archaeologically marginal. On the contrary, the parish contains enough archaeology to keep a project like SHARP busy for a millennium. We have sampled only a tiny fraction of the buried remains. We are locating new sites far faster than we can explore old ones; the archaeological resource is growing rapidly as desktop research, fieldwalking, metal-detecting and geophysical survey add to the list. Many of the sites are deep, complex, and of superb quality, so excavating even a small part of one of them can take years.

Equally rapid is the accumulation of unanswered questions. We are learning all the time, but each increment of knowledge immediately spawns a dozen new lines of enquiry. Knowing little, you do not know what to ask. Knowing much, you know how many questions remain to be answered.

Instead, then, of moving towards some sort of closure, SHARP's ambition continues to expand. We have more information, more ideas and more questions than ever before. So we need more surveys, more excavations and more analysis than ever before.

Let us summarise what we know and, in that context, consider our priorities for new research in the years ahead.

We know there was human activity in Sedgeford before *c.* 50 BC, but the evidence, so far, is thin. We know that Mesolithic hunter-gatherers were active, that Bronze Age farmers were working the land and burying their dead in barrows and that their Iron Age successors were building farmsteads on wind-swept downland. This is a start, but much of the job of understanding thousands of years of Sedgeford's prehistory remains.

We know a little more about the Late Iron Age, or, more specifically, the period *c.* 50 BC to AD 60. We can visualise Sedgeford as part of a more heavily populated zone extending over several miles, dotted with farmsteads and also with sanctuaries rich with gold and silver; a zone that likely as not was ruled by some fraction of the Icenian tribal elite of warlords and druids. Something of these overlapping landscapes of production, power, and ritual seems to have been revealed on Polar Breck, in the Late Iron Age levels on Boneyard-Reeddam, and more widely in the evidence of aerial photos, fieldwalking survey and metal-detecting.

But if our working hypothesis is correct – that Sedgeford at this time was part of an Icenian tribal centre – our knowledge of it extends little beyond what can be gleaned from the many rich hoards of coins, torcs and other offerings that have come to light, both in Sedgeford and adjacent parishes. Just how densely settled was the area? What types of people lived there 2,000 years ago? How did they make their living? And what connections did they maintain with the wider world?

Then it seems likely that there was some sort of hiatus. Instead of growing over into something else, the archaeological imprint of the Iceni is extinguished, and what appears some time later is an Early Roman landscape of new farmsteads, and then a Late Roman landscape of villa-estates.

These, at least, are our working hypotheses, based on the evidence from the Upper Chalkpit-Lower Polar Breck site. But they remain to be fully tested. Is it really the case that no settlements continue through the trauma of AD 60/61 and its aftermath? Are all destroyed by Roman 'fire and sword'? Is Sedgeford returned to Year Zero? And is the transition from farmstead to villa-estate so stark, with its implication, perhaps, if we read into the archaeological record the grim testimony of the Roman law codes, that once-free farmers working mainly for their own subsistence were transformed into agricultural serfs chained to the demands of a ruthless military-supply economy?

Sedgeford's 'body in an oven' may or may not be evidence of the breakdown of Roman authority and order in the 4th century AD. What is certain is that the archaeological imprint of Roman imperial culture ends as definitively in Sedgeford as it does across Britannia as a whole. Imported coinage, mass-production pottery, life in grand houses, Romano-British rural settlements, and all the other material expressions of *Romanitas* seem to vanish in a single generation.

Then we are in the dark. For a while, perhaps half a century or so, there is quite literally no evidence of any kind. For the later 5th century AD (at the earliest), we have antiquarian reports of Early Anglo-Saxon cemeteries, a couple of urns salvaged from a gravel quarry in the local museum, and one known cemetery of late 5th to early 7th century AD date from which 180 artefacts have been recovered in metal-detector survey. But no Early Anglo-Saxon cemetery has been sampled by modern excavation, and no associated Early Anglo-Saxon settlement sites have been located.

The Middle Anglo-Saxon cemetery and settlement on the Boneyard-Reeddam/Lower Chalkpit site seems to appear suddenly, *de novo*, in the years around AD 650/700. Major questions immediately arise. Where were people living before this, and why did they move to this new location? What was the old settlement (or settlements) like? How did it compare with the new? Can the change be related to wider economic, social, political and cultural developments? More precisely, what is the relationship between changes in human settlement in Sedgeford and the development of the Kingdom of East Anglia, the growth of the Church and Christian confession and the division of the land into great estates?

There are, moreover, further transitions which pose more such questions.

The Middle Anglo-Saxon settlement was not fixed in form. In the early 8th century, when the cemetery was first in use, the settlement seems to have been loosely structured within a curving boundary. In the later 8th century or perhaps early 9th century, it was completely reorganised, having a rectilinear grid imposed upon it, creating a series of individual plots. The implication may be that centralised authority, whether ecclesiastical or secular (or both), was becoming more assertive, and that society was increasingly preoccupied with regulating space and defining responsibilities.

Then it changed again, probably in the early 10th century, with the creation of a huge D-shaped enclosure. The boundary ditches of the settlement grid were still there, sometimes re-cut wholesale, sometimes on the same line, but the settlement was henceforward dominated by a monumental enclosure higher up the slope, presumably with rampart, palisade and some sort of entrance-way. As such, it would have some of the features required for the residence of a thegn, an Anglo-Saxon lord of the manor, or perhaps someone grander still, an ealdorman, the master of a great estate. And was this monument simply designed to impress, to assert rank and status, or was it also a defence-work in a frontier zone during turbulent times? For Sedgeford faced the Kingdom of Lindsey on the far side of The Wash and the Viking-infested North Sea.

Turbulent times may also be the context for the sudden termination of the Boneyard-Reeddam/Lower Chalkpit settlement – what we call 'South Sedgeford' – and the relocation of the main focus a few hundred yards to the north-west on the opposite side of the river ('North Sedgeford'). This 'Late Anglo-Saxon shift' was perhaps made possible by falling sea-levels, since the West Hall area appears to have been marshland in the Early and Middle Anglo-Saxon periods, but then to have been drained and reclaimed in the later 10th or early 11th century, perhaps when a great causeway was constructed to create the Reeddam.

But were abandonment and relocation simultaneous processes and a single event, or was there a hiatus or, perhaps, a more drawn-out period of relocation? Did one or another of the wider conflicts of the period result in the arrival of new lords able to impose their imprint on a landscape from which earlier settlement had been largely erased? We do not know. We need more evidence from West Hall, the historic core of the Medieval village.

We know of a demolished building, which we interpret as a chapel of 10th or 11th century date under West Hall Paddock. We are confident that the extant church was built in the 13th century, though whether this building is the direct replacement for the West Hall Paddock structure we are uncertain. We have documentary references of similar date to two Medieval manors immediately to the south, one eventually held by Norwich Cathedral Priory, the other belonging to the de Secheford family; and we have seen some foundations of the latter in small excavations in Ladywell Field.

But so many details elude us. When exactly did the shift occur? What were the original components of the new settlement? When and in what sequence were the four moated courts of the two manor complexes created? And, with a wider perspective, what was the relationship between these high-status facilities and the evolving economy and society of Medieval Sedgeford? In particular, how was water dammed, canalised and managed as a productive resource, communications route and /or source of power?

The picture becomes a little clearer thereafter. The subsequent growth of the village can be tracked in documentary records, in the evidence of standing buildings and other landscape features, and in the pottery assemblages recovered from the Sedgeford Village Survey's garden test-pits. We can see the old settlement at West Hall fusing with later settlements at Cole Green and Eastgate and, to a degree, with Littleport and Sedgeford Hall, to form the present village. At the same time, we bear witness to the apparent 'failure' of two distant outliers, Eaton and Gnatingdon, and wonder why. And more generally, we would like to know how these settlements differed and interacted as components of the parish-wide economy of the High Middle Ages and later.

Because of these and many other questions – because, indeed, we have far more than when we started – we plan on returning to Sedgeford each summer for years to come. You, the reader, may already be involved. If so, this, our first full-length archaeological monograph, will have given you a better idea how all the pieces fit together and provided a fair summary of what we have done and what we know so far. If you are not involved, but fancy trying some hands-on archaeology – surveying the landscape, digging a trench, studying the finds, or doing any one of a dozen other things that are part of the archaeological process – you may like to join us. There is a lot to do and work for all.

The Sedgeford Timeline

The Sedgeford Timeline comprises: a) general time periods b) historical events; and c) Sedgeford 'events' (usually broad developments as revealed by archaeology). The time periods represent a combination of Norfolk HER (Historic Environment Record) periods with SHARP-specific periods to create a timeline that works in relation to our investigations and data-set. Sometimes we can date only within broad bands, e.g. Roman. Sometimes we can be more specific, e.g. Early Roman. Sub-periods are given in brackets and indented, and Sedgeford 'events' are then set against either the broad band or the sub-period depending on the accuracy of our dating.

Periods and sub-periods	Historical events	Sedgeford events
Palaeolithic *c.* 900,000-8,000 BC		
(Lower Palaeolithic) *c.* 900,000-250,000 BC		
(Middle Palaeolithic) *c.* 250,000-40,000 BC		
(Upper Palaeolithic) *c.* 40,000-8000 BC		
Mesolithic *c.* 8000-4000 BC		
(Early Mesolithic) *c.* 8000-6000 BC		
(Late Mesolithic) *c.* 6000-4000 BC		Worked flint indicates small groups of hunter-gatherers present and perhaps one or more temporary camps.
Later Prehistoric *c.* 4000-100 BC		Icknield Way comes into use.
Neolithic *c.* 4000-2350 BC		Worked flint indicates early farmers at work.
(Early Neolithic) *c.* 4000-3000 BC		A flint axe is lost or discarded.

(Late Neolithic) *c.* 3000-2350 BC		
Bronze Age *c.* 2350-700 BC		A series of round barrows are constructed, some of them forming a tight cluster on rising ground.
(Early Bronze Age/ Beaker) *c.* 2350-1700 BC		A crouched burial is made on Lower Chalkpit.
(Middle Bronze Age) *c.* 1700-1200		
(Late Bronze Age) *c.* 1200-700		
Iron Age *c.* 700 BC-AD 60		
(Early Iron Age) *c.* 700-450 BC		
(Middle Iron Age) *c.* 450-100 BC		A crouched burial is made on Lower Chalkpit.
(Late Iron Age) *c.* 100 BC-AD 60		A sanctuary exists in Polar Breck and Shernborne Breck, with a gold torc, a gold stater and a bronze chariot fitting among the deposits. A sanctuary also exists on Boneyard-Reeddam, with a hoard of 39 gold staters and a horse burial among the deposits. A farmstead exists on Upper Chalkpit.
	Boudican Revolt and Roman Conquest AD 60/61	There is a possible hiatus in activity.
Roman *c.* AD 60-400		Peddars Way comes into regular use.
(Early Roman) *c.* AD 60-100/125		A farmstead exists on Lower Polar Breck and Upper Chalkpit.
(High Empire) *c.* AD 100/125-250/275		
(Late Roman) *c.* AD 250/275-400	End of Roman Imperial control, *c.* AD 400/410	A probable villa is constructed at Eaton. An agricultural processing plant is established on Upper Chalkpit. Sedgeford may be supplying Brancaster Roman Fort. A body is cremated in a ruinous grain-drying oven on Upper Chalkpit.

Anglo-Saxon *c.* AD 400/450-1100		
(Early Anglo-Saxon) *c.* AD 400/450-650/700		Both cremation and inhumation cemeteries are established.
(Middle Anglo-Saxon) *c.* AD 650/700-850/875	Christian conversion of Kingdom of East Anglia. AD 630 onwards	A new village and cemetery are established on the Boneyard-Reeddam/Lower Chalkpit site. The village is reorganised on a regular rectilinear grid pattern. A monumental D-shaped enclosure is constructed on the southern side of the village.
(Late Anglo-Saxon) *c.* AD 850/875-1100	Danish Supremacy AD 871 Anglo-Saxon Reconquest AD 917 Danish Conquest AD 1016 Norman Conquest AD 1066	The Boneyard-Reeddam/Lower Chalkpit village and cemetery are abandoned. A new settlement focus is established at West Hall. 'Red Rose' is interred in a chapel at West Hall (now or a little later).
Medieval *c.* AD 1100-1500		Moated manorial courts established at West Hall and in Ladywell Field. Expansion of settlement to Cole Green and Eastgate.
(Early Medieval) *c.* AD 1100-1250		
(High Medieval) *c.* AD 1250-1500		Major rebuilding of St Mary the Virgin Church.
Early Modern *c.* 1500-1750/1800	English Reformation 1530s English Revolution and Civil Wars 1640s.	First surviving map of Sedgeford created. Expansion of settlement to Littleport and Sedgeford Hall. Powder magazine or armoury built in 1640s
Late Modern *c.* 1750/1800-present	First World War 1914-1918 Interwar 1918-1939 Second World War 1939-1945 Postwar 1945-present	Sedgeford Tithe award 1840. RNAS/RFC aerodrome established 1915, developed into RAF fighter training base. Dummy airfield in Second World War. Ribbon development links previously separate settlement foci.

Index